The Handbook of Energy Trading

For other titles in the Wiley Finance series
please see www.wiley.com/finance

The Handbook of Energy Trading

Stefano Fiorenzani
Samuele Ravelli
Enrico Edoli

WILEY
A John Wiley & Sons, Ltd., Publication

This edition first published in 2012

Registered office
John Wiley & Sons Ltd, The Atrium, Southern Gate, Chichester, West Sussex, PO19 8SQ, United Kingdom

For details of our global editorial offices, for customer services and for information about how to apply for permission to reuse the copyright material in this book please see our website at www.wiley.com

Library of Congress Cataloging-in-Publication Data

Fiorenzani, Stefano.
The handbook of energy trading / Stefano Fiorenzani, Samuele Ravelli, Enrico Edoli.
p. cm.
ISBN 978-1-119-95369-2
1. Energy industries. 2. Power resources. 3. Commodity exchanges. I. Ravelli, Samuele. II. Edoli, Enrico. III. Title.
HD9502.A2.F567 2012
332.64′4–dc23

2011043012

ISBN 978-1-119-95369-2 (hbk), ISBN 978-1-119-95454-5 (ebk),
ISBN 978-1-119-95456-9 (ebk), ISBN 978-1-119-95455-2 (ebk)

A catalogue record for this book is available from the British Library.
Typeset in 10/12pt Times by Laserwords Private Limited, Chennai, India
Printed in Great Britain by TJ International Ltd, Padstow, Cornwall

To our families

Contents

List of Figures xi

List of Tables xv

Preface xvii

Acknowledgements xix

1 Energy Markets as Efficient Markets 1

1.1 The "Efficient Market Hypothesis" 1

1.1.1 Trading Implications 2

1.1.2 Informational and Mathematical Implications 3

1.2 Mathematical Framework 3

1.2.1 Information Set: σ-algebras 3

1.2.2 Conditional Expectation 5

1.3 Martingale Hypothesis 7

1.3.1 The Random Walk Hypothesis 8

1.3.2 Sequences and Reversal, Cowles Jones Test: Theoretical Framework 10

1.3.3 Variance Ratio Tests 11

1.4 Violations of EMH and Behavioural Finance 13

1.5 Information Asymmetries and Accelerating Processes 15

1.6 The Peculiar Structure and Nature of Energy Commodities Markets 17

1.7 EHM in Energy Commodities Markets: Some Evidence from Data 19

1.7.1 Efficient Market Hypothesis: Testing the Intraday Returns 26

1.8 Subordination, Trading Volume and Efficient Market Hypothesis 27

1.9 Subordination and Stochastic Timescales 28

2 Directional Trading 33

2.1 Definitions and Main Features 33

2.2 Market Products for Directional Trading 35
2.3 Price Trend Determination 37
2.3.1 Fundamental Trading Models 37
2.3.2 Statistical Trading Models 42
2.3.3 Technical Trading Models 49
2.3.4 Case Studies 51
2.4 Strategic Asset Allocation Methods 57
2.4.1 Traditional Asset Allocation Models 57
2.4.2 Single Period Asset Allocation Model 58
2.4.3 Inter-temporal Asset Allocation Problems 59
2.4.4 Solution Methods – Dynamic Programming 62
2.4.5 Asset Allocation with Capital Constraints 76

3 Spread Trading 81
3.1 Spread Definition and Identification 82
3.2 Non-Stationarity and Cointegration 84
3.3 Empirical Analysis of Energy Spread Trading Strategies 89
3.4 Empirical Analysis of Energy Spreads and Spread Trading Strategies 92
3.4.1 Cross Commodities Spread Trading (Spark Spread) 92
3.4.2 Time Spreads on Brent 95
3.4.3 Location Spread: Italy vs. Germany 96
3.5 Combining Directional and Spread Trading Strategies 98

4 Options and Non-Linear Derivatives 101
4.1 The Essence of Non-Linearity 101
4.1.1 Factors that Influence Option Value 103
4.1.2 Option Traders 104
4.1.3 Energy Option Markets 105
4.2 Exotic Options 105
4.3 Combinations 109
4.4 Value Bounds and Parity Relationship 112
4.5 Basics on Option Pricing 115
4.6 The Greeks 119
4.6.1 Delta and Delta Hedging 120
4.6.2 Gamma 120
4.6.3 Theta 121
4.6.4 Vega 121
4.7 Adjusting the Continuous Time Dynamic Hedging Framework 122
4.7.1 Discrete Δ and Extreme Market Moves 122
4.7.2 Gamma and Shadow Gamma 123
4.7.3 Vega and Volatility Surface Movements 124
4.7.4 Theta, and the Greek's Importance for Exotic Option Traders 125

4.7.5 Futures and Forwards to Hedge the Risk: Structured Products 125
4.8 Case Study 126

5 Structured Products on Energy 131
5.1 Structured Products on Energy: Main Typology 131
5.2 Retail Structured Products 133
5.2.1 Profiled Forward Contracts 133
5.2.2 Full Requirements Contracts 134
5.3 Wholesale Structured Products 135
5.3.1 General Pricing Issues on Structured Products 135
5.3.2 Virtual Power Plants: Structure and Pricing Techniques 140
5.3.3 Virtual Refinery: Structure and Pricing Techniques 142
5.3.4 Virtual Gas Storage: Structure and Pricing Techniques 144
5.3.5 The Structure of Swing Contracts and *Make-up* Clause 146
5.4 Hedge in Incomplete Markets 149
5.5 Case Study: Structured Products 152
5.5.1 Virtual Power Plants 152
5.5.2 Swing on Gas 155
5.5.3 Virtual Refinery 158

6 Metatrading Strategies and Capital Allocation Techniques 163
6.1 Metatrading Definition and Fundamental Elements 163
6.2 Macroeconomic Megatrends: Understanding and Analysis 164
6.2.1 Keynesian Business Cycle Theory 166
6.2.2 Real Business Cycle Theory 167
6.2.3 Austrian Business Cycle Theory 168
6.2.4 Risk-based Business Cycle Theory 170
6.3 Trading Business Organizational Issues 172
6.3.1 Book Structuring 173
6.3.2 Internal Market 175
6.4 Capital Management Principles 177
6.4.1 Economic Capital Definition and Initial Allocation 177
6.4.2 Risk Measurement and Integration Approaches for Energy Portfolios 178
6.4.3 Performance Assessment 188
6.4.4 The Dynamics of Capital Allocation (Capital Reallocation Process) 192

Bibliography 195

Index 199

List of Figures

1.1	Residual normal fit on WTI series	21
1.2	Residual normal fit on HH series	22
1.3	Residual normal fit on EEX series	23
1.4	Henry Hub gas futures: empirical analysis	30
1.5	Subordinated model test result	31
2.1	ICE Brent crude oil future	34
2.2	Cash position versus market value December 2010	36
2.3	Energy aggregated demand supply	38
2.4	Demand/supply shocks	39
2.5	Winter gas demand/supply	41
2.6	Summer gas demand/supply	42
2.7	Power demand/supply	43
2.8	Intensity of long-memory process	46
2.9	Deterministic versus stochastic trend	48
2.10	Technical analysis on ICE Brent: moving averages	50
2.11	Technical analysis on ICE Brent: channels	51
2.12	Calendar ahead vs Calendar oil-linked formula	52
2.13	PSV bid stack model	56
2.14	Optimal controls obtained at the first step	69
2.15	Optimal controls obtained at the second step	70
2.16	Binomial tree	71

3.1 Optimal buy and sell with mean reversion 83
3.2 European spark spread 84
3.3 Two strongly correlated series and their spread, which is clearly non-stationary 85
3.4 Optimal control of a mean-reverting asset as a function of price and speed of mean-reversion 90
3.5 Spark spread in Italy calendar 2011 91
3.6 Time spread on ICE Brent 95
3.7 Location spread Germany-Italy Q1 2011 97
3.8 API2/API4 spread vs Best Freight, obtained as the minimum between freights Panama Bolivar, Cape Bolivar, Panamax Indonesia, Cape Rich Bay, Panamax Rich Bay 99
3.9 Empirical distribution of gasoil crack spread returns 100

4.1 Combinations between one options and the underlying. (a) long position on a call and short on the asset; (b) long position on the asset and on a put 110
4.2 Upwards spread combinations. (a) upwards spread with call; (b) upwards spread with put 110
4.3 Straddle and strangle. (a) straddle; (b) strangle 111
4.4 Short call (96), long call (104), long asset 123
4.5 Gamma surface (time & price) of a 95–110 strangle 124
4.6 Historical relative percentage changes in a portfolio's value from 01/04/2011 to 29/04/2011 for the naked and hedged position on a call with strike 120, maturity at 11/06/2011 and as underlying the future on Brent for July 2011 129

5.1 Forward curves as of 03/12/2011 153
5.2 Payoff distribution of naked position 154
5.3 Volumetric and MinVariance hedged payoff distributions 154
5.4 Trees for prices for different values of parameters. (a) strong mean reversion, low volatility: $a^P = 3, a^I = 10, \sigma^P = 0.3, \sigma^I = 0.1$ (b) small mean reversion, high volatility: $a^P = 0.1, a^I = 0.1, \sigma^P = 0.7, \sigma^I = 0.2$ 155
5.5 Prices term structures scenarios 156
5.6 Swing hedging 158
5.7 Virtual refinery case study 161

6.1 Economic cycle, risk and money supply 173
6.2 Book structure scheme 174
6.3 VaR, ES and CVaR graphical representation 182
6.4 PaR and CFaR graphical representation 184

List of Tables

1.1 ADF on WTI daily prices 20

1.2 ADF on WTI daily returns 20

1.3 ADF on Henry Hub daily prices 21

1.4 ADF on HH daily returns 22

1.5 ADF on EEX daily prices 23

1.6 ADF on EEX daily returns 23

1.7 WTI Cowles Jones 24

1.8 HH Cowles Jones 25

1.9 EEX Cowles Jones 25

1.10 WTI variance ratio 25

1.11 HH variance ratio 26

1.12 EEX variance ratio 27

1.13 ADF on WTI intraday returns 27

1.14 Estimation results variance linear regression 30

2.1 Statistical trading strategy on ARMA 54

3.1 ADF on Italian spark spread level 93

3.2 Italian spark spread strategy 95

3.3 ADF on oil time spread level 96

3.4 Oil time spread strategy 96

3.5 ADF on location spread level 97

3.6 Location spread strategy 98

3.7 Target function computed as the strategy result in case of success (scenario up) minus 10 times (e.g. generically n) the risk limit overused (risk limit €5) 100

4.1 Factors influencing call and put values. The symbol ↗ represents an increasing value, while ↘ represents a decreasing value 104

4.2 Value of a portfolio composed of a long position on a call (with underlying futures ICE Brent 3 months, strike \$120) and the underlying. For every trading date the value of the portfolio, calculated as described, is shown, both before and after the rebalancing 127

5.1 Main features of structured products 132

5.2 Merchant vs proprietary perspective on structured products 132

5.3 Virtual power plant's operational constraints 141

5.4 Parameters of a Virtual Gas Storage 145

5.5 VPP parameters 152

5.6 Swing parameters 157

5.7 Summary of test case characteristics 159

5.8 Summary of test case characteristics 160

Preface

Over the past ten years energy trading has proved one of the most capital attractive of businesses. Both in the US and in Europe energy trading has become a fundamental activity for utilities (vertically integrated energy companies), investment banks and hedge funds, enticing a lot of experienced staff from other (more established) trading sectors such as equity, FX or fixed income. Probably due to this fast, and perhaps unexpected, growth in importance, energy trading has developed without the support of either precise or ad hoc benchmarks in terms of organization, management and control, something its complex nature desperately requires.

Energy trading is not just of interest to energy traders, it is also relevant to a very wide range of other professionals engaged in the business, such as energy analysts, risk managers and, last but not least, energy trading managers. This book is intended to cover in a detailed way all the various aspects of energy trading from the most macro to the most micro. Dealing so thoroughly with every topic gave us the chance to analyze many aspects of the business in depth with the aim of providing support to energy trading managers, energy traders and energy trading analysts as well as trying to bridge the worlds of practitioners and academic research. Obviously, in order to be at the cutting edge of every topic discussed we could not avoid the occasional use of technical language or a pretty complex mathematical one. But, we genuinely believe that anyone choosing to read this book is ready for something more than the basics and we wanted to provide them with something more advanced.

Trading in general and energy trading in particular is not a pure science but rather a complex mix of scientific techniques and emotional behaviours. It is impossible to gain a complete understanding of the topic using just one approach. For that reason we will try to explore and critically revise all the potential trading approaches that can result in profits in the energy sector. In particular, the book condenses our combined professional experience in the field, covering quantitative analysis, trading, risk management as well as the managerial aspects of the energy trading business.

In order to keep our readers on their toes in every chapter we alternate theoretical discussion with practical applications and examples. In our view practical applications are important to clarify and exemplify theoretical discussion and sometimes also to show that the use of mathematical complexity is justified and not merely an exercise in aesthetics. We have tried hard to avoid unnecessary complexity, just as we have always tried to avoid dangerous simplifications.

The book seeks to answer questions like: *why is energy trading different from any other trading business? Where are those differences? Are energy markets efficient markets or do inefficiencies allow for extra profits? How should we structure an energy trading business in order to maximize the probability of being successful? How many energy trading strategies and energy trading instruments can we use and how should we use them in order to be successful?*

The book consists of six chapters, ranging from practical studies of the efficiency of energy markets to quantitative analysis of derivatives and portfolio strategies. Despite the highly theoretical nature of some of the topics analyzed, we have been careful not to lose sight of the practical aspects. The first chapter gives a detailed analysis of the efficiency of energy markets, combining traditional statistical analysis tools with our own market insight. Next follow the presentation and critical revision of the most used energy trading strategies, focusing on different approaches, different markets and trading instruments. The presentation is tailor-made for energy markets, and not merely a simple application of existing theory to energy markets. With many factual examples, and numerical schemes for practical implementation, we intend to provide helpful insights for readership in both academia and industry.

The book ends by dealing with the more macro aspects of energy trading (designated as metatrading elements) such as macroeconomic trends determination, organizational, capital allocation and risk management issues. We believe that this book is comprehensive in setting out for the reader all the relevant problems connected with an energy trading business. On some issues firm solutions to problems have been provided, on others we were simply happy to be the first to engage in discussion!

Stefano Fiorenzani
Samuele Ravelli
Enrico Edoli

The views, opinions, positions or strategies expressed by Samuele Ravelli are his alone, and do not necessarily reflect the views, opinions, positions or strategies of E.ON Energy Trading SE.

Acknowledgements

We would like to express our gratitude to the following people for their conceptual and material help.

to *Carlo Occhiena* for many profitable discussions on technical trading techniques, which helped us fine tune the details of directional trading strategies;

to *Tiziano Varigiolu* for his generous advise on both conceptual and technical matters.

Writing a book together means continuously challenging each other, reviewing every section and try to organize the various constituent parts into a whole. So we would like to thank one another for the common collaborative effort aiming at the very best result.

We are also grateful for the challenging comments we received from our anonymous referees preparatory to publishing.

The responsibility for any remaining errors is ours alone.

Stefano Fiorenzani
Samuele Ravelli
Enrico Edoli

1
Energy Markets as Efficient Markets

1.1 THE "EFFICIENT MARKET HYPOTHESIS"

Are energy markets efficient markets? In what sense can a commodity market be considered efficient? And what are the trading implications of market efficiency? These are the questions we would like to answer in this introductory chapter. The third question, in particular, has a strong impact on the overall meaning of the book, but obviously, before discussing the trading implications of market efficiency we need to define the concept formally and to try to understand if energy markets can be considered efficient in some sense.

The theoretical origins of the Efficient Markets Hypothesis (EMH) are connected with pioneering studies of modern financial economics. The first formal definition and in depth analysis must surely refer to the studies of Roberts (1967) and Fama (1970). Whenever we say that a market, a financial market particularly, is efficient we basically refer to efficiency in the informational sense. In fact, in a competitive market, asset prices dynamically reflect relevant information flows and consequently a certain market is more informationally efficient if it is able to reflect more relevant information in its asset prices. Information is thus relevant if it can predict future price dynamics. According to Fama's original definition, a capital market is said to be efficient with respect to a certain information set if security prices would be unaffected by revealing that information to all market participants. Hence, the description of the information set is the base for the definition of market efficiency.

The classic taxonomy of the information set exposed by Roberts (1967) characterizes three different forms of market efficiency: weak, semistrong and strong.

In weak form market efficiency the information set considered includes only the history of prices themselves. If the market we are considering is efficient in the weak form, revealing the whole history of security prices to market participants wouldn't impact their behaviour in the market. In other words, future prices cannot be predicted by analyzing prices from the past. Under this framework, price realizations are time independent of each other. Knowing last price realization or the whole history of prices wouldn't change the ability to predict future prices. This form of market efficiency has strong mathematical and trading implications and will be discussed throughout the chapter.

In its semistrong form, the information set includes all the so-called "publicly available information", while in the strong form of market efficiency private information is also considered as a part of the available information set. Under these two frameworks, price adjustments to new information should be immediate and of a reasonable size. Consistent upward or downward adjustments after the initial change should be interpreted as informational inefficiencies.

Independently of the nature of the information set used for the definition of a particular market efficiency form, it is clear that the only way information should be reflected in prices is through real market transactions. Hence, even if the information flow is huge and fast in its development but the frequency of effective transactions is not proportional, the market efficiency paradigm loses its importance. In other words, a market can be efficient only if it is sufficiently liquid, otherwise the information flow cannot be reflected in price signals. Market efficiency is strictly connected to perfect competition between a wide universe of market operators (no single one of which is able to impact price dynamics). If this were not the case, information would be uploaded into prices as discrete packages resulting in sizable price jumps. Often energy or other commodity markets suffer when liquidity problems arise and this is something that has to be seriously considered when testing for market efficiency.

1.1.1 Trading Implications

The efficient market hypothesis has aroused interest in the public debate not because of its theoretical appeal, but mainly for its trading implications. In fact, if the disclosure of a certain information set to market participants does not affect their price forecast, no extra profits can be extracted on the basis of that information set. In the weak-form efficiency case the information set is basically the complete knowledge of price history. This implies that if a market is efficient in weak form, trading based on technical or statistical analysis cannot provide expected excess returns, while fundamental trading can still be profitable. In a semi-strong efficient market not even fundamental trading can be expected to overshoot the market, while the strong efficiency form is that theoretical situation in which not even with private information can we expect consistently to realize extra returns. Obviously, the last situation is a purely theoretical one since if a strongly efficient market were to exist, trading would be meaningless in it (as also a book on trading!).

Looking at how many people work in the trading industry around the world we might well be inclined to say that, in general, financial markets are far from being efficient. But, what is a market in practice? Is it possible that a market can be considered efficient for a certain asset class and not for another? It can happen that information fully reflected into a certain security's price (and hence irrelevant for its better prediction) can be useful to better predict the future price of an other security. It can be that (especially in those markets characterized by a mix of financial and industrial investors) market segmentation allows for an inefficient mechanism of transmission of information and consequently potential excess profits.

A full understanding of the degree of efficiency of the market we are operating in, conditional on the information set we are endowed with, allows us to understand which trading activity is worth setting up and what is the best way of allocating our risk capital. It is interesting to analyze in depth and specify the concept of market efficiency within different market sectors in order to verify the concrete possibility of making money out of our energy trading activity.

1.1.2 Informational and Mathematical Implications

So far we have defined and analyzed the EMH as an information-based concept. In practice, a market is considered efficient if it is able to reflect the information flow immediately into asset price dynamics. However, we have not really formally defined the concept of information. We said that a market framework is efficient at time t with respect to a certain information set $\varphi(t)$ if revealing that information to market players will not change their future price forecast. This implies, obviously, that market players are already endowed with an information set $\Phi(t)$ already containing $\varphi(t)$ [formally, $\Phi(t) \supseteq \varphi(t)$]. If we imagine that agents formulate their future price forecast by means of the conditional expectation operator, we may write the following expression using the *Law of Iterated Expectations*:

$$E\left[E\left[P_T|\Phi_t\right]|\varphi_t\right] = E[P_T|\varphi_t] \xrightarrow{yields} E\left[P_T - E[P_T|\Phi_t]|\varphi_t\right] = 0 \quad T \geqslant t$$

which formally states that redundant information is worthless in improving (or at least changing) forecasting errors. Discussing the classic taxonomy of information sets related to market efficiency forms we saw that our information set can be the whole history of asset prices or, equally, the whole set of publicly available information. We need to give a formal definition to all those sets before analyzing the mathematical and statistical implications of EMH.

1.2 MATHEMATICAL FRAMEWORK

In this section we introduce the mathematical and statistical background useful to describe and analyze the EMH and briefly present some mathematical theory.

1.2.1 Information Set: σ-algebras

From a mathematical point of view the concept of "information set" (available at time t) is given by the definitions of *σ-algebra* and *filtration*: let Ω be an abstract space, that is with no special structure, and let 2^Ω denote all subsets of Ω, including the empty set $\emptyset$. Let $\mathcal{F} \in 2^\Omega$ be a subset of Ω. $\mathcal{F}$ is a σ-algebra if it satisfies the following properties:

i. $\emptyset \in \mathcal{F}$ and $\Omega \in \mathcal{F}$
ii. If $A \in \mathcal{F}$ then $A^c \in \mathcal{F}$, where A^c denotes the complement of A

iii. $\mathcal{F}$ is closed under countable unions and intersection: that is if $A_1, A_2, \ldots$ is a countable sequence of events in $\mathcal{F}$ then $\bigcup_{i=1}^{+\infty} A_i$ and $\bigcap_{i=1}^{+\infty} A_i$ are both also in $\mathcal{F}$.

The pair $(\Omega, \mathcal{F})$ is called a measurable space.

Even if the general definition does not require a special structure for Ω, we will always consider Ω as the space of all possible *events* for a given experiment. In probability theory, an event is a set of outcomes to which a probability is assigned. For example, if the experiment is the roll of a dice, an event is "a five appears", and it is intuitive that the probability assigned to this event is $\frac{1}{6}$.

Now the problem is how to describe spaces of events that have a complex structure, with an infinite and uncountable number of events, collected in the σ-algebra $\mathcal{F}$. First of all we have to define a probability measure.

Given a measurable space $(\Omega, \mathcal{F})$ we say that the real-valued function $\mathbb{P} : (\Omega, \mathcal{F}) \longrightarrow [0, 1]$ defined on $\mathcal{F}$ is a probability measure if it satisfies:

i. $\mathbb{P}(\Omega) = 1$
ii. For every countable sequence $\{A_n\}_{n \in \mathbb{N}} \subseteq \mathcal{F}$ of pairwise disjoint elements (i.e. $A_i \cap A_j = \emptyset$ whenever $i \neq j$) one has:

$$\mathbb{P}\left(\bigcup_{n=1}^{+\infty} A_n\right) = \sum_{n=1}^{+\infty} \mathbb{P}(A_n)$$

The triplet $(\Omega, \mathcal{F}, \mathbb{P})$ is called a probability space.

The last mathematical object needed to describe the price evolution of an asset in a mathematical framework is the *random variable* (and the *stochastic process*). A random variable X is an unknown quantity that varies with the outcome of a random event. Before the random event, we can know which values X *might possibly* assume, but we do not know exactly which one it will take: let $(\Omega, \mathcal{F}, \mathbb{P})$ be a probability space and let $(E, \mathcal{E})$ be a measurable space. A random variable is a $\mathcal{F}$-measurable function $X : (\Omega, \mathcal{F}) \to (E, \mathcal{E})$, i.e. such that $\forall H \in \mathcal{E}$ one has:

$$X^{-1}(H) := \{\omega \in \Omega | X(\omega) \in H\} \in \mathcal{F}$$

Since $X^{-1}(H) \in \mathcal{F}$ we can consider the following probability on E, named the *law of* X:

$$\mu_x(H) = \mathbb{P}(X \in H) = \mathbb{P}(\{\omega \in \Omega | X(\omega) \in H\})$$

An interpretation of this definition is that the preimages of the "well-behaved" subset of E (the elements of $\mathcal{E}$) are *events*, i.e. elements of $\mathcal{F}$, and hence are assigned a probability by $\mathbb{P}$. One can prove that μ_x is a probability measure on $(E, \mathcal{E})$ in the sense of the definition given above.

At this point it seems clear that a price in the market can be viewed as a *realization* of some random variable: at time t, given a suitable set of information $H \in \mathcal{F}$, the price realization will be described by $X(H)$. But how to describe the sequence of prices and the flows of information? A possible way might be to model a sequence of information sets and a sequence of random variables.

Let us start with the sequence of information: given a measurable space $(\Omega, \mathcal{F})$, a *filtration* is an increasing sequence of σ-algebras in $\mathcal{F}$, i.e. $\{\mathcal{F}_t\}_{t\geqslant 0}$ is a filtration if

i. $\mathcal{F}_t \subseteq \mathcal{F}$ for each t
ii. if $t_1 \leqslant t_2$ then $\mathcal{F}_{t_1} \subseteq \mathcal{F}_{t_2}$

Let us assume that the σ-algebra $\mathcal{F}_t$ is the information set available at time t, which is increasing. If we want to have a mathematical description of the information set given by the history of prices we have to introduce the concept of σ-algebra generated by a set and by a random variable: if $C \in 2^{\Omega}$ is a subset of Ω then the σ-algebra $\sigma(C)$ generated by C is the smallest σ-algebra containing C; if $X : (\Omega, \mathcal{F}, \mathbb{P}) \to (E, \mathcal{E})$ is a random variable then the σ-algebra generated by X, denoted by $\sigma(X)$, is the σ-algebra $\sigma(X^{-1}(\mathcal{E}))$, generated by the subset $\{\omega \in \Omega | X(\omega) \in \mathcal{E}\} \subseteq \Omega$.

A *stochastic process* is a sequence of random variables indexed by a set $\mathcal{T}$: $\{X_t\}_{t\in\mathcal{T}}$. In particular, for each fixed t, the mapping $w \to X_t(\omega)$ is a random variable; for each $\omega \in \Omega$ fixed the mapping $t \to X_t(\omega)$ is a deterministic function of t, called the *trajectory* of X for the outcome ω.

We are now (finally) ready to describe the evolution of a price in the market: at every time t a certain information set $\mathcal{F}_t$ is given and a certain event $H \in \mathcal{F}_t$ happens; then the realization of the stochastic price $x = X_t(H)$ follows and the market operator can see it.

If we are in a *weak efficient* market then the only information available at time t is the history of the prices in the time interval $[0, t)$, so the information set at time t is given by the σ-algebra $\mathcal{F}_t^X = \sigma\left(\{X_u\}_{u\leqslant t}\right)$ that is the **smallest** σ-algebra generated by the history of the process.

In *semi-strong* form efficiency the information set is clearly bigger than $\mathcal{F}_t^X$: we also have to consider the public information $\mathcal{P}_t$; in this case the σ-algebra is given by $\bar{\mathcal{F}}_t = \sigma\left(\mathcal{F}_t^X \cup \mathcal{P}_t\right)$; in *strong efficiency* the information set $\hat{\mathcal{F}}_t$ is given by the history of prices $\left(\mathcal{F}_t^X\right)$, the public information $(\mathcal{P}_t)$ and also the private $(\mathcal{R}_t)$ information, so $\hat{\mathcal{F}}_t = \sigma\left(\mathcal{F}_t^X \cup \mathcal{P}_t \cup \mathcal{R}_t\right)$. It follows that

$$\mathcal{F}_t^X \subseteq \bar{\mathcal{F}}_t \subseteq \hat{\mathcal{F}}_t \tag{1.1}$$

1.2.2 Conditional Expectation

Another important concept in probability theory, useful here to describe the *efficiency* of the market, is that of *conditional expectation*. Let $(\Omega, \mathcal{F}, \mathbb{P})$ be a probability space, $X : \Omega \to \mathbb{R}$ a random variable and consider a σ-algebra $\mathcal{G} \subseteq \mathcal{F}$ included in $\mathcal{F}$. We would characterize $\mathbb{E}\left[X|\mathcal{G}\right]$, i.e. the expectation of X given that we have access to the information in $\mathcal{G}$. It is not trivial to formalize this notation, so we start with a simple intuition. Recall that the unconditional expected value is given by

$$\mathbb{E}[X] = \int_{\Omega} X(\omega) \cdot \mathbb{P}(d\omega)$$

which is a weighted average of the values of X with respect to the weights given by $\mathbb{P}$. Suppose now that we have access to this *extra information*: we know that all the possible events lie in a subset of Ω (in particular, a subset of $\mathcal{F}$), i.e. the only possible events one can observe form a subset $B \subset \mathcal{F}$ such that $\mathbb{P}(B) > 0$. It seems reasonable to normalize our probability measure $\mathbb{P}$ so that we have the total mass equal to unity on the space B. Thus we normalize the probabilities as $\frac{\mathbb{P}(d\omega)}{\mathbb{P}(B)}$ and consider the following *conditional expectation of X given B*

$$\mathbb{E}[X|B] = \frac{1}{\mathbb{P}(B)} \int_B X(w) \cdot \mathbb{P}(d\omega)$$

The next step, useful for understanding the "random aspect" of $E[\cdot|B]$ is the following. Suppose we have access to the information contained in a finite partition $\mathcal{P} = \{A_1, \ldots, A_N\}$ with $A_n \in \mathcal{F}$. Having access to $\mathcal{P}$ is equivalent to knowing in exactly which of the components $A_i \in \mathcal{P}$ the possible events one can observe lie. Once we know in exactly which component A_i of the partition the events lie, we can compute $\mathbb{E}[X|A_i]$. We may therefore define a mapping $\omega \to \mathbb{E}[X|A_n]$ if $\omega \in A_n$. This shows that the conditional expectation is itself a random variable and this leads to the following definition:

$$\mathbb{E}[X|\mathcal{P}](\omega) = \sum_{n=1}^{N} \mathbf{1}_{A_n}(\omega)\mathbb{E}[X|A_n]$$

We note also that $\mathbb{E}[X|\mathcal{P}]$ is $\sigma(\mathcal{P})$-measurable, being constant on each component of $\mathcal{P}$.

What happens when $\mathcal{P}$ is not only a finite partition, but a σ-algebra? The major problem is that $\mathbb{P}(A_n)$ could be 0 for some elements of $\mathcal{P}$. We have to take a more indirect approach, based, however, on the property previously obtained: let $(\Omega, \mathcal{F}, \mathbb{P})$ be a probability space and X a random variable s.t. $\mathbb{E}[X] < +\infty$. Let $\mathcal{G}$ be a σ-algebra in $\mathcal{F}$, i.e. $\mathcal{G} \subseteq \mathcal{F}$. We say that the random variable Z is the conditional expectation of X given the σ-algebra $\mathcal{G}$ if

i. Z is $\mathcal{G}$-measurable
ii. $\forall G \in \mathcal{G}$ it holds that

$$\int_G X(\omega)\mathbb{P}(d\omega) = \int_G Z(\omega)\mathbb{P}(d\omega)$$

We denote Z by the symbol $\mathbb{E}[X|\mathcal{G}]$.

There is an important property of the conditional expectation useful to describe and analyze the three forms of efficient market: assume that the σ-algebras $\mathcal{G}$ and $\mathcal{H}$ satisfy $\mathcal{H} \subseteq \mathcal{G} \subseteq \mathcal{F}$. Then the following equalities hold:

$$\mathbb{E}\left[\mathbb{E}[X|\mathcal{G}]|\mathcal{H}\right] = \mathbb{E}[X|\mathcal{H}] \tag{1.2}$$

$$\mathbb{E}[\mathbb{E}[X|\mathcal{G}]] = \mathbb{E}[X] \tag{1.3}$$

If X is $\mathcal{G}$-measurable then

$$\mathbb{E}[X|\mathcal{G}] = \mathbb{E}[X] \tag{1.4}$$

Let us consider the first property, called the *Law of Iterated Expectations*. It states that if we have two types of information sets $\mathcal{G}$ and $\mathcal{H}$ such that one is finer than the other (the information in $\mathcal{H}$ is also included in $\mathcal{G}$) then the knowledge of the extra information in $\mathcal{G}$ is useless for calculating the conditional expected value of X given the (smaller) information set $\mathcal{H}$.

Let us consider the three forms of market efficiency and the respective σ-algebras as in formula (1.1) and let R_t be the return of an asset at time t. We are now able to derive the following implications of market efficiency: strong form implies semi-strong form, which implies weak form. In fact, suppose the strong form of efficiency holds. Then:

$$\mathbb{E}[R_t|\hat{\mathcal{F}}_t] = 0$$

Now we can apply the rule of iterated expectations to obtain the semi-strong form:

$$\mathbb{E}[R_t|\bar{\mathcal{F}}_t] = \mathbb{E}[\mathbb{E}[R_t|\hat{\mathcal{F}}_t]|\bar{\mathcal{F}}_t] = 0$$

an analogous case to weak efficiency, implied by semi-strong efficiency.

1.3 MARTINGALE HYPOTHESIS

In the following we are going briefly to introduce the notion of *martingale*, which is a stochastic process with some peculiar properties. The role of this process in the Efficient Markets Hypothesis comes directly from the notion of *fair game*, basically a game which is neither in your favour nor in that of your opponent. In the classic financial literature the property of this kind of process represents well the *ideal* condition of an efficient market, where no players are supposed to have the rational chance to profit from trading activities. Historically, the martingale hypothesis has been the earliest model for financial asset prices and, under some assumptions, it still has important applications in modern theories.

Let's start with the definition. Given a probability space $(\Omega, \mathcal{F}, \mathbb{P})$ and a filtration $\{\mathcal{F}_t\}_{t\geqslant 0}$ a stochastic process $(X_t)_{t\geqslant 0}$ is said to be a *martingale* if the following conditions hold:

i. the process is *adapted to* $\mathcal{F}_t$, i.e. the random variable X_t is $\mathcal{F}_t$-measurable $\forall t \geqslant 0$. This condition is always verified if we consider the filtration generated by the process itself
ii. the process has a finite expectation: $\mathbb{E}(X_t) < \infty \quad \forall t \geqslant 0$
iii. $\mathbb{E}(X_t|\mathcal{F}_s) = X_s \qquad \forall s, t \quad s.t. \quad s \leqslant t$

Until now we have always considered the general case of continuous time models, i.e. models in which the time t belongs to an uncountable set $\mathcal{T}$ (for example, when $\mathcal{T}$ is an interval of the real line, $\mathcal{T} = [0, T]$). In some applications, in particular for statistical analysis, it is more convenient to consider *discrete* models, i.e. models in which the time t belongs to a countable set $\mathcal{T}$, for example, $\mathcal{T} = \{0, t_1, t_2, \ldots, t_i, \ldots T\}$. Even if this assumption appears a bit restrictive (discrete time models are a subset of continuous time models), modelling reality as a series of discrete events is not completely wrong: many events occur at discrete time points such as transaction ticks. In what follows we will continue to use the notation "t", meaning, however, that the set $\mathcal{T}$ to which t belongs is discrete, for simplicity $\mathcal{T}$ has the form $\mathcal{T} = \{0, 1, \ldots, t, t+1, \ldots, T\}$.

Let us now introduce P_t, defined as the price of an asset at time t; assume the asset's price behaves as a martigale. Condition iii in discrete time is rewritten as

$$\mathbb{E}[P_{t+1}|\mathcal{F}_t] = P_t$$

Now we introduce the process of returns (or errors) $(e_t)_{t \geqslant 0}$:

$$e_{t+1} = P_{t+1} - P_t$$

Using formula (1.4) and the fact that $\mathbb{E}[P_t|\mathcal{F}_t] = P_t$ we obtain:

$$\begin{aligned}\mathbb{E}[e_{t+1}|\mathcal{F}_t] &= \mathbb{E}\left[P_{t+1} - P_t|\mathcal{F}_t\right] = \\ &= \mathbb{E}\left[P_{t+1}|\mathcal{F}_t\right] - \mathbb{E}[P_t|\mathcal{F}_t] = \\ &= P_t - P_t = 0\end{aligned}$$

So the martingale hypothesis implies the following:

i. the best prediction of tomorrow's price P_{t+1}, given the asset's price history $\mathcal{F}_t$ available in t, is the current asset's price;
ii. the asset's expected returns, conditional on the asset's price history (or not conditional, using formula 1.3), is zero; which means that positive and negative returns are equally likely.

1.3.1 The Random Walk Hypothesis

The concept of martingale leads us to a closely related model: the Random Walk hypothesis. Basically this is the way to model an asset's price consistently with the efficient market hypothesis; in fact, if the EHM hypothesis holds, there is no reason to expect changes in the price level between t and $t+1$ because the price P_t, currently observable on the market, contains all the available relevant information. The unique reason that could lead to a change in the price level is the arrival of "news", prediction errors, that are supposed to be zero mean and not correlated to all the past information available at time t. In formula, the model is described by the following equation:

$$P_{t+1} = P_t + e_{t+1}$$

where e_t are supposed to be pairwise independent and identically distributed with mean 0 and variance σ^2, i.e. $e_t \sim \text{iid}\left(0, \sigma^2\right)$. However, observation of financial markets suggests that we should assume a positive trend in the price process in order to allow an asset's price to yield a non-zero expected return; so it is necessary to include a non-zero expected return for modelling an asset's price (see Keith Cuthbertson and Dirk Nitzsche, 2004). To include this property, we can consider a slightly different process called Random Walk with drift:

$$P_{t+1} = P_t + \mu + e_{t+1}$$

with μ denoting the expected price change. Using formulas this leads to the following relationship:

$$\mathbb{E}[P_{t+1}|\mathcal{F}_t] = P_t + \mu$$

The independence of the increments implies not only the uncorrelation between increments, but also the uncorrelation of any other non-linear function of these increments. We may observe that a random walk process with drift can be described as an AR(1) process with drift:

$$P_t = \mu + \theta P_{t-1} + \varepsilon_t$$

where P_t denotes the price of an asset at time t, μ stands for the drift and $\theta = 1$ corresponds to a unit root. When $\theta = 1$ the process can also be seen as

$$\Delta P_t = \mu + \varepsilon_t$$

showing that a random walk process with drift is a difference stationary process, which means a first-differencing produces a stationary time series $\mathbb{E}[\Delta P_t] = \mu$. To verify that the random walk is the true process of a given asset's price time series, it is necessary to test this hypothesis empirically. The non-stationary of a time series can also be given by the presence of a deterministic time trend process. This happens when a general AR(1) model is extended to be

$$Y_t = \mu + \theta Y_{t-1} + \gamma t + \varepsilon_t$$

In this case non-stationary could be caused by the presence of time trend ($\gamma \neq 0$). This non-stationary process can be removed by regressing the dependent variable against t. So a general procedure to test whether P_t follows a random walk process, against its opposite, involves running a regression for the differentiated series of a general random walk (known to be a difference stationary process). In formulas:

$$P_t = \mu + \theta P_{t-1} + \gamma t + \varepsilon_t$$

$$\Delta P_t = \mu + \theta P_{t-1} - P_{t-1} + \gamma t + \varepsilon_t$$

$$\Delta P_t = \mu + (\theta - 1) P_{t-1} + \gamma t + \varepsilon_t$$

So, considering the last equation, the null hypothesis we would like to test corresponds to

$$H_0 : \mu = \gamma = (\theta - 1) = 0$$

Avoiding testing these conditions jointly, assuming that restrictions on deterministic trend and deterministic time trend are satisfied, it is enough to compare the t-ratio of the associated coefficient $(\theta - 1)$ upon the critical values of the Augmented Dickey-Fuller test.

1.3.2 Sequences and Reversal, Cowles Jones Test: Theoretical Framework

Recalling the random walk without drift, it is possible to formulate an equivalent model for the natural logarithm of prices P_t as

$$p_t = \mu + p_{t-1} + \varepsilon_t \qquad \varepsilon_t \approx \text{IID}(0, \sigma^2)$$

where $p_t = \log(P_t)$. Let us now define the continuously compounded return of an asset as

$$r_t = p_t - p_{t-1}$$

We can test if these are really distributed as a white noise process, as postulated. If we introduce a binary function I_t that returns 1 if at time t the compounded returns of an asset are positive, and 0 if the reverse holds (in formula 1 if $r_t < 0$, and 0 if $r_t > 0$), it is possible to recover the number of sequence (pair of returns with the same sign) and reversals (pair of returns with the opposite sign) in historical returns. Given the fact that the error component, ε_t, of a driftless martingale is symmetric and with zero mean, the test aims to check if the number of positive returns equals the number of negative returns (as implied by the random walk hypothesis). A way to test this hypothesis, proposed by Cowles and Jones (See Campbell, lo and MacKinley (1997) for more details on this and the following tests), is to compare the frequency of sequences and reversals in a time series. Considering a sample of $T + 1$ returns for a given asset, the number of sequences should be expressed as a function of I_t. Let Y_t be defined as

$$Y_t = I_t I_{t+1} + (1 - I_t)(1 - I_{t+1})$$

then the number of sequences (N_s) and the number of reversals (N_r) are defined as follows:

$$N_s = \sum_{t=1}^{T} Y_t \qquad N_r = T - N_s$$

and the estimator of the probabilities to observe sequences and reversals are respectively defined as

$$\hat{\pi}_s = \frac{N_s}{T}$$

and

$$\hat{\pi}_r = \frac{N_r}{T}$$

So the Cowles-Jones (CJ) statistic is defined as

$$\widehat{\text{CJ}} = \frac{\hat{\pi}_s}{1 - \hat{\pi}_s}$$

and should be equal to 1 according to the martingale hypothesis. Empirically the test should consider both overlapping and non-overlapping returns leading to the derivation of different distributions for the null hypothesis. Moreover, the assumption of zero drift in price pattern is not realistic; so including a positive drift in the model sequences becomes more likely than reversal simply because the drift introduces a positive trend into the process. For this reason the CJ has to be bigger then 1 in this case and, consequently, the theoretical distribution of the statistic should be corrected. In general for a random walk model with drift, considering overlapping returns, the CJ statistic is distributed according to

$$\widehat{\text{CJ}} \approx N\left(\frac{\pi_s}{1 - \pi_s}, \frac{\pi_s(1 - \pi_s) + 2(\pi^3 + (1 - \pi)^3 - \pi_s^2)}{T(1 - \pi_s)^4}\right)$$

where

$$\pi = Pr\,(r_t > 0) = \Phi\left(\frac{\mu}{\sigma}\right)$$

taking μ and σ as empirical average and standard deviation of the sample considered.

1.3.3 Variance Ratio Tests

The random walk hypothesis has a great impact on the variance and covariance structure of returns. We are going to show how under this model, the variance of a certain increment, over a given time interval, is simply a linear function of the time interval under consideration. Recalling that the continuously compounded return of an asset is defined as

$$r_t = p_t - p_{t-1}$$

considering a series obtained by adding n consecutive returns observations, the n-period continuously compounded return is given by

$$r_{t,t+n} = r_{t+1} + r_{t+2} + r_{t+n}$$

and we show that

$$\begin{aligned} \text{var}(r_{t,t+n}) &= \text{var}(r_{t+1} + r_{t+2} + \ldots + r_{t+n}) \\ &= \text{var}(e_{t+1} + e_{t+2} + \ldots + e_{t+n}) \end{aligned}$$

$$= n \ \mathrm{var}(e_t)$$
$$= n \ \mathrm{var}(r_t)$$

So if the random walk hypothesis holds the variance of a multiperiod return as n times the variance of a single period return, where n denotes the numbers of time interval considered. Suppose we now want to assess whether a given series behaves as a random walk process. One way of doing this is to definc a variance of a two-period compounded return and test if the first-order autocorrelation coefficient differs from 0. In fact, consider that a two-period compounded return is defined as

$$\begin{aligned}\mathrm{var}(r_{t,t+2}) &= \mathrm{var}(r_{t+1} + r_{t+2}) \\ &= 2 \ \mathrm{var}(r_t) + 2 \ \mathrm{cov}(r_t, r_{t+1})\end{aligned}$$

So, if we define a "VR" as the ratio between the variance of a two-period return and two times the variance of the corresponding one-period return, under the random walk model this ratio must have some defined properties. In particular, considering the variance ratio for a two-period compounded return we can show that

$$\begin{aligned}\mathrm{VR}(2) &= \frac{\mathrm{var}(r_{t,t+2})}{2 \ \mathrm{var}(r_t)} \\ &= \frac{2 \ \mathrm{var}(r_t) + 2 \ \mathrm{cov}(r_t, r_{t+1})}{2 \ \mathrm{var}(r_t)} \\ &= 1 + \rho_1\end{aligned}$$

As discussed under the random walk model the returns are pairwise independent, so the first-order autocorrelation coefficient must be zero. The presence of a positive or negative autocorrelation coefficient leads to different VR values denoting different behaviour for the series, in particular:

- $\rho_1 > 0$ leads to $VR(2) > 1$ and denotes Mean Aversion
- $\rho_1 < 0$ leads to $VR(2) < 1$ and denotes Mean Reversion

and so distance from the random walk model. It is possible to generalize this analysis and the general rule for an n period Variance Ratio follows:

$$\mathrm{VR}(n) = \frac{\mathrm{var}(r_{t,t+n})}{n \ \mathrm{var}(r_t)} = 1 + 2\sum_{k=1}^{n-1}\left(1 - \frac{k}{n}\right)\rho_k$$

According to the above formula it is possibile to see that even for high order multi-period returns the variance is still a particular linear combination of the first n-1 autocorrelation coefficient of the considered series. The null hypothesis of white noise can be tested computing the standardized statistic for the variance ratio that, for overlapping returns, is distributed as follows:

$$\sqrt{nT}(\mathrm{VR}(n) - 1) \approx N\left(0, \frac{2(2n-1)(n-1)}{3n}\right)$$

So we can test if the standardized statistic for the Variance Ratio:

$$\sqrt{\frac{nT}{\text{theoretical} \quad \text{variance}}}\left(\widehat{\mathrm{VR}}(n) - 1\right) \approx N(0, 1)$$

lies outside the interval $[-1.645, 1.645]$ at 95% confidence level. If it lies outside the interval, the random walk hypothesis can be rejected.

1.4 VIOLATIONS OF EMH AND BEHAVIOURAL FINANCE

Traditional financial theory teaches us that market participants are rational subjects endowed with a certain homogeneous informational set; are to be considered irrational all those behaviours that deviate from this interpretation.

Market models defined according to this kind of traditional approach should be characterized by a large proportion of market players acting rationally with respect to their information set and a smaller proportion of irrational agents acting inconsistently. The rational majority should realize higher returns than the irrational minority and in any case no extra returns with respect to the market as a whole can be realized by anyone if the market is somehow efficient (in fact, we cannot imagine that the majority of market players retain relevant private information not reflected in market prices). Under this framework, after a certain period of time the minority of irrational players should be eliminated from the market and simultaneously an increasing quantity of relevant information should be reflected in prices, making the market ever more efficient. The final results should be the end of trading activity since extra returns cannot even be expected and realized by market participants.

However the reality of financial trading of the past century does not say that. Trading activity has grown consistently through time in terms of both transacted volumes and number of participants.

Should we imagine that the world (at least the financial one!) is full of irrational people? Obviously not. In reality, traditional financial theory does not say anything about the real cognitive and decision-making process (or a realistic representation of them). If we consider realistically those aspects we can explain market distortions, albeit without being able to forecast them.

Traders are human beings with their own perception of the surrounding reality, their own psychology and fears of failure. The economic consequences of those deviating behaviours cannot be explained under the framework of traditional theories and are usually labelled anomalies. Behavioural finance is the discipline (formally born in the 1970s) which tries to integrate individual behavioural attitudes into financial theory.

After the pioneering work on behavioural economics by Kahneman and Tversky (1974; 1979) we can say that Richard Thaler (1999) has definitely closed the gap between the normative approach of traditional financial theory and the descriptive one of behavioural financial economics. The first milestone of behavioural theory deals with the way information is gathered and elaborated to support the decision-making process. Typically, financial agents use an heuristic approach.

Heuristic rules generally work well but can sometimes create serious systematic errors. Three typical heuristic behaviours can be identified and studied: similarity, availability and anchoring. Similarity is the tendency of market agents to refer to stereotypes (a similar situation in the past) before taking decisions. This attitude often drives analysts to "overreact" (in positive or negative ways) to real information, by being over optimistic in all those situations that had a positive outcome in the past, and vice versa. Overconfidence is also connected with similarity since positive past performances induce an overestimate of our forecasting capacity.

Availability is a cognitive model studied in depth by Kahneman and Tversky (1974). It is related to the fact that single agents estimate the likely of occurrence of a certain event based on the frequency and clarity of memories of similar events "available" in their minds. The availability cognitive model tends to be incorrect whenever a structural change affects the market. The third heuristic behaviour is anchorage, which is the natural propensity of agents to be unconsciously influenced by remote axioms or hypotheses. Anchorage helps to explain some recurrent errors in decision-making processes such as the overestimate of the probability of joint events and the underestimate of the probability of disjoint events. Anchorage is also linked to some forms of decisional conservatism.

In general, economic agents tend to prefer the status quo to the purchase of a new position. Various heuristic behaviours tend to combine, sometimes producing smoothing effects and at other times exponential effects. In any case, what occur are behavioural deviations from the expected rational approach.

The cognitive mistakes examined so far deal with heuristic models of information, research and elaboration. Together with these there are other factors affecting the decision-making process that belong rather to the strict emotional sphere of the decision maker. One of them is aversion to ambiguity. Aversion to ambiguity is related to fear of the unknown and the preference that agents display for what is somehow familiar. A particular case of aversion to ambiguity is represented by aversion to regret. The knowledge that a certain decision will result ex-post facto in wrong decisions ingenerates inactivity in many market players. Inactivity is only one of the important implications of aversion to regret; another is the attention to what the other players are doing. The same wrong decision made by the majority of market players is less important than a wrong decision taken by a single agent.

Another field of interesting research into behavioural finance concerns the analysis of the way operators express their preferences. In orthodox financial theory all decisions should be made according to the so-called expected utility principle. Nevertheless, empirical evidence shows that investors evaluate investment decisions under uncertainty violating expected utility theory. In particular, Kahneman and Tversky (1979) analyze three principal deviations from the expected utility scheme. Namely: certainty effect, reflection effect and isolation effect. All three effects reflect an incorrect way, displayed by agents, of assessing probabilities. The certainty effect leads people to overevaluate certain events and, on the other hand, to take extremely risky decisions when the associated probabilities are low. Certainty effect is very evident in asset allocation processes. Empirically, a lot of wealth is allocated (beyond any rational expectation) to low volatility assets. On the other hand, observation of national lotteries shows that when the success probability is extremely low people's attention is mainly focused on the potential gain. The higher the jackpot the lower is the importance of objective probability of success. Empirical evidence also shows that, despite traditional risk definition embedded in expected utility theory, potential losses and gains are not considered symmetrically by agents (reflection effects). Typically, in the face of potential gains market players show risk aversion, while facing potential losses they show more risk vocation. In other words, the "reflection" of potential returns around the zero changes subjects' attitude to risk. The isolation effect is the natural inclination of market participants to neglect common elements among different decisional options and to concentrate their attention uniquely on differential aspects. This way of processing information may lead an to inconsistent preference structure.

To complete the list of violation of the EMH, we will now look briefly at the limitation of the no arbitrage principle as the equilibrator principle of financial market dynamics. The over-efficient Markets Hypothesis is based on the concept that free lunches are not allowed consistently through time. When they exist, arbitrageurs exploit them immediately, pushing back the market to the original equilibrium situation. Empirical evidence shows that risk-free arbitrages are extremely rare and difficult to exploit because of market frictions, lack of liquidity and other constraints that may limit the operational activity of market players (e.g. they are not allowed short selling, or tight stop loss limits). The simultaneous lack of effective and efficient arbitrageurs and the presence of non fully rational operators may determine inefficient market situations.

1.5 INFORMATION ASYMMETRIES AND ACCELERATING PROCESSES

The violations of EMH examined in the previous section deal in the main with the lack of rationality of market participants. Those deviations of empirical evidence from mainstream theory are not the only ones. One of the most important premises of traditional financial theory is the assumption of perfect (or almost perfect) information. The relaxation of this assumption was introduced into traditional neoclassical economic analysis by eminent economists such as Joseph Stiglitz as soon as it became evident how unrealistic this assumption was. Nevertheless, even today, many trained economists and particularly financial economists continue to consider the relaxation of the assumption of perfect information as unusual. To assume perfect information is a monstrous distortion of reality. All economic activity is based on the fact that information is not perfectly and equally created and distributed. In a world with perfect information there would no need for firms such as Bloomberg or Reuters to exchange information. Analysts would not spend time studying corporate figures. The entire financial sector, including the banking sector, would not exist since all players would always be perfectly endowed with the exact quantity of goods or assets they needed. Economists and traders would not exist either. Information is the very heart of economic activity.

People and companies make money out of other people and companies just because they use information that the others do not have. The existence of financial markets is evidence of the fact that information asymmetries cannot be eliminated just by intense trading activity. It is also interesting to analyze the essence of information.

It is usually assumed, or at least perceived, that the nature of information is independent of the subject that is observing or using it. Even assuming that the root of information is independent of the first subject that is observing it, the flow of this information signal, from one subject to another, will change the original signal into a new one. Hence, information can be created, and the process of information creation reflects the relative importance of the subject through which the information is passing. In essence we can say that information creation is a social process and, like every social and human process, it cannot be mapped exactly with a simple model.

In financial markets, a very important phenomenon related to the dynamics of information is the class of so-called feedback loop processes, in other words all those processes connected to acceleration (or deceleration) of information flow speed. There are many factors connected to the way information is processed by people (and hence new information is created), which act as accelerators for the normal speed of information flow. Especially in recent times, due to the improvement of information technology and the increase in the relative importance of finance and financial markets in our lives, accelerating factors are becoming extremely important for the explanation of financial market dynamics.

The growing interest that public information media have recently accorded finance is one of the most important accelerating factors today. Almost all newspapers and TV news now dedicate significant tranches of column space or air time to financial news, often reporting analysts' opinions together with facts. In doing so they necessarily transmit in a simplified way an information signal created in a professional environment to a non-professional one, a simplification that often leads to bias of the original content or message. Moreover, the simple fact that common mass media discuss financial issues induces in ordinary people the idea that finance should necessarily be a part of their lives.

In addition, we should also note that the border-line between reporting a fact and commenting on it is thin, especially if the comment emanates from people who have an interest in conveying a certain message instead of another one. At their very heart, financial services are products which have to be sold. Marketing tools and publicity work for financial services as for all other products. Not surprisingly, the increase of interest in finance shown by ordinary people is often accompanied by an increase in the tools for accessing financial services.

Other accelerating factors relate more to individual or social psychology, such as excess of confidence; some others relate more to the cultural model that predominates at that particular time; others again are purely economic factors like credit expansion processes or liquidity illusions.

The common feature of many of the accelerating factors is that they usually induce a feedback loop process. Initial increase or decrease of financial asset prices (due, for example, to one of the accelerating factors described) causes an additional increase or decrease which retroactively again pushes prices up or down. Basically, what one has is a *vicious circle*. Feedback loop processes are often considered a main cause of the speculative bubbles that have characterized recent financial history. At other times, feedback loop processes are also induced by powerful financial operators in order to take advantage of the creation of a bubble and when it bursts.

1.6 THE PECULIAR STRUCTURE AND NATURE OF ENERGY COMMODITIES MARKETS

All the concepts, theories and deviations described so far do not refer directly to energy commodities markets but have been developed and tested in depth (if not exclusively) in traditional and mature financial sectors like stocks or fixed income markets. When we try to approach the study of energy commodities markets from the perspective of traditional (or less traditional) efficiency analysis, we need to consider carefully and evaluate the following factors:

a) energy global market liberalization is recent and largely incomplete; hence energy commodities trading is a relatively recent and immature business (excluding oil);
b) the financial energy industry is fundamentally linked to its physical production industry.

Without considering oil trading, which is a long-established trading business, most energy markets have only recently liberalized and consequently trading activities have only recently started on them. The gas and power liberalization process only started in the late 1990s, and only in more advanced countries is it really possible to conduct proper trading activity. Carbon markets are also a recent phenomenon since officially they only started up in Europe after 2005. Basically, in a very short period of time we have observed an increasing flow of capital and interest towards energy markets as a whole, but obviously not all the subsectors have received the same attention and not all of them have followed the same path of development in the same time frame. Hence, some fields like oil (which traditionally is characterized by significant trading volumes) basically behave and interact like a typical financial market with a high degree of efficiency and information fluidity. Some other sectors or local markets, like most European power markets, still suffer from scarce liquidity and information asymmetries which prevent them from being examples of efficient markets.

The observed tendency is towards integration between different sectors of the global energy market but the speed and direction of this process are still uncertain. Even sectors which have traditionally been considered as local markets, like natural gas (due to production and transportation constraints), are becoming more and more global commodity markets. Market integration together with growing interest of financial investors and traders lead to a growing number of transactions and hence to an increasing efficiency of energy markets as a whole.

Lack of integration leads to market niches which is equivalent in trading language to potential persistent arbitrage conditions which are evident violations of the EMH as discussed in this section. We may hence expect that in the energy sector, some markets like oil, where we can try to apply and test for the traditional efficient market hypothesis, to be manifest, and some others like gas or power where we should expect to observe this hypothesis fail to represent real market dynamics. Another important source of inefficiency of energy markets may relate to the significant link that some energy commodity prices display with respect to the underlying physical production process. This link brings forth two significant (for our purposes) implications: industrial processes represent fundamental exogenous variables for price dynamics; and market segmentation.

The first implication is trivial but also tremendously important. Energy is a commodity that has to be produced, extracted, transformed and physically transported by means of complex and capital intensive industrial processes. Moreover, the industrial energy sector is dominated by a few big players who in effect determine (in some circumstances) market conditions. It is clear that the dynamics and the variability of the energy production process impact on the dynamics of the energy price. Obviously, depending on the kind of energy commodity we consider, we may find that the impact is more evident in the short term, as in power spot markets, or in the medium long term, as in oil or gas markets.

When the degree of efficiency of the energy market we are considering is insufficiently developed, we can have a scenario where the energy price signal does not immediately reflect relevant shocks in the production system. This translates immediately into a trading advantage for those players who can access this kind of information sooner than others. Moreover, since most energy markets are physically and financially interrelated, we usually observe a propagation of fundamental shocks among different energy sectors, so that the same informational advantage can be multiply exploited before becoming public (i.e. before being completely reflected by a price change). The second implication is less trivial but still extremely important for explaining potential arbitrages that can emerge and persist in energy markets. Energy markets participants can be divided into two groups: industrial players willing to hedge their natural exposure and traders willing to make profits from trading energy commodities (physically or financially). Industrial players usually try to reach their economic goals with their industrial activity, using trading only for optimization or risk reduction purposes. Many of them (obviously, not the most advanced) participate in the market only occasionally even if the exposure they manage is not negligible at all. Clearly, they cannot have the same informational level and operational efficiency as a professional trader who stays in front of their screen 10 hours a day. Naturally, the value of the arbitrages they can introduce into the market is the shadow price of the informational and professional lack they decided to have. On the other hand, professional traders (sometimes called speculators, giving the word a bad name) take advantage of potential arbitrages but their activity is not strong or significant enough (in terms of traded volumes) to push back prices to their equilibrium level. This situation is typical of an energy market dominated by industrial players. In some cases, oil markets in particular, the number and the relative importance of professional traders representing the interests of non-industrial players are so huge that market price dynamics can be completely disconnected from industrial fundamentals being mainly driven by financial market sentiment. Usually, this kind of deviation should not be very persistent because the physical link between physical demand–supply interaction cannot be ignored or overturned indefinitely. Market segmentation in the energy field is pretty natural especially considering that energy markets are largely emerging markets. This phenomenon can be expected to gradually disappear as markets and market participants mature, but for today it is an important fact that has to be carefully considered.

1.7 EHM IN ENERGY COMMODITIES MARKETS: SOME EVIDENCE FROM DATA

As previously discussed, the random walk model implies unit root process in level and difference-stationary processes. To test this hypothesis we would like to run the Augmented Dickey-Fuller (ADF) test on given series for three different commodities prices: oil, natural gas and power. Again, the purpose of this analysis is to understand how information is worked out by agents in different energy markets. We would like to start by checking the EMH, by means of the well-known ADF test, in a market which is considered the most "financial" of these three: the oil market.

Starting from the oil side, we use a data set of 5,933 observations on WTI (West Texas Intermediate) 1 month ahead futures prices, considering the closing price series starting from 01/07/1986 up to 01/03/2010 (source: Bloomberg). We start by testing for the presence of unit root in the level, including constant and linear trend in the regression run, and so we would like to test the unit root presence by regressing the oil price via the following equation:

$$P_t = \mu + \theta P_{t-1} + \gamma t + \varepsilon_t.$$

The null hypothesis we are going to test is

$$H_0 : \theta = 1$$

over the alternative hypothesis:

$$H_0 : \theta < 1.$$

The test is taken comparing the standard t-statistic $t_\theta = \frac{\hat{\theta}}{(\mathrm{se}(\hat{\theta}))}$ against critical t-statistic value as per the original paper by Dickey-Fuller (1979).

As per the output in Table 1.1 the t-statistic of the estimated coefficient is greater than the critical level, so we cannot reject the null hypothesis, and the test gives the evidence for unit root presence in the true process governing the price pattern.

Table 1.1 ADF on WTI daily prices

		t-statistic
Augmented Dickey-Fuller test statistic		−2.230870
	1% level	−3.959584
Test critical values:	5% level	−3.410562
	10% level	−3.127053
Kolmogorov-Smirnov	95% level	P-value 3.1075e-097

As we know, unit root implies a difference-stationary process, as we can test by regressing the following equation, and we shall verify that the reverse does not hold; hence some series are difference-stationary but not unit root process. Starting with the WTI series, we regress the equation:

$$\Delta P_t = \mu + (\theta - 1)P_{t-1} + \gamma t + \varepsilon_t$$

Defining "α" as $(1 - \theta)$, the null hypothesis we are going to test now is:

$$H_0 : \alpha = 0$$

over the alternative hypothesis:

$$H_0 : \alpha < 0.$$

The regression outputs shown in Table 1.2 are under the critical level, so we reject the null hypothesis in the direction of $H_0 : \alpha < 0$ and the test thus gives evidence of stationary-difference series, implying that random walk properties are likely in the true process underlying the WTI prices. Finally, let us consider the residual of the regression; according to the random walk model, the error components are supposed to be i.i.d. A common assumption in financial literature is that logarithmic returns basically the errors of the random walk model as defined, are normally distributed. A Kolmogorov-Smirnov taken on the error series at 95% level, as the Normal fit illustrated in Figure 1.1, shows instead distance from the Gaussian assumption. Moreover, the i.i.d. assumption also implies homoscedasticity of the errors, and we should also verify distance from this assumption by performing a Breusch-Pagan test. As is generally assumed, the hypothesis of efficient markets seems to be realistic for the oil market. And, as previously stated, this kind of product is now perceived by investors to be a financial rather than a physical asset and not

Table 1.2 ADF on WTI daily returns

		t-statistic
Augmented Dickey-Fuller test statistic		−58.71645
	1% level	−3.959584
Test critical values:	5% level	−3.410562
	10% level	−3.127053

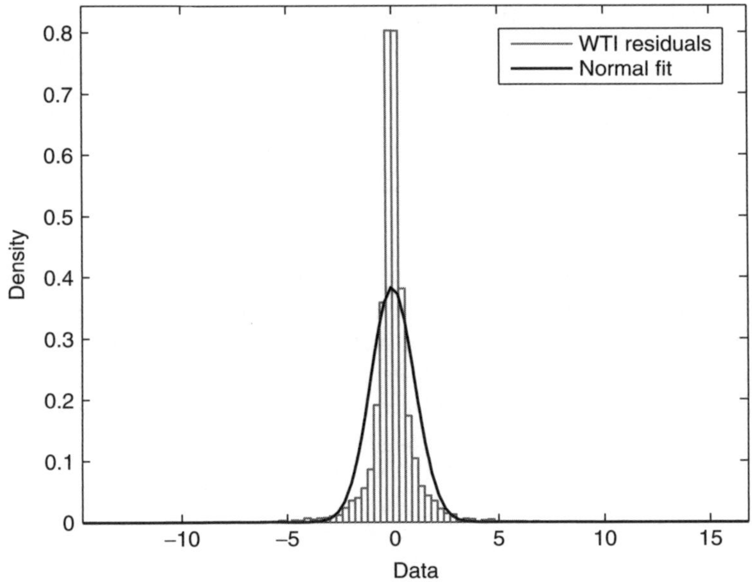

Figure 1.1 Residual normal fit on WTI series

only industrial but purely financial operators also access this market. Obviously, the ways these different classes of agent elaborate the flows of information coming from the market are different, and so the price pattern of this commodity has been widely affected by the advent of this class of operator.

It is interesting now to run the same analysis on the gas market and verify what kind of efficiency level is in place. In particular, we use a data set of 4,960 observations on Henry Hub 1 month ahead futures prices, considering the closing price series starting from 01/04/1990 up to 01/03/2010 (source: Bloomberg). Let us start by testing the presence of unit root in the level, as we did before, including the constant and linear trend in the regression run. This led us to reject, even if near the threshold, the null hypothesis of unit root, excluding the random walk model, as the true process (Table 1.3).

We know that if a series is a unit root process the first difference series is stationary, but the reverse does not hold. In fact, on the first difference series the

Table 1.3 ADF on Henry Hub daily prices

		t-statistic
Augmented Dickey-Fuller test statistic		−3.673155
	1% level	−3.959592
Test critical values:	5% level	−3.410712
	10% level	−3.127143
Kolmogorov-Smirnov	95% level	P-value 0.0121

Table 1.4 ADF on HH daily returns

		t-statistic
Augmented Dickey-Fuller test statistic		−71.25818
Test critical values:	1% level	−3.959592
	5% level	−3.410712
	10% level	−3.127143

regression outputs, shown in Table 1.4, are below the critical level, so we reject the null hypothesis in the direction of $H_0 : \alpha < 0$ and the test thus gives evidence of stationary-difference series, as for the oil series. So the series is stationary-difference, but not a random walk because it does not exhibit unit root in the level.

Again, the residuals of the model are not Gaussian according to Kolmogorov-Smirnov taken on the error series, as the normal fit chart shows in Figure 1.2. Moreover, the i.i.d assumption of homoscedasticity of the errors is rejected according to the Breusch-Pagan test.

Finally, the same analysis has been under taken on the more liquid European power market: the EEX (German power market). In particular, we have used a data set of 2,000 observations on EEX power contract month ahead futures prices, considering the closing price series starting from 12/03/1999 up to 01/03/2010 (source: Bloomberg). Again, we test for the presence of unit root including constant and linear trend in the regression. The results, shown in Table 1.5, satisfy the null hypothesis, even if near to the threshold.

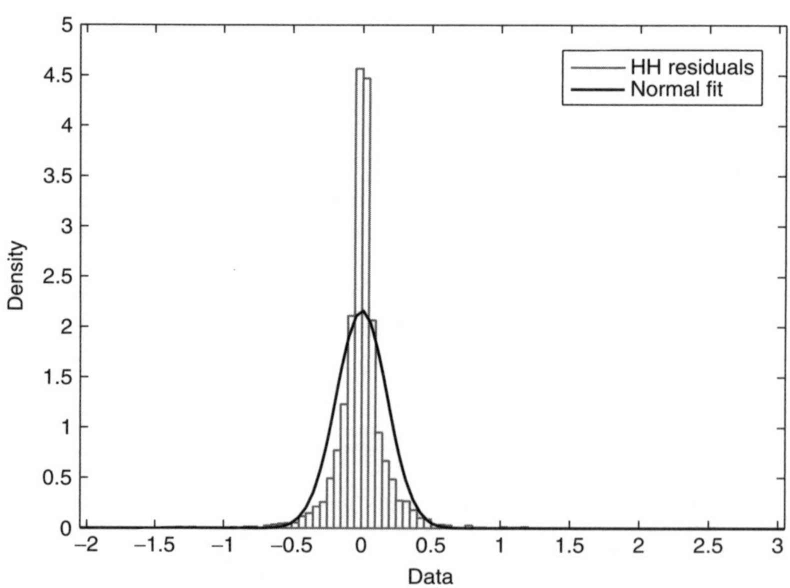

Figure 1.2 Residual normal fit on HH series

Table 1.5 ADF on EEX daily prices

		t-statistic
Augmented Dickey-Fuller test statistic		−2.786220
Test critical values:	1% level	−3.962641
	5% level	−3.412059
	10% level	−3.127941
Kolmogorov-Smirnov	95% level	P-value 0.0231

Table 1.6 ADF on EEX daily returns

		t-statistic
Augmented Dickey-Fuller test statistic		−40.43467
Test critical values:	1% level	−3.962641
	5% level	−3.412059
	10% level	−3.127941

On the first difference series the regression outputs, shown in Table 1.6, are below the critical level, so we reject the null hypothesis in the direction of $H_0 : \alpha < 0$. The test thus gives evidence of stationary-difference series, as for the oil series. So the series is stationary-difference, and likely to be governed by a random walk model, even if the test gives results closer to critical levels. Again, the residuals of the model are not Gaussian (see figure 1.3), and the homoscedasticity of the errors

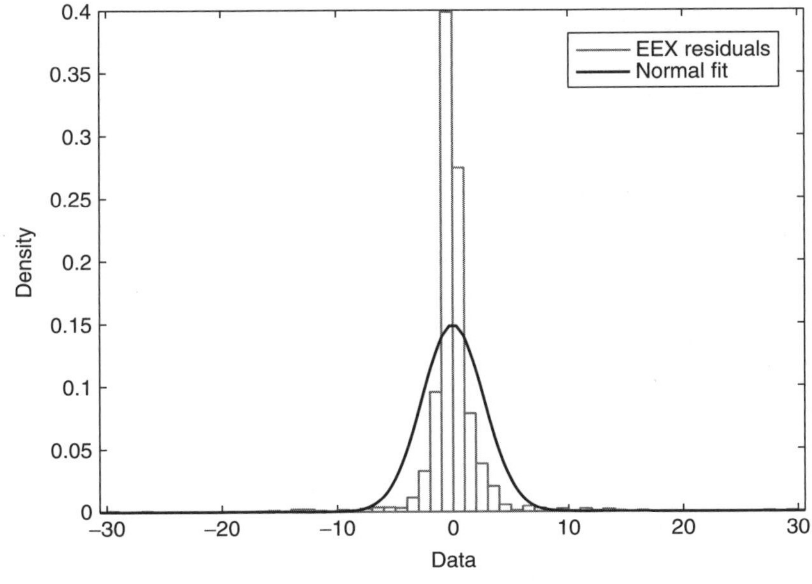

Figure 1.3 Residual normal fit on EEX series

is rejected. In conclusion, we could state that the oil market is the unique market that shows clearly a price series likely to be generated by a random walk model, while gas and power markets do not reach the same efficiency level according to the same model. This is basically consistent with the market segmentation and the different operators involved across different markets. Local or not perfectly integrated markets (like gas and power) are characterized by industrial or commercial agents that manage their natural exposure, but not necessarily by taking positions on pure information/price signal on a regular basis. So a highly integrated market such as the oil one, shows a higher degree of efficiency than the power or gas market. In respect of residuals of the equations considered for the three markets, we may note distance from normality and homoscedasticity assumptions, while a graphical inspection suggests the need to consider almost leptokurtic distributions.

Another way to test the efficiency level of a market is by the Cowles-Jones (CJ) test which aims to check whether, statistically, positive trends are more likely than negative ones. In efficient markets, financial operators should be able to elaborate immediately relevant information that justifies a rally or downside in prices; so over long time periods the possibility of observing pairs of consecutive positive (negative) returns have to be negligible under the EMH assumption. In the following we are going to run the Cowles-Jones test on the data set presented in the previous section (Oil WTI, Gas Henry Hub and Power EEX). For each time series we show the empirical CJ value and the theoretical CJ value with the standard deviation of its distribution in order to verify if the in-sample test differs statistically from 1. For the oil time series the test returns a value of 0.990949 (see Table 1.7); the distance from the theoretical CJ value is smaller than the standard deviation of the statistic distribution. This leads us to reject the hypothesis that the difference is statistically different from 0, and so the oil market is shown to be an efficient market according to this test.

Running the same test on gas and power time series we get respectively values of 1.031071 and 1.191886 for the CJ statistic (see Tables 1.8 and 1.9); in both cases the distance from the theoretical CJ value is greater than the standard deviation of the statistic distribution. This leads us to accept the distance from the theoretical value as statistically different from 0, and to state that the gas and power markets are not efficient according to the random walk hypothesis when set against the CJ test. Again this reinforces the general assumption, which is also confirmed by

Table 1.7 WTI Cowles Jones

Mean	0.000319	
Std. Dev.	0.025044	
π	0.505081	
π_s	0.500052	
Theoretical CJ at 95%	1.000207	
Empirical CJ	0.990949	
Difference	−0.009258	
	Mean	Variance
CJ theoretical distribution	1.000207	0.00067
CJ Std. Dev.	0.025958	

Table 1.8 HH Cowles Jones

Mean	0.000183	
Std. Dev.	0.037021	
π	0.501975	
π_s	0.500008	
Theoretical CJ at 95%	1.000031	
Empirical CJ	1.031071	
Difference	0.031040	
	Mean	Variance
CJ theoretical distribution	1.000031	0.000805
CJ Std. Dev.	0.028368	

Table 1.9 EEX Cowles Jones

Mean	0.000145	
Std. Dev.	0.080724	
π	0.500715	
π_s	0.500001	
Theoretical CJ at 95%	1.000004	
Empirical CJ	1.191886	
Difference	0.191882	
	Mean	Variance
CJ theoretical distribution	1.000004	0.002001
CJ Std. Dev.	0.044733	

the previous test, of different market segmentation between a global and financial market (such as the oil market) and more local and physical ones (gas and power).

The final test we would like to run on these series is the "Variance Ratio"; here the underlying assumption relies on the autocorrelation structure implied by the random walk model. Again, the assumption is that operators must have a rational chance to forecast future trend observing price history. Does that assumption hold true for energy markets? Hence, in the following, we report the results for a Variance Ratio test on the Brent, gas and power data set used above. We report the Variance Ratio value on two-period overlapping returns for each series and the associated values for the confidence statistic level at 95%. For the oil time series we get the parameters in Table 1.10, while Table 1.11 and 1.12 report results for gas and power.

The variance of asymptotic distribution is 4, and the associated standardized statistic is −0.706841192, which falls inside the boundaries at 95% confidence

Table 1.10 WTI variance ratio

n selected period	2
T number of observations	5939
1 period returns variance	0.000627244
2 period returns variance	0.001238217
Variance Ratio	0.987028799
H_0 standardized statistic	−0.706841192

Table 1.11 HH variance ratio

n selected period	2
T number of observations	4958
1 period returns variance	0.001372447
2 period returns variance	0.002656375
Variance Ratio	0.96775136
H_0 standardized statistic	1.605645493

level. So we cannot reject the null hypothesis and we confirm that the random walk assumption is validated for the oil series. The same statistic applies for the gas series.

For the gas series, the variance of asymptotic distribution is 4, and the associated standardized statistic is −1.605645493, which falls again inside the boundaries at 95% confidence level, even if near the boundaries. So we cannot reject the null hypothesis and we confirm the random walk assumptions for the gas series under a certain level of uncertainty.

For the power series the variance of asymptotic distribution is 4, and the associated standardized statistic is −10.50823493, which falls outside the boundaries at 95% confidence level. So we cannot accept the null hypothesis and we cannot confirm the random walk as a true model for the power series. As shown by other tests, the power market is the unique commodities market, in light of the different tests we have carried out that clearly show distance from the efficiency markets hypothesis and structure in price patterns. The oil market is clearly the more liquid and efficient; there is no evidence of a systematic possibility of making a profit, in a statistical sense, through directional trading due to the high degree of informational efficiency that characterize this market. Gas and power show lower efficiency levels, and more explicit structure in price pattern, which confirms that these markets are still influenced by operators with greater industrial/commercial perspective.

1.7.1 Efficient Market Hypothesis: Testing the Intraday Returns

Discussion of EMH hypothesis has led us to test, across the chapter, different statistical properties that a random walk process is supposed to display. In particular, we have referred to the ADF test that aims to detect the presence of unit roots in the price's process. Bearing in mind the previous, it was clear that the EMH hypothesis, according to the aforementioned unit root test, can only be accepted when run to take into account daily returns and over a long time horizon. In fact the test on daily prices for WTI shows a t-statistics value of estimated coefficient greater than the critical level; actually, we cannot reject the null hypothesis and need to accept the presence of unit root. That confirms for us that the market is efficient in a statistical sense when we observe daily movements; but what happens if we look at the series through a magnifying glass? What if we get closer to a change in prices by looking at hourly, or even deeper resolutions, instead of on a daily basis?

To address this question we have performed the same ADF test on intraday series for the oil market (the most liquid commodity market of the three considered).

Table 1.12 EEX variance ratio

n selected period	2
T number of observations	1998
1 period returns variance	0.006516366
2 period returns variance	0.008699794
Variance Ratio	0.66753416
H_0 standardized statistic	10.50823493

In particular, we have considered the series of intraday prices for the WTI first monthly futures quoted at Nymex, over a period starting from 04/01/2010 (00.03) up to 13/04/2010 (15.15) (tick size movements), for a total of 51,951 observations.

Again, we would like to test for the presence of a unit root in the level, including constant and linear trend in the regression run, and so we would like to test the unit root presence by regressing the oil intraday prices over the following equation:

$$P_t = \mu + \theta P_{t-1} + \gamma t + \varepsilon_t.$$

The null hypothesis we are going to test is:

$$H_0 : \theta = 1$$

Table 1.13 reports the results obtained.

As is evident from the above results, we reject the null hypothesis given the fact that the t-statistic is below the critical values for the test, and so it seems that the price series is no longer consistent with the random walk hypothesis when observed on intraday movements. This suggests to us that the same market could become inefficient, in the way information is worked out, over thinner time intervals, which is evidence of how different kinds of operator, working at different frequencies, can impact the market microstructures and trading flows.

1.8 SUBORDINATION, TRADING VOLUME AND EFFICIENT MARKET HYPOTHESIS

So far we have seen how many energy markets fail to satisfy the assumptions and the consequences of EMH. In the last section (1.7.1) we noted that sometimes the same efficiency test applied to the same market can lead to acceptance or rejection,

Table 1.13 ADF on WTI intraday returns

		t-statistic
Augmented Dickey-Fuller test statistic		−171.5392
Test critical values:	1% level	−3.958210
	5% level	−3.409888
	10% level	−3.126654

depending on the time resolution of price series we currently observe. For example, the WTI Oil Future market passes efficiency tests when we observe time series with a daily granularity, while it fails to pass it when we analyze intraday price series.

The reasons for such an outcome may be related to market segmentation but also to the characteristics of information flow dynamics. On one hand, it is true that, even if WTI Oil is a very liquid market, only a portion of all market operators who have their capital invested there, really operate frequently within the day. This attitude makes them inefficient with respect to the relevant information which may become public within the day. On the other hand, as we have said earlier, it is also true that information is revealed in asset prices only at discrete times, particularly when big trading volumes are transacted in the market. Most of the time, the lack of efficiency is reflected in a deviation from normality of returns distribution. It is a well-known stylized fact that returns distributions (also when market liquidity is extremely high as for oil or US gas markets) deviate from normality especially in the level of kurtosis.

This last point may be related to, or explained by, trying to acquire an in-depth understanding of how really relevant information flows into prices. Actually, a discontinuous flow of information can bias returns distribution without compromising EMH. Transactions are taking place at discrete (even if very small) intervals of time, hence information reflected in transaction prices is discontinuous by definition and flows according to a timescale that differs from the natural one. If we then assume the existence of a business time (or operational time) which replaces the natural timescale in financial markets activity, it is natural to assume that the financial timescale is closely related to the level of market activity, measured by different indicators as trading volume or number of transactions per unit of time. The close relationship between the level of market activity and the variations occurring in financial asset prices has been studied in depth and documented over the last thirty-five years in many theoretical and empirical studies, and obviously has a deep impact on the standard way we usually test and investigate for market efficiency. In fact, we know from previous discussions that EMH is very closely related to the hypothesis of normality of asset price returns. Recently Ané and Geman (2000) and some years ago, Clark (1973) hypothesized and proved empirically that trading volume and transaction number somehow determine the stochastic timescale which allows the asset return process to be expressed as a classical Arithmetic Brownian Motion. This result is very important since, conditionally to the observation of the stochastic timescale process, the assumption of normality of asset returns is recovered, together with EMH.

1.9 SUBORDINATION AND STOCHASTIC TIMESCALES

Monroe's theorem (1978) states that each semimartingale process $Y(t)$ can be represented as a time-changed Brownian motion

$$Y(t) = B(A(t))$$

where B represents a standard Brownian motion and A is an increasing right continuous process such that $A(0) = 0$. This representation is called subordination and the process $A(t)$ is called the subordinator. In the financial literature the concept of subordination was first introduced by Clark (1973), who represented financial asset returns as the subordinated version of an arithmetical Brownian motion:

$$Y(t) = \mu A(t) + \sigma B(A(t)).$$

In finance, to assume that the asset return process is a semimartingale under the natural probability measure P is pretty standard and one of the most important prerequisites of the no-arbitrage theory. Clark's representation implies that the marginal density of $Y(t)$ conditioned on $A(t)$ is a Gaussian one. In other terms, the unconditional marginal density of returns $f(Y(t))$ can be written as a mean variance mixture of normals, where the subordinator process A works as the mixing variable. Obviously, from asset price time series, the subordinator process cannot be directly observed. We can only indirectly speculate about its characteristics. Clark (1973) suggested the existence of a close relationship between cumulated volume and stochastic timescale, while Ané and Geman (2000) found more explanatory power in cumulated number of transactions as proxy for the subordinated process. We will try to verify the subordination theory for the Henry Hub gas future market, using daily log-returns, cumulated volume and number of transactions in order to see whether in the energy field too the presence of a stochastic timescale may be considered a plausible assumption.

For the sake of our analysis we have considered the same time series of first line Henry Hub gas future contracts (865 observations from 02/01/2007 to 26/04/2010). Figure 1.4 shows the time series daily return's marginal distribution graph. Transacted volumes and number of transactions have also been taken into consideration. We will denote as:

- $P(t)$ the future price observed daily;
- $Y(t)$ the price return observed daily (calculated as usual $Y(t) = \log(P(t)) - \log(P(t-1))$);
- $T(t)$ the cumulated number of transactions observed daily;
- $V(t)$ the cumulated volume observed daily.

The best candidate for the role of subordinator, among cumulated volume and transaction number, can be selected using the method proposed by Schwert (1990) and subsequently endorsed by Ané and Geman (2000). According to this method, we first need to obtain a return's variance estimate for the selected time series running the following regression:

$$Y(t) = c + \sum_{i=1} \delta_i Y(t-i) + \varepsilon(t) \rightarrow \widehat{\sigma^2}(t) = \left(\sqrt{\frac{\pi}{2}} |\widehat{\varepsilon(t)}|\right)^2$$

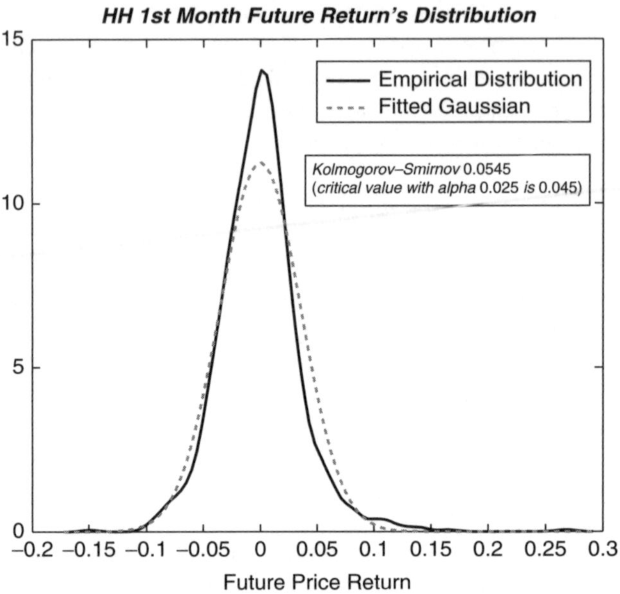

Figure 1.4 Henry Hub gas futures: empirical analysis

Second, we can measure the power of explaining volatility changes of the variables $T(t)$ and $V(t)$ by running the following regressions and comparing their results (see Table 1.14):

1. $\widehat{\sigma^2}(t) = \alpha + \beta \Delta V(t) + \sum_{i=1}^{12} \rho_i \widehat{\sigma^2}(t-i) + \eta_t$
2. $\widehat{\sigma^2}(t) = \alpha + \gamma \Delta T(t) + \sum_{i=1}^{12} \rho_i \widehat{\sigma^2}(t-i) + \eta_t^2$
3. $\widehat{\sigma^2}(t) = \alpha + \beta \Delta V(t) + \gamma \Delta T(t) + \sum_{i=1}^{12} \rho_i \widehat{\sigma^2}(t-i) + \eta_t^3$

Concisely, we can state that both volume and transaction number have similar explanatory power on volatility changes. Hence, both can be considered good candidates for the role of subordinator. For the rest of the analysis we will consider the volume $V(t)$ as our subordinator variable. Once we have identified the subordinator proxy we can test the proposed subordinated model (Clark's model) by analyzing the properties of the marginal density of $Y(t)$ conditioned on the observation of

Table 1.14 Estimation results variance linear regression

Equation	α	β	γ	R-squared
1	2.52 e^-07	1.01e-09	–	0.0879
	(1.66e-08)	(5.94e-11)		
2	3.27e-07	–	1.95e-09	0.0885
	(1.67e-08)		(1.08e-10)	
3	2.20e-07	−1.96e-09	5.47e-09	0.0890
	(1.7e-08)	(3.68e-10)	(6.67e-10)	

the subordinator process $V(t)$. According to Clark's model we should be able to verify that

$$f(Y(t)|V(t)) \sim N(\mu \cdot V(t), \sigma^2 \cdot V(t)) \rightarrow f(Y(t)|V(t) = n) \sim N(\mu \cdot n, \sigma^2 \cdot n) \quad \forall n \varepsilon R_+$$

Considering that the estimates we usually obtain for the mean parameter are not statistically different from zero, we have that the two elements we really ought to consider in our test are:

a) the normality of all the conditional densities;
b) the positive linear relationship between the variances of those distributions.

A prerequisite for that kind of testing is to have an estimate of the sequence of conditional densities $f(Y(t)|V(t) = n) \sim N(\mu \cdot n, \sigma^2 \cdot n) \quad \forall n \varepsilon R_+$. Classical Gaussian Kernel methods can be used to estimate the joint distribution

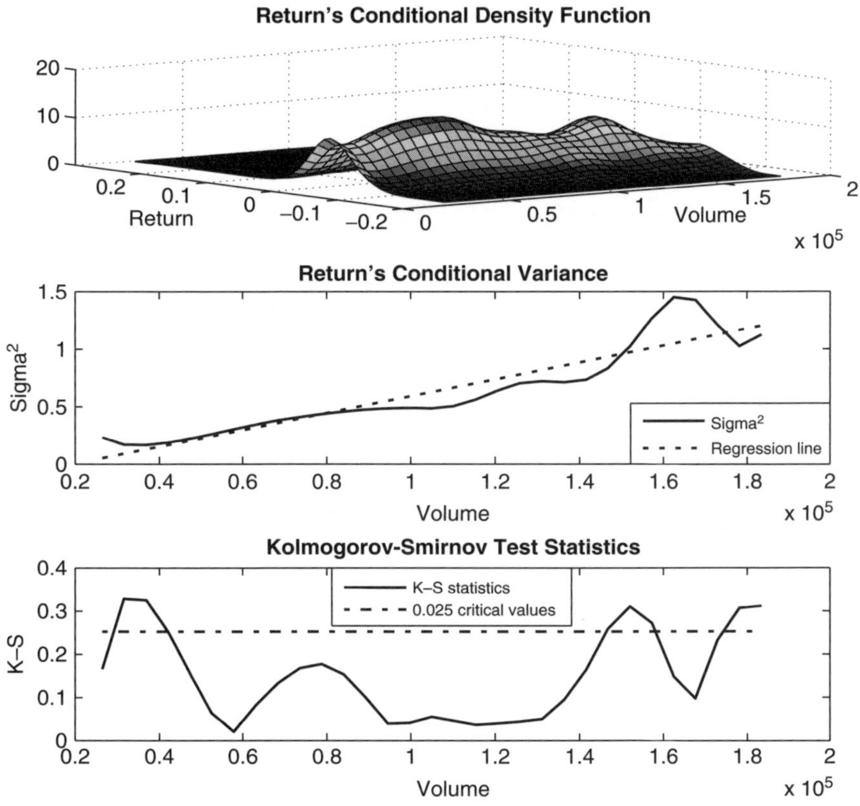

Figure 1.5 Subordinated model test result

$f(Y(t), V(t))$. By applying the well-known theorem of conditional probabilities we can get the conditional distribution function we are looking for as follows:

$$f(Y(t)|V(t)) = \frac{f(Y(t), V(t))}{f(V(t))}$$

From results given in Figure 1.5 we can clearly see that the return's distribution conditioned on volume is mostly normally distributed (Kolmogorov-Smirnov test almost always satisfied) and that the return's variance and volume are linked by a positive linear relationship. Hence, we can conclude that, at least for the case analyzed, the subordination model is able to reconcile non-normal returns distributions and EMH.

2 Directional Trading

2.1 DEFINITIONS AND MAIN FEATURES

Directional trading strategies are almost the simplest trading strategies that can be implemented by a professional trading player. Basically, a trading strategy can be defined as directional if it simply considers the direction (in terms of prices) the investor believes the market will follow in a given future time horizon. The determination on the future market price direction or trend will then determine the buy or sell decision. The essence of directional trading can be synthetised in the classic phrase *buy low, sell high*.

We mention professional trading players, since only for them (or most of them) is short selling allowed, and consequently only professional traders can buy or sell assets considering only their market view without any other constraint.

As may be inferred from the general definition given, directional trading has two main variables that have to be considered: time and trend. Decision timing is important for obvious reasons. The optimal timing of a buy decision is obviously the early stage of an ascending price trend while the opposite is valid for the optimal decision timing of a sell decision. But, time is also important for reasons that many trading players sometimes neglect or at least underestimate. In fact, an optimal evaluation of the time horizon a certain directional strategy will pay back is just as important as the optimal decision timing. Just as for almost all economic and financial activities, trading is not an unconstrained game. In trading activities time is capital and capital is, for most of the players, a limited resource. We can have the best view on market trends but if we do not have enough capital to cope with potential losses we may incur, before my view can be realized (and paid back), my strategy is condemned to failure. Whenever we try to determine or forecast market direction we also need to determine the time horizon my forecast will realize and, consequently, assess our capital endowment before taking any trading decision (see Figure 2.1 for a clear example of short and long trend). The time horizon also affects the investor's ability to accept risk: on the one hand, an investor with a long time horizon may have a greater ability to accept risk, having a longer time period to recoup any losses; on the other hand, with a shorter time horizon the ability to accept risk may be lower because the investor would not have time to recoup any losses.

The importance of the proper time window selection for our directional trading strategy is clearly highly connected with the other basic feature of a directional trading strategy, the trend identification. Actually, we cannot set the time window

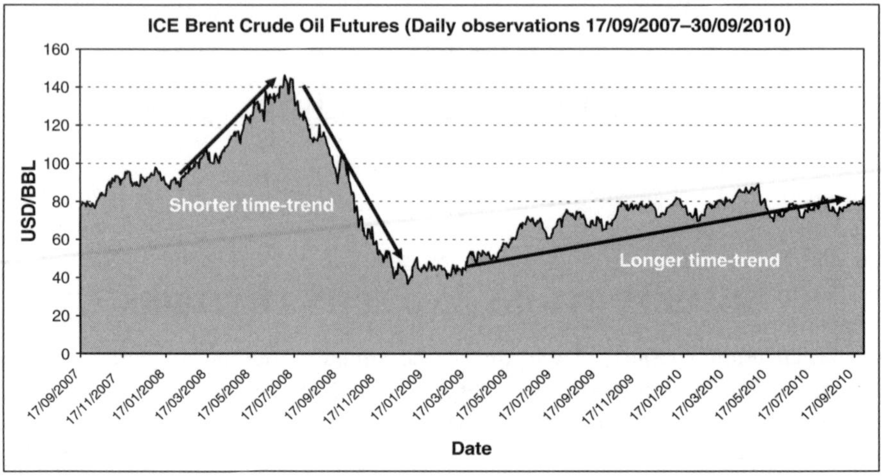

Figure 2.1 ICE Brent crude oil future

in disjunction with respect to the trend identification or vice versa. Moreover, most of the typical capital constraints usually set up in professional trading activities are jointly based on market direction in a given time horizon (e.g. within day stop loss or daily VaR). Trend identification or market dynamics forecast is a topic we have discussed briefly in the previous chapter in connection with the so-called Efficient Market Hypothesis (EMH). We have emphasized the linkage between price forecasts by market players and the information set available to the same market players. Every individual investor tries to subjectively project their own information in order to forecast future market dynamics and set up their own trading strategy.

We have defined a certain market framework as efficient with respect to a certain information set if, basically, the same information set is useless to better predict market behaviour than would be the case simply by observing the current price signal. The way a certain investor elaborates available information in order to construct their own forecast can be defined as a model. In this chapter we will try to identify and describe the principal class of models used by market operators in order to establish their directional trading strategies. Bearing in mind that usually the information set under consideration and available to almost all market players is the publicly available one (price history, volume history, demand dynamics, supply dynamics, etc.), the model classes we will consider are only those related to price or fundamental data analysis.

It should already be clear that the effectiveness of a certain model implemented to support a directional trading strategy has links with and implications for the general level of market efficiency. At the limit, if the market is close to a theoretical situation of semi-strong market efficiency, none of the approaches we will present in the remainder of the chapter should be able to generate consistent excess returns.

2.2 MARKET PRODUCTS FOR DIRECTIONAL TRADING

We have stated that directional trading is based on market price trend identification. Hence, in order to perform the strategy, we need to select instruments whose value proportionally reacts to market price dynamics. We usually refer to the class of instruments which generate a payoff that is a linear function of the underlying asset price dynamics in order to have a simple proportion between the overall payoff of our directional strategy and the identified (and hopefully realized) market trends. Essentially, our attention will focus on linear derivative instruments like forwards, futures, swaps and contracts for differences (cfd), as well as on the underlying asset itself (spot trading). In traditional financial markets, such as stock markets, a directional trader can either take a position on the stock itself or on a forward contract written on it, in the end obtaining the same payoff structure. The unique difference is related to cash exposure and to the counterparty risk which usually push market operators towards term contracts instead of spot ones. This is also the reason why term markets (futures or OTC forward markets) are typically much more liquid than spot ones.

In the energy field the possibility of implementing a directional trading strategy using spot instruments is in many cases physically prevented for reasons that have to be described on a case by case basis. Let's start with the case of physically storable commodities like oil or gas. The first consideration concerns the difficulty of accessing the physical market. Trading physical oil or gas entails being a professional operator in the field of energy with the proper organizational structure including physical logistics. This kind of organization has a cost that a pure trader tries to avoid. The second important fact to be considered is the cost of storage which we need to face when trading the physical commodity directly. Storage facilities for either gas or oil are extremely scarce and consequently expensive, hence their use for setting up a directional trading strategy only is quite often not justified. For some other energy commodities or energy related commodities like electric power or weather variables, physical storability is almost impossible, hence the only way of making profits out of a price trend identification is by taking a position on the term market.

The kind of directional trading we would like to do (Section 2.3 is dedicated to the analysis of different approaches) will determine a different frequency of market activity. From this point of view market liquidity is an extremely important topic. Liquidity is important to prevent big intermediation costs and bid/ask spreads that impact on the overall trading performance, especially when market activity is intense. Liquidity is also important in order to estimate the proper time horizon from our directional trading strategy since the downside risk can be enlarged within a thin (scarcely liquid) market. In fact, if the size of the position we hold is big with respect to the normal market liquidity, we can no longer be considered a price taker for that market. In such a case we would seek to close up our position urgently. We will intensify price trend, worsening the closing up overall cost.

Among the group of linear derivatives with the same degree of liquidity (term instruments) the decision on which instrument is optimal to operate depends upon subjective decisions concerning cash or credit exposure. From the economic point of view, forward and futures contracts have the same function: both types of contract allow people to buy or sell a specific type of asset at a specific time at a given price. However, it is in the specific details that these contracts differ. First of all, futures contracts are exchange-traded and, therefore, are standardized contracts. Forward contracts, on the other hand, are private agreements between two parties and are not as rigid in their terms and conditions. Because forward contracts are private agreements, there is always a chance that a party may default on its side of the agreement. Futures contracts have institutional clearing houses that guarantee the creditworthiness of the transactions, which drastically lowers the probability of default to almost never. The different credit risk exposure may or may not have an explicit associated cost (explicit credit charge) which, in any case, has to be accounted for in the overall trading strategy performance. Secondly, the specific details concerning settlement and delivery are quite distinct. For forward contracts, financial settlement occurs at the end of the contract. Futures contracts are marked-to-market daily, which means that daily changes are financially settled day by day until the end of the contract. A different settlement or margin call rule implies a different cash exposure and consequently a different associated cost (refer to Figure 2.2 for an example of cash exposure related to a future position). Obviously, cash and credit exposure costs should never be so large as to significantly impact overall trading performance, but they have to be considered when selecting the appropriate trading instrument for our strategy for the sake of cost optimization.

In principle, non-linear instruments as options could also be used in order to perform directional trading strategies. In Chapter 4 we will examine this possibility in relation to options trading. For the moment it is sufficient to stress that the non-linearity (with respect to the underlying asset's price) related to an option's payoff can induce undesired effects in the overall directional strategy

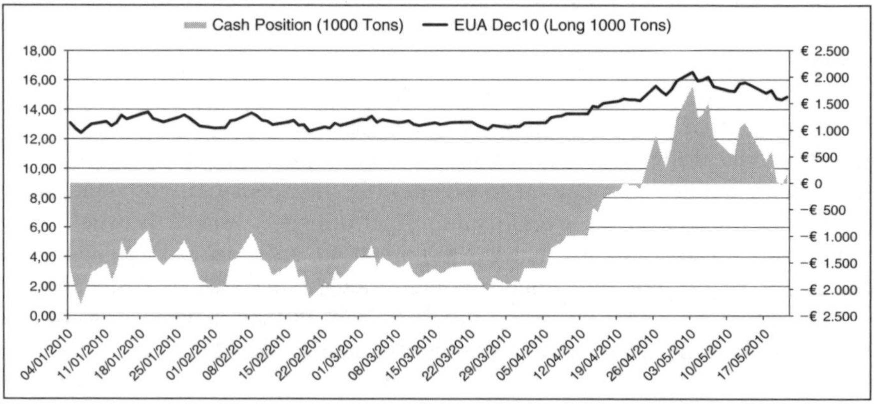

Figure 2.2 Cash position versus market value December 2010

performance (effects related to volatility movements or secondary option price effects). Hence, for straightforward directional strategies, the use of linear instruments is strongly suggested.

2.3 PRICE TREND DETERMINATION

One of the most commonly heard statements about directional trading is *the trend is your friend*. We should definitely agree with this statement. Once the trend is determined, most of the directional trader's job is done. The way a certain trader aims to determine price trend can be defined as his trading approach or model. In this section we will examine alternative ways or approaches to predict price dynamics and how we can try to gain a profit from them.

Usually, trading approaches are grouped into three different classes: fundamental trading; statistical or mathematical trading; and technical trading. We believe that this kind of classification is still valid in the energy sector even if within the energy field some approaches are more commonly used than others.

By fundamental trading we mean the trading approach (directional or not) based on the analysis of the fundamental economic relationship between relevant variables. Typically, a fundamental analysis is strictly related to the analysis of aggregated demand/supply dynamics for that market, hence price trend determination in fundamental directional trading strategies is based on more or less simplified demand/supply models. In the energy sector, fundamental trading is fairly diffuse, especially in those subsectors like power or gas markets characterized by a relatively low liquidity (and so relatively low informational content in price signals) and extremely local dynamics.

Statistical or mathematical trading approaches are all those methods where trend identification is based on a statistical or, more generically, a mathematical model while by technical trading we mean the trading approach based on the use of technical analysis tools.

It is worth noting that, despite this typical classification (useful for the sake of a concise presentation of directional trading), many operators often combine and compare different approaches in order to enforce or stress test their price forecast. Moreover, many fundamental models make deep use of mathematical or statistical tools for their implementation exactly as many technical analysis tools are basically *hidden* statistical tools.

In the remainder of this section we will examine the three categories in detail, focusing on their specific applications and potential in the energy sector.

2.3.1 Fundamental Trading Models

Many common features characterize the demand/supply dynamics and drivers of energy commodities markets, at least those fully open to competition. Economic theory has it that in a free and competitive market the price of any traded good or service is entirely determined by the interaction between aggregated demand and aggregated supply. Because of this, the analysis and full comprehension of aggregated demand and supply dynamic interaction are necessary in order to set up a fundamental trading approach.

For example, in the electricity spot market the concept of System Marginal Price has a fundamental importance (also in *pay as bid* markets). The System Marginal Price is exactly determined, hour by hour, by the interception of the system merit order curve and system aggregated demand.

The aggregated energy supply function is by definition upward sloping (see Figure 2.3), but its shape will obviously depend on the inner physical characteristics of the productive system of the particular energy commodity and sometimes also on that of its substitutes. Global energy supply is of course limited in the medium and short term by technological and physical constraints. Oil and natural gas extraction is limited by physical availability and technological capability, and also by transportation constraints. Power production (a derived energy form) is also constrained by energy transformation capability. This implies that the upward shape of the curve of the energy supply function necessarily has a vertical asymptote at some point, and that this point can be modified very slowly through time. On the other hand, effective energy supply can be impacted by contingent factors, such as production outages, that may reduce it significantly or modify its curve.

Aggregated energy demand is typically assumed to be price inelastic, at least in the short run, and obviously reflects the energy consumption of a certain area or country. This assumption is surely true for the overall energy sector, but can be misleading for particular sub-sectors where substitution effects can determine demand sensitivity to price.

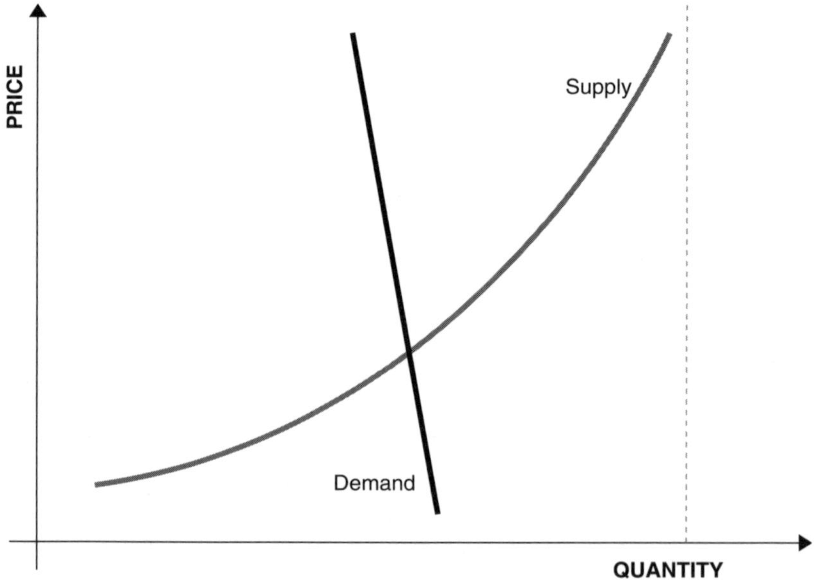

Figure 2.3 Energy aggregated demand supply

Typically, energy demand can be divided into industrial demand and domestic demand. Industrial and domestic demand have different behaviours and mostly they display different price elasticity. Hence, the dynamics and the shape of the curve of the aggregated energy demand function of a certain country or region is influenced by the proportion within aggregated demand of industrial and domestic consumption.

As mentioned, demand and supply are subject to fluctuations and shocks (expected or unexpected) due to more or less permanent changes (see Figure 2.4) in their main drivers. Given the non-linear nature of the interaction between energy demand and supply, small changes in demand/supply conditions will not necessarily always produce small price changes. Small shocks to demand in conditions of *constrained* supply (due to production outages, for example) can produce significant price reactions that would not appear under *normal* supply conditions.

Usually, aggregated or even individual energy demand and supply cannot be observed directly, but must be inferred from other economic variables. In power and sometimes in gas sectors, where organized spot markets are effectively operating, energy demand and supply can be directly observed simplifying the construction of a fundamental model for price forecasting.

Gas demand/supply drivers

Natural gas is a natural energy resource in the sense that it is naturally present in the ground and technology only has to be employed for extraction. In any case, for many countries, extraction fields are not the main source of natural gas and

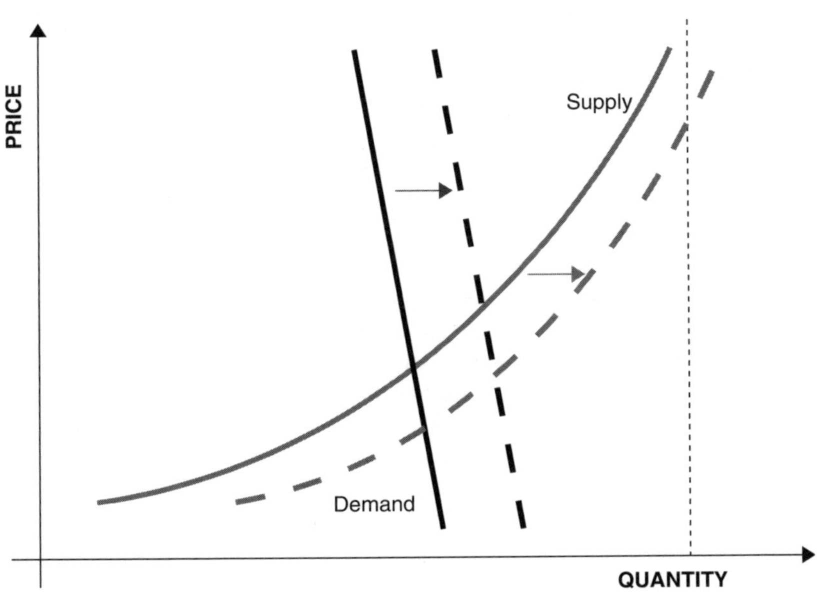

Figure 2.4 Demand/supply shocks

make up only a very limited proportion of the overall gas supply. Hence, the identification of natural gas supply main drivers concerns extraction facilities as well as transportation and storage facilities.

Theoretically, production facilities should offer their product at marginal cost of production, but often opportunity cost may be different and more attractive as reference price for suppliers. While gas transportation pipelines or even LNG (liquefied natural gas) infrastructures are tools for moving gas from one particular geographical area to another, gas storage is, rather, a facility tool for moving gas through time. In both situations transportation and storage facilities can contribute to the aggregated demand and supply of a certain area.

Concerning transportation facilities, it is easy to understand that opportunity cost arguments can divert gas from one country to another, hence in the supplier country there will be a demand component related to export linked to foreign gas price and in the consumer country there will be a corresponding gas supply. Obviously, this is not the case if the transportation facility joins a production unit (or a production country) to a consumption unit.

A similar situation applies for gas storages with a yearly seasonal cycle: they are gas demanders during summer and gas suppliers during winter. Obviously, their value is related to the winter–summer price differential.

By analyzing the peculiar gas infrastructure of a certain country or area and applying opportunity cost arguments we can (at least in a simplified setting) construct and represent aggregated gas supply and its evolution through time. The same approach can be used to analyze gas demand components.

Gas demand can usually be divided into a domestic component and an industrial one. Every single country has its own demand structure related to the particular role natural gas plays in its domestic and industrial usage. Also, on the aggregated demand side, the opportunity cost approach is a reasonable tool for understanding how gas demanders formulate their bids. In fact, natural gas can be (at least partially) substituted by other energy sources if its price is too high; conversely, gas can replace other energy commodities if its price is lower with respect to the other energy commodities. However, substitution effects that may occur between gas and other energy commodities can only happen to a limited extent and in any case not in real time with respect to price movements, hence aggregated gas demand can still be considered locally rigid with respect to price.

By ranking and combining together the evolution of the gas supply and demand drivers and respective bid prices we should be able to identify a demand-supply equilibrium price and use it as reference price in order to identify potential directional trading opportunities within our fundamental trading approach (see Figures 2.5 and 2.6). Later on in this chapter we will present a case where a simple fundamental gas model is constructed for the Italian market and used in a simulated fundamental trading strategy.

Power demand/supply drivers

In general, bearing in mind what was stated for natural gas aggregated demand/supply interactions, there are two substantial facts we need to consider

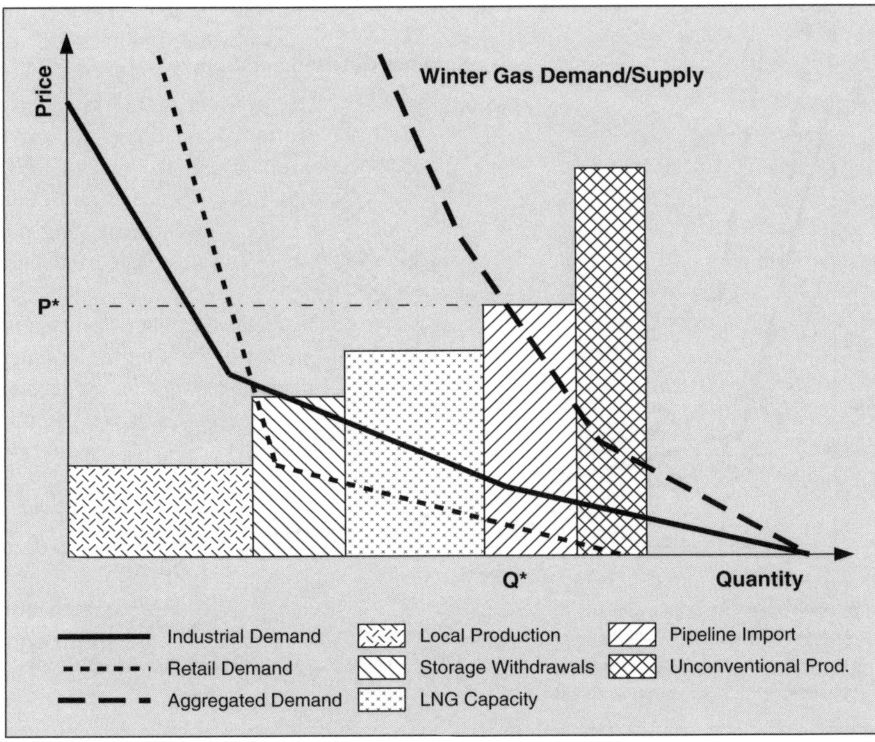

Figure 2.5 Winter gas demand/supply

in order to define electric power demand/supply. The first is that electric power is a derived energy commodity (often derived directly from natural gas) and the second is the lack of storability of electric power. The first point implies that in every single market there are several power generation facilities (which differ from one another in terms of the technology employed), competing with each other for production. Every single technology differs in both fixed costs (initial investment which has to be repaid) and marginal cost (related and not related to fuel cost and efficiency). Refer to Figure 2.7 to have an example of economic merit order in power markets.

Every single power producer (including those characterized by the use of the same technology) adopts different strategic bidding approaches. The diversity described makes power aggregated supply function (also called merit order or stack curve) extremely dynamic and reactive with respect to demand unexpected shocks. The more a certain market is composed of a diversified set of generating technologies, the more it is flexible in reacting to sudden changes in power demand and the less a price-based mechanism should be emphasized in order to push the market towards equilibrium.

Non-storability implies that, once produced, electric power has to be consumed or it will be lost, so it represents a lack of flexibility of the production system that may be responsible for significant price spikes; on the other hand, non-storability

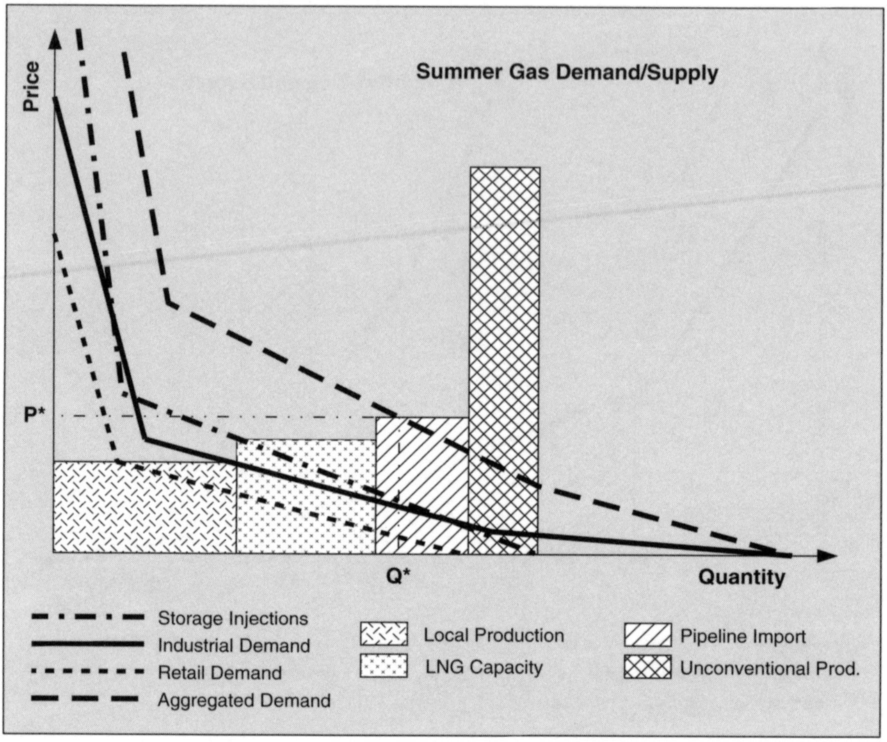

Figure 2.6 Summer gas demand/supply

combined with typical operational constraints of some generation technologies may result in strange bidding strategies characterized by negative bid prices.

As for natural gas, power demand can be for industrial or residential uses and every single country may be characterized by a different combination of the two demands. The particular kind of industrial production of a certain country may induce a significant baseload industrial demand with no substantial daily peak loads, while other countries may display more *peak-shaped* industrial load. Residential power demand is typically influenced by its usage. Where power is used for heating and cooling purposes its impact on overall demand may be extremely significant and its time evolution and sensitivity to weather conditions may have an important impact on prices. Once these main drivers of power demand and supply have been analyzed in depth, a more or less simplified fundamental model can be constructed and a fundamental directional trading strategy can be adopted based on it.

2.3.2 Statistical Trading Models

As discussed in Chapter 1, in a market that operates efficiently, according to the EMH hypothesis, the possibility of forecasting the direction of the next movements of a given asset is simply a guess. All the information useful to understand

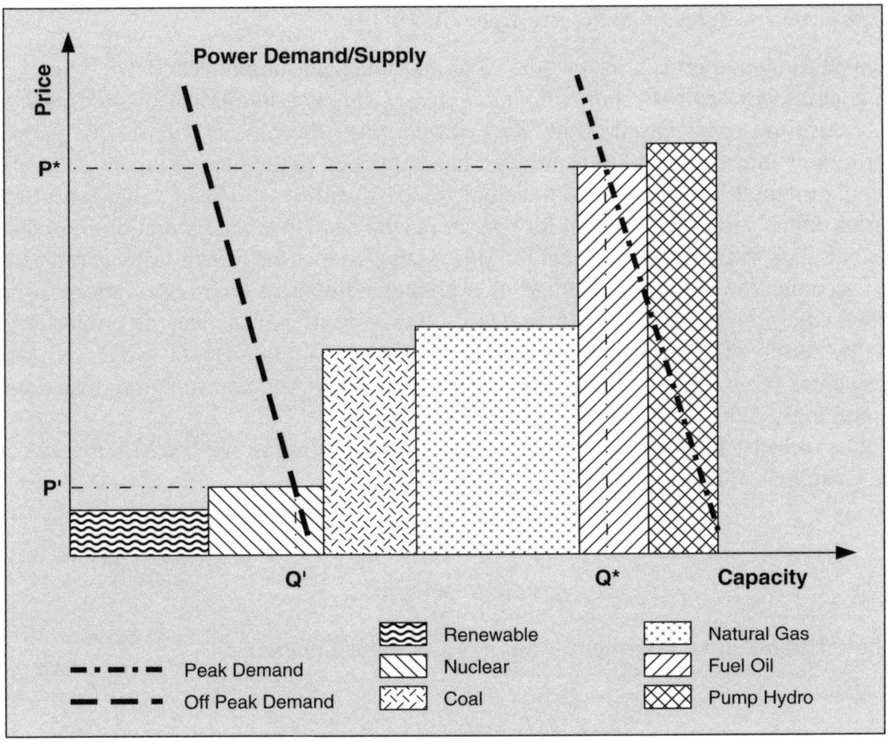

Figure 2.7 Power demand/supply

the financial and economic fundamentals, and so to take trading decisions, is instantaneously and rightly reflected in the market prices. Basically, it is possible that some structure or recursive autoregressive component is still present in the price pattern and by using an econometric and statistical model one may be able to predict the short-term price movements. The classic statistical approach to the analysis of time series aims to detect and model recursive structure in a series and detect trend, seasonality, cycle and autoregressive components. As noted, a series should have numerous components, and a general understanding of the economic phenomena that goes beyond the series will be a determinant in the correct identification of series behaviour. The choice of the data window to consider in order to estimate parameters should not be made ex-ante, without having an idea of the series we are exploring or the possible seasonal effect to be detected, i.e. the presence of an economic cycle. The message is that a simple *statistical* aseptic analysis of financial time series, without a clear perception of what kind of economic fundamentals govern the series, may well lead to a misleading indication and to detection of the wrong statistical components. For these reasons a deep understanding of econometric methods, and theory, is essential. In the following we will briefly summarize the main econometric approach used to detect short-term trends in financial time series.

Exponential weighted moving average (EWMA)

A well-known approach in the statistical and financial literature to detect tendency in a series is so-called *exponential smoothing*. This is a traditional method used to forecast time series based on the idea of *adaptive expectations* – basically, people form their future expectations on what has happened in the past. It is a popular and simple method for obtaining a punctual forecast of the step-ahead value for a time series that is particularly useful for operators who need to make predictions based on a small data sample. The idea behind this method is that the forecast of a given asset p_t becomes the weighted average of a greater number of past observations p_{t-n}, where the weights assigned to previous observations are in general proportional to the terms of a geometric progression $(1, (1-a), (1-a)^2, (1-a)^3, \ldots.)$. A geometric progression is the discrete version of an exponential function, hence this averaging method has been termed *exponential*.

The forecast for the step-ahead, $\mathbb{E}[p_t] = f_t$, according to the EWMA model can be written as follows:

$$\begin{aligned} f_t &= a(p_{t-1} - f_{t-1}) + f_{t-1} \\ &= ap_{t-1} + (1-a) f_{t-1} \end{aligned}$$

The relation can be rewritten in the more familiar notation:

$$\mathbb{E}[p_t] = f_t = a \sum_{s=1}^{t} (1-a)^{s-1} p_{t-s}$$

with a parameter bounded to exist between $0 < a < 1$.

This smoothing method is a particular kind of general moving average formula and is particularly appropriate for a series that moves around a constant average level, without showing trend or seasonal structure. The model itself can be extended to account for other components such as local trend or additive/multiplicative seasonality. The basic version of this smoothing method is called *single smoothing*.

A modified version suitable for analyzing series that clearly exhibit linear trend is the so-called *double smoothing*, where the forecast is made up of two different components, f_t and s_t, that in formula are defined by the equations:

$$\begin{aligned} f_t &= ap_{t-1} + (1-a)(f_{t-1} + s_{t-1}) \\ s_t &= g(s_t - s_{t-1}) + (1-g)s_{t-1} \end{aligned}$$

which means that expectation for a generic $t + k$ step-ahead will be given by the following equation:

$$\begin{aligned} \mathbb{E}[p_{t+k}] = f_{t+k} &= \left(2 + \frac{gk}{1-a}\right) f_t - \left(1 + \frac{gk}{1-a}\right) s_t \\ &= 2f_t - s_t + \frac{g}{1-a} (f_t - s_t)k. \end{aligned}$$

Another possibility is to consider a smoothing method that takes into account linear trend and a seasonal multiplicative component; a suitable extension of this method is *multiplicative smoothing*, where an estimate of a generic $t + k$ step-ahead will be given by the following equation:

$$\mathbb{E}[p_{t+k}] = f_{t+k} = (a + bk)c_t + k$$

where a stays for the intercept, b captures the linear trend and c_t the multiplicative seasonal component. On the other hand an additive seasonal component could be fit using another extension of the basic model, the so-called *additive smoothing* (three parameters exponential smoothing), that in equation is described by the following expression:

$$\mathbb{E}[p_{t+k}] = f_{t+k} = a + bk + c_{t+k}$$

So, as we have seen this class of method is widely used in finance for trend and seasonal components individuation, especially when only small data sets are available and there is insufficient history to back test a more complex model. Obviously, this approach seems to work well in the really short-term period, but these methods are totally unable to account for any *economic* implications and there is no possibility of linking the forecast to other, meaningful, economic variables.

ARMA model

This class of model is among the most widely used in the financial literature. It is possible to combine basic econometric processes such as the autoregressive and the moving average into an ARMA model. Let us now briefly recall the basic components definitions underlying an ARMA process. A basic moving average process of order one (MA (1)) should be defined as a constant mean μ plus the sum of a random variable ε_t and α times its lagged value. Denoting with p_t the price of a given asset at time t, the model can be formally defined as

$$p_t = \mu + \alpha\varepsilon_{t-1} + \varepsilon_t \, , \quad \varepsilon_t \sim \text{IID}(0, \sigma^2)$$

An autoregressive process of order one (AR(1)), is a process where the current value p_t equals θ times its previous values plus an unpredictable error component:

$$p_t = \theta p_{t-1} + \varepsilon_t \, , \quad \varepsilon_t \sim \text{IID}(0, \sigma^2)$$

The AR model, depending on the value assigned to the θ parameter, is said to be a long-memory process. We can see that the intensity of the autoregressive parameter affects the way the series reverts towards its unconditional mean. A quick way to see this graphically is to compare three series generated with three different values of the autoregressive coefficient (Figure 2.8).

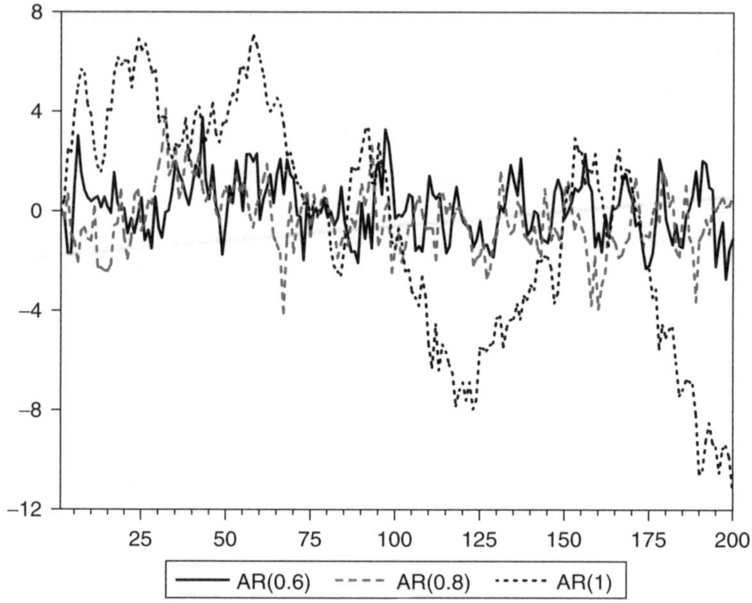

Figure 2.8 Intensity of long-memory process

Generally speaking, an MA(q) process is a moving average process of order q defined as

$$p_t = \mu + \varepsilon_t + \alpha_1 \varepsilon_{t-1} + \ldots + \alpha_q \varepsilon_{t-q}$$

and an AR(n) process of order p can be defined as

$$p_t = \theta_1 p_{t-1} + \theta_2 p_{t-2} + \ldots + \theta_n p_{t-n}$$

We can now combine the autoregressive and moving average specification into an ARMA(n, q) model that is consistently defined as

$$p_t = \theta_1 p_{t-1} + \ldots + \theta_n p_{t-n} + \varepsilon_t + \alpha_1 \varepsilon_{t-1} + \ldots + \alpha_q \varepsilon_{t-q}$$

This class of model, one widely used in the financial literature, gives the possibility (with a relatively small complexity) of capturing most of a time series' structure in an easy way.

Deterministic versus stochastic trend

In order to explain the impact of a *stochastic trend* on a time series and the statistical implication for process that shows this feature we need to introduce the formal definition for *deterministic trend* (also called *trend stationary* process) and *stochastic trend* process (random walk with drift model has been chosen). A classic example of *deterministic trend* series may be described by a simple model with a linear (deterministic) time trend:

$$p_t = a + bt + \varepsilon_t \tag{2.1}$$

Conversely, a classic example of *stochastic trend* is the well-known random walk with drift model, described by the following equation:

$$p_t = b + p_{t-1} + \varepsilon_t \tag{2.2}$$

Now, taking the expectation for the step-ahead of a *trend stationary* process, the value is given by the following equation:

$$\begin{aligned}\mathbb{E}_t(p_{t+1}) &= a + b(t+1) + \mathbb{E}_t(\varepsilon_{t+1}) \\ &= a + b(t+1)\end{aligned}$$

and generic expression for a k step-ahead forecast is given by the equation:

$$\begin{aligned}\mathbb{E}_t(p_{t+k}) &= a + b(t+k) + \mathbb{E}_t(\varepsilon_{t+k}) \\ &= bk + (a + bt)\end{aligned}$$

The above clearly shows how all the values forecast stay on a deterministic linear trend implied by the fixed parameters of the equation. On the other hand, if we consider the random walk with drift model, the equations that describe the expectation of the model are:

$$\begin{aligned}\mathbb{E}_t(p_{t+1}) &= b + \mathbb{E}_t(p_t) + \mathbb{E}_t(\varepsilon_{t+1}) \\ &= b + p_t\end{aligned}$$

which means that the forecast of the step-ahead observation is strictly linked to the more recent realization observed at time t, and this exploits the property of a stochastic trend. Another significant way to look at the difference between deterministic and stochastic trends is the way the *errors* component affects the behaviour of the series. In a local trend series the noise component has a local temporary effect on the model, while in a stochastic trend the errors component has a permanent effect. Working backwards the equation for the random walk with drift model it is possible to exploit this persistence property of the errors:

$$p_t = bt + p_0 + \sum_{k=1}^{t} \varepsilon_{t-k} + \varepsilon_t$$

It is thus easy to see that the more recent shock not only affects the future observations, but the model retains even the older shocks, which is why it is called long-memory process.

Looking at the first difference in both processes it is possible to individuate another important difference between trend stationary and stochastic trend series. Look at the definition of the series' first difference:

$$\Delta p_t = b + (1 - L)\varepsilon_t \quad \text{deterministic trend}$$

$$\Delta p_t = \quad b + \varepsilon_t \quad \text{stochastic trend}$$

The component $(1 - L)$ in the first equation, where L represents the Lag operator, is essential in order to understand the main difference between these two processes. This component allows a trend stationary series to vary according to the shock at time t but conversely, the same perturbation will be absorbed at time $t + 1$ because the process will take into account the same shock with inverted sign, reverting to the initial value. That means that the series is reverting to its long-term level which, in the case of trend presence, is the trend itself. Alternatively, the first difference of a stochastic trend series is affected at each step by a random component with a permanent effect that does not lead to a reversion along a trend; that is why the random walk with drift model, even if graphically similar to a deterministic trend series, is considered a series that shows a stochastic trend (see Figure 2.9 for a graphical representation).

These statistical properties obviously have an important implication for trading models. In fact, when analyzing financial time series, the detection of a statistical trend on which to base any trading decision may well be misleading if we are dealing with a stochastic trend series because, especially in the short term, random

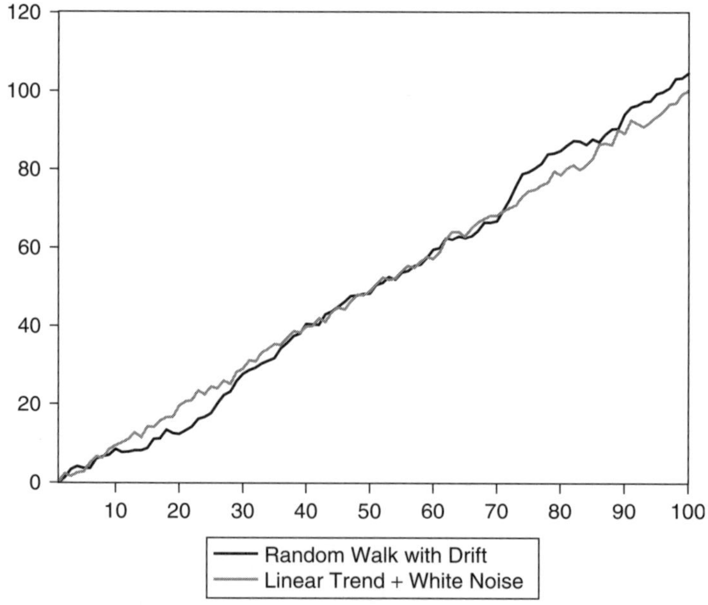

Figure 2.9 Deterministic versus stochastic trend

deviations from the individuated trend are highly probable. In conclusion, as shown, the detection of a stochastic trend (ADF and other similar statistical tests are available) is fundamental in terms of trading model implementation before proceeding with the fit of any model; the use of a classic statistical model fit on a non-trend stationary is non-coherent with basic econometric assumptions.

2.3.3 Technical Trading Models

This book is mainly dedicated to *scientific approaches* to energy trading so relatively little space will be devoted to technical analysis methods. It is important to emphasize that technical analysis is diffuse and popular with trading players, a fact which makes it important to be taken into consideration even by those who do not believe in its reliability. Neverthless, it is worth noting that behind many technical analysis indicators basic statistical methods apply.

In today's literature there are literally hundreds of definitions of so-called *technical analysis*. In recent years, some self-styled *market guru* tried to extrapolate from this a pretty simple and quick way to approach the market and get the best out of it. Principles of technical analysis in a raw form have been studied since the seventeenth century, their best-known exponent being Joseph de la Vega in his *Confusion of Confusions* (1688), while, in the same year in Japan a rich merchant, Homma Munehisa, was working on a forerunner of what had come to be known as the Japanese Candlestick, also trying to detect cyclical patterns in the market.

In modern times technical analysis has developed mainly in computerized trading systems, such as neural networks and automated fast trading software. In essence, technical analysis is the graphical and statistical study of historical market prices and volumes. In fact, using these techniques traders try to forecast future market directions assuming that markets will move through the same path as has already occurred historically.

Primary technical analysis is based on the study of charts. The methodology has recognized various graphical archetypal patterns, called figures, that markets aim to follow and which should occur in the intraday activity as well as in mid- or long-term trading. In the main, figures are the head and shoulders of path formation, wedge, double tops, as well as triangles or gaps. In any case, the literature has seen the development of many of these figures, for which, in some cases, the statistical evidence of the path still needs to be proved.

Figures and charts are often supported by indicators and overlays (or at least they should be). Indicators are mathematical elaboration of volumes and prices, such as Relative Strength Index, Momentum, Stochastic, MACD. Overlays assist in the reading of charts, emphasizing key figures. They span from the basic moving averages and their hundreds of derivations, to more elaborate Bollinger Bands, Pivot Point, Parabolic SAR, Elliot waves and so on. Often channels, support and resistance or trend lines are also graphically added to the chart (see Figure 2.11). A whole chapter could easily be devoted to Candlestick Indicators, also known as the Japanese Candlestick. Each candle is made up by using opening and closing prices and max and min prices for the relevant time delay chosen. Here the technicians

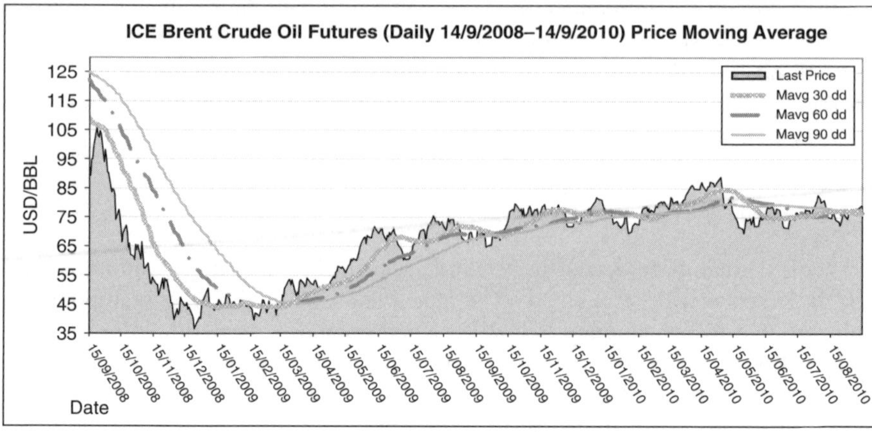

Figure 2.10 Technical analysis on ICE Brent: moving averages

recognize a whole bunch of figures, often given esoteric or dramatic names such as Hanged Man, Morning Star, Hammer or Dark Clouds. Other exotic techniques have been developed, such as the line chart or the point and figures technique.

Below is a brief overview of the most common instruments of technical analysis.

Simple Moving Averages (SMA) are among the simplest indicators (see Figure 2.10). They are simple averages of n previous periods before (usually days), such that a SMA10 would be the average of the 10 previous data sets. While periods may vary considerably, in a stock chart we usually find a short SMA (e.g. 5 periods) and a longer one (e.g. 14 periods). The intersection between charts and the SMA itself gives us the indication on market trend.

Bollinger Bands, created by J. Bollinger around 1980, consist in a SMA supplemented by adding an upper band at k times the n-period standard deviation above the middle SMA and a lower band at k times the n-period standard deviation below the middle SMA. The purpose is to give a definition of a low limit and what a high limit might be.

The Relative Strength Index (RSI) is used to indicate whether the market is in a weak phase or a strong phase, assuming that a series of declining closing prices indicates a weak market and a series of rising closing prices indicates a strong market. Calculation methods start from price variation of the selected time period. These data are classified as positive or negative and then an average of the absolute value is taken. This means all values are also a positive number for decreasing values. Obtained values are then imputed to a ratio so the RSI value stays in a range from 0 to 100. Sometimes an analyst might individuate a channel in which RSI values are considered standard (usually values between 30 and 70). An RSI of more than 70 basis points means the market is going overbought, while an RSI of less than 30 basis points means the market is going oversold. In each of these cases the assumption is of a change of trend.

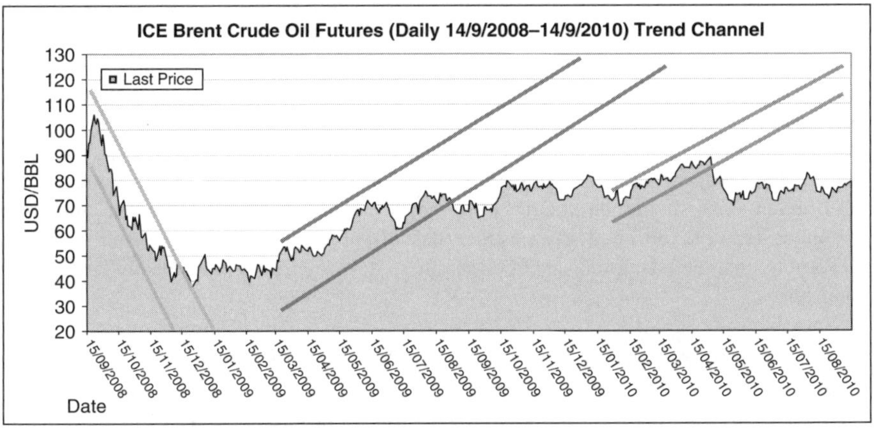

Figure 2.11 Technical analysis on ICE Brent: channels

Momentum shows the absolute difference between today's price and n-lagged price, in order to recognize a price pattern. Rate of change (ROC) is simply the ratio of those variations and the starting price (ROC = momentum/n-period before price).

2.3.4 Case Studies

Case study 1: Statistical trading

The aim of this section is to test how the statistical trend identification techniques presented so far should be implemented in order to forecast price movement and take trading decisions. First of all it is important to look at the *idea* behind the statistical model adopted. The classic approach to time series analysis aims to detect structure (seasonality, cycle, etc.) and autoregressive movements in the variable. How good the estimate is is evaluated taking into consideration both the ability of the model to explain historical series patterns and the degree of freedom of the model itself given by the numbers of parameters. This measure of *statistical performance* can be misleading if trading decisions are not taken coherently with the assumptions of the estimated model. This means that in order to use a model *coherently*, a trader must consider three factors related to the model used, before taking a decision: time horizon, sample window and structural market change.

- *Time horizon*: an econometric model (like ARMA) that aims to forecast a punctual value in the short term. The structure of the model itself is built up in this spirit: evaluate how recent market movement will impact the step-ahead observations, and not the *long-run* level. That means one may use coherent forecasting while taking a trading decision: a long or short position needs to be taken and closed in the time interval considered. An autoregressive model on daily observation will provide a signal for daily *in & out* strategy; different strategies holding the same position for a longer time interval, without updating the forecast, are not statistically coherent.

- *Sample window*: the data set for parameter's estimation needs to be accurately selected, considering market conditions; time series may be affected by significant changes in liquidity levels (especially in emerging markets) impacting price dynamics. Price distortions should be removed from the historical sample so as to obtain a more meaningful parameter's estimation.
- *Structural market change*: related to the previous point, a last warning is to pay attention on market break or structural change in the economic fundamental of the series. Years of market data should be totally meaningless if the economic rationale underlying relations between different asset values has disappeared or has significantly changed (example: market decoupling or coupling due to new regulatory rule, technology changes and others).

So, bearing in mind the previous consideration, a statistical trading model should be easy to set up by building a strategy based on an econometric model.

A case study has been prepared, working on a classical ARMA. Let us consider a product tradable on the Italian power market forward: a contract on calendar ahead for Italian power. We consider a series of closing prices assessments on a daily basis, on a time window starting from 23/02/2009 up to 30/06/2010, for a total of 320 observations (source: Bloomberg) see Figure 2.12 for more detail. We have built an econometric model to forecast the $t + 1$ price level of the calendar ahead forward. In order to do so we have fitted an ARMA (1,1) model on the time series considered. Moreover, to empower the performance of the model, we have included an exogenous economic variable that impacts the value of power in Italy: the forward calendar level of an oil-linked formula (in particular, the level of the ENIGR07[1] formula, adjusted for an average efficiency level of CCGT power plant, which is a benchmark for the gas price in Italy). Including the level of an oil-linked formula, which is a proxy for the variable cost for gas-fired thermal

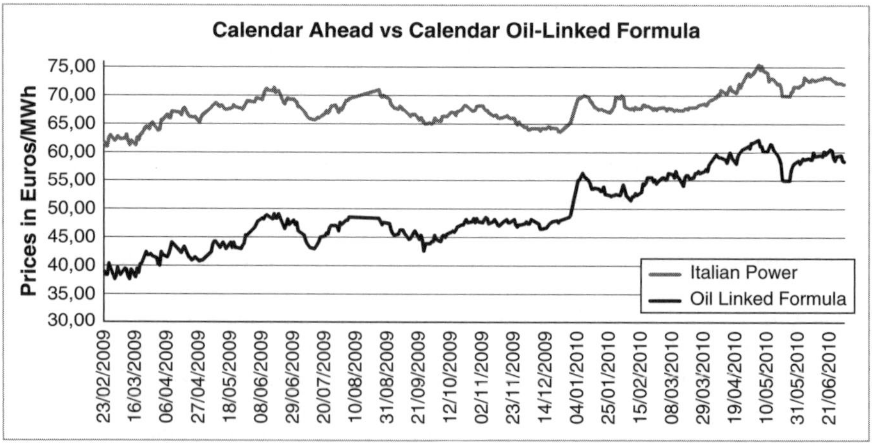

Figure 2.12 Calendar ahead vs Calendar oil-linked formula

[1] Eni Gas Release 2007 is the name of an oil-linked formula used mainly in Italy by Eni for the compulsory release of gas.

power plant in Italy, we have an economic variable that allows us to better detect the long trend level; autoregressive movements of the series are managed by the ARMA components.

The aim of the statistical trading strategy implemented is to obtain a trading signal comparing the forecast price for the day ahead with the closing price observed at time t. Generally speaking, a statistical trading strategy is a system that, based on a set of rules, automatically compares current and historical price levels of a certain financial product with the forecast price level (in this case, as the output of an econometric model). For our case study, in formulas, using p_t we have defined the observed closing price level of the calendar ahead forward, and using $\widehat{p_t}$ the price forecast of the calendar ahead closing price for the same trading day. Hence the system compares the observed closing price level at time t with the forecast price level at time $t+1$, and the statistical boundary level at a certain confidence level α. The statistical calculations for the confidence level are obtained by adding/subtracting the standard deviation of the model residuals times the quantile of normal standard distribution at a chosen confidence level α:

$$\hat{p}_{t+1}^{\text{up}} = p_t + \alpha(N(0,1))\sigma_{\text{residuals}} \qquad \hat{p}_{t+1}^{\text{down}} = p_t - \alpha(N(0,1))\sigma_{\text{residuals}}$$

So the trading decision is taken according to the following rules:

- if $p_t < \hat{p}_{t+1}^{\text{down}}$ then the observed closing price is significantly disaligned under the price lower bound confidence level for the following trading day, and so this results in a *BUY* signal;
- if $p_t > \hat{p}_{t+1}^{\text{up}}$ then the observed closing price is significantly disaligned above the price upper bound confidence level for the following trading day, and so this results in a *SELL* signal;
- where $\hat{p}_{t+1}^{\text{down}} \leqslant p_t \leqslant \hat{p}_{t+1}^{\text{up}}$, this designates a closing price level that falls inside the confidence levels, there is no clear sign of statistical disalignment, so this results in a *DO NOTHING* signal.

The strategy compares the current value against the up and down boundaries around the forecasted price in order to take a decision; that means that the disalignment from the level forecast has to be significant from a statistical point of view to result in a trading signal. If the current closing price is included between the up & down boundaries this results in a *do nothing* trading signal results.

As noted, the position needs to be taken and closed within the same trading day in order to be consistent with the estimated model. The control parameter α allows us to set the statistical confidence level to calculate the boundary around the forecast: the higher α is set, the wider the boundaries and so the number of wrong trading decisions is expected to be lower. On the other hand, the more distant the boundaries are, the less the strategy will take positions. Table 2.1 sums up the statistical results of the business case.

The *statistical ratio* is calculated as the ratio between profit positions and the total number of positions taken along the strategy time horizon. The control parameter α affects the number of trading signals and hence obviously the reliability of

Table 2.1 Statistical trading strategy on ARMA

Confidence level	Statistical ratio	Total position taken
@ 99%	93%	30
@ 90%	88%	98
@ 80%	84%	145
@ 70%	80%	211
@ 60%	75%	264

the model in terms of performance. A more aggressive trading strategy will result in a higher number of transactions affecting the profit ratio, while the reverse holds. This business case does not take into account transaction costs and bid-ask spread (even if thin for a liquid product like a calendar), and no P&L figures have been calculated: in terms of a *statistical* evaluation, a simple P&L number would be misleading. In fact, a positive final cash flow should result from a low number of *profit* positions with large (unpredicted) market movements and so is not indicative from a statistical perspective. The plain calculation of the profit ratio for the implemented strategy gives nice results, even considering a low confidence level.

Case study 2: Fundamental trading

The aim of this section is to implement and back test a strategy based on a fundamental model for trend individuation. Again, as we saw in the previous section, an understanding of the idea and the assumptions on which the model is based will help us take coherent trading decisions. The time horizon of the strategy as well as *in and out* trading timing are totally different with respect to a short-term trading strategy, such as the statistical one presented in the previous case study. Our fundamental approach aims to model the price movements based on the long-run economic relationship, and for this reason short-term deviations or other autoregressive movements will not be considered. This implies, as stated, that the strategy's time horizon is longer, and that a *buy/sell and hold* strategy for the amount will be the best solution for trading according to this kind of model.

The Italian gas market has been considered for the development of a fundamental bid stack model. The idea of a fundamental model is to find the *equilibrium* price as the market price at which the supply of a commodity equals the quantity demanded, and so we need to model supply and demand separately for the Italian gas market.

On the supply side, we have selected the relevant sources of gas in Italy. We have considered national production, which is negligible in terms of quantity, and the importers that play the most important role in the Italian market. Specifically, the entry points considered for Italy are: Mazara del Vallo, where gas coming from North Africa is imported; Passo Gries, where gas coming from the North Sea is imported through the TENP pipeline; Tarvisio, where Russian gas is imported through the TAG pipeline; the LNG terminals; and national storage. Each gas entry point is characterized by a different marginal cost of extraction and different opportunity cost, so we have tried to make some assumptions in order to assign a reasonable price reference level to each. In particular, when considering the gas imported from Algeria, for instance, we only need to cover the transportation cost since that country's suppliers have no opportunity to sell gas to other buyers because interconnection facilities are only available with Italy; hence their opportunity cost is basically zero. Gas imported from the North Sea has been priced at the same level as TTF (the Dutch gas market exchange) adding the cost of carrying gas to the Italian hub. The Russian gas has been priced with a common Oil Index formula at which the import LTC with Russian suppliers is generally supposed to be indexed. The LNG has been priced at the maximum between NBP (UK Gas market exchange), TTF and Zeebrugge (Belgian gas market exchange), taking into account that this class of supplier is really reactive to price signals with the possibility of delivering gas to different countries (almost in the medium term). Finally, a specific consideration needs to be made on storage, which represents the opportunity to carry gas through time, profiting from seasonality in gas prices between winter and summer. So gas operators inject gas into the storages during the summer and withdraw it in winter. For these reasons we need to consider the storage as a supply component during the winter, and as a demand component during summer. When considered as supply, we have chosen to price the storage at the average of the PSV price observed during the previous summer when the gas was injected into the storages.

On the other hand, the demand can be broken down into three main types of consumer: domestic, industrial and power generator. As stated in the previous section, a substitution effect between different commodities sources can occur just for a portion of the aggregated demand and, moreover due to physical constraints, not in real time with respect to price movements. For these reasons the aggregated demand has been considered locally price insensitive, and we have modelled each component of the demand separately taking into account seasonal structure of consumption and expected growth rate for each.

Ranking suppliers by reference price, from the cheapest to the most expensive, together with aggregated demand, we can ascertain the equilibrium (marginal) price, with monthly granularity, as the reference price associated with the last gas supplier to satisfy the aggregated demand. The Italian PSV market is not a regulated market, which is why the marginal price should not be taken as the equilibrium price of the market. We can also consider a *weighted average sourcing price* (wasp) as the average of the reference prices at which each supplier is supposed to be willing to sell (the prices are obviously weighted to the capacity of carrying gas to the Italian hub for each entry point). Finally, the model gives two price indications for determining marginal price (opportunity cost) and average price of gas sources in the future. We could state that, according to the model assumptions, an equilibrium PSV value (see Figure 2.13 as an example) must fall within the

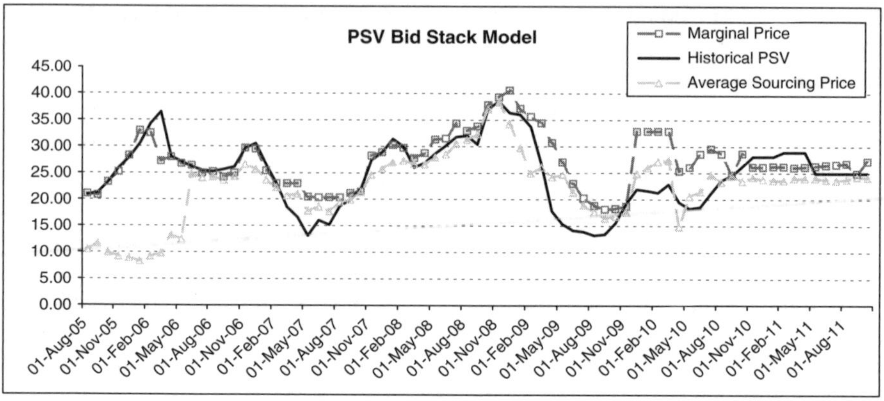

Figure 2.13 PSV bid stack model

range upper bounded by the marginal price and lower bounded by the wasp:

$$\text{PSV}_{\text{weighted average sorcing price}} \leqslant \text{PSV}_{\text{equilibrium price}} \leqslant \text{PSV}_{\text{marginal price}}$$

In order to back test the model, forward and futures gas prices listed on the different European gas exchanges have been used.

An example of a trading strategy based on this model is not possible for a dynamic and continuous *in & out* strategy that is not consistent with the idea of the model itself. Short-term deviations are not detected by this kind of model and trade in the short term is totally inconsistent. We simulate a trading case where a position has been opened months before delivery, with a *buy and hold* strategy.

During September 2008 the forward contract SUMMER 2009 was traded on average at 30.5 Euros/MWh; for the same period the fundamental model presented worked out a forecast price range of 23 to 20 Euros/MWh (marginal price to wasp price) for the delivery of gas during summer 2009. The model was wrong in absolute terms, because in the end the average price forward quotation on month ahead products (for each of the months of summer 2009) was about 14.5 Euros/MWh, but absolutely right in detecting which decreasing trend the market was following. So a short position on summer 2009, taken during September 2008 when forward quotation was clearly above the marginal price, resulted in a huge profit (even better than what the model itself expected).

Again, during January 2009 the forward contract WINTER 2009 (intended as the winter season starting in October 2009 and ending in March 2010) was traded on average at 25 Euros/MWh; for the same period the model worked out a forecast price range of between 23 and 21 Euros/MWh (marginal price to wasp price) for the delivery of gas during winter 2009. The final average price forward quotation on month ahead products (for each of the months of winter 2009) was even lower, around a level of 20 Euros/MWh, and the model was again right in detecting which decreasing trend the market was following. Once more, a short position on winter 2009 will have resulted in a positive P&L.

2.4 STRATEGIC ASSET ALLOCATION METHODS

2.4.1 Traditional Asset Allocation Models

One of the main problems faced by a subject who has an amount to invest in a market is the choice of how to invest in the assets in an *optimal way*. *Utility functions* are the expedient used to define which is the *optimal way*.

From an economic point of view utility is a measure of relative satisfaction: given two packages x, y of a consumption set, if the consumer prefers package x to package y then the utility associated with package x must be greater than the utility associated with y. It is well known from classic economic theory that there exist different classes of utility function (such as CARA, CRRA, CES) divided according to the risk aversion attitude they express.

From a mathematical point of view a utility function is a function $U : [0, +\infty] \longrightarrow \mathbb{R}$ that is strictly increasing and concave. The most used utility functions are, for example,

$$u(v) = \log v$$

$$u(v) = \frac{v^{\gamma}}{\gamma} \quad \gamma < 1, \gamma \neq 0$$

$$u(v) = -e^{-\beta v} \quad \beta > 0$$

The doctrine of utilitarianism saw the maximization of utility as a moral criterion for the organization of society, and this becomes the *optimal way* that an investor wants to pursue. He has an initial capital, w_0, and he tries to allocate this capital in the market in order to maximize some utility deriving either from increased terminal capital, by additional intermediate consumption capability, or both.

Obviously, in an uncertain environment where return on investment is unknown at the time of investment, a rational investor can only try to maximize its expected utility by choosing its optimal asset allocation strategy.

Traditionally, in the financial literature this problem has been tackled from two different perspectives. The first and simplest one is the static single period problem, while the second is the dynamic multi-period one. Under the first problem's framework, the investor only focuses on the terminal result of their strategy, assuming no actions or significant events occur from the time of the investment to the end of the investment period (which can be tomorrow or the end of the year). The framework depicted is extremely simplistic compared with reality. In fact, in the real world market players continuously re-adjust their capital allocation in order to cope with intermediate results and capital constraints. The mathematical complexity related to the two approaches is obviously different, for which reason it is better to treat them separately.

2.4.2 Single Period Asset Allocation Model

Let us try to formalize the single period problem. Let the investor's decision time be $t = 0$, while strategy's end is T.

The static (single period) asset allocation problem can then be written as follows:

$$\max_{(\theta_1,\ldots,\theta_N)} \mathbb{E}\left[e^{-\rho T} U(V_T)\right]$$

where

- $U(w)$ is the utility function connected to terminal wealth;
- θ_i, $i = 1, \ldots, N$ is the capital allocated on investment assets;
- V_T is the wealth variable produced by the portfolio's strategy;
- ρ is the continuously compounded risk-free rate.

Historically, Markowitz was among the first to tackle the problem of strategic asset allocation (1952). The problem he faced was slightly different from the generic one described above but can be thought of as a special case of it. Markowitz's problem, proposed in 1952, can be summarized in the following way: an investor can allocate his capital into N assets and must decide how much to invest in each asset, trying to balance expected return and risk of the portfolio. The model uses the portfolio's variance as the measure of its risk and its expected return as the measure of the investor's long-term prospects.

The objective is to minimize the overall variance of the portfolio's return while taking into consideration the following constraints: the fact that the expected return of the portfolio is fixed at a target level/$\{\tilde{r}\}$, and the fact that the investors cannot invest more than their initial monetary endowment. An efficient portfolio is defined as the portfolio that maximizes the expected return given a fixed level of risk (standard deviation), or the portfolio that minimizes the risk subject to a given expected return.

Let $r = (r_i)_{i=1,\ldots,N}$ be the expected return of the assets, $\Sigma = \left[\sigma_{i,j}\right]_{i,j=1,\ldots N}$ the variance–covariance matrix between the assets, and $\theta = (\theta_i)_{i=1,\ldots,N}$ the amount invested in every asset. The expected return of the portfolio is given by $r^T\theta$ and the variance by $\theta^T \Sigma\theta$, which is the quantity we want to minimize given a fixed rate of return $\tilde{r}$; the total amount invested in each single asset must add up to the initial amount w_0.

The problem is:

$$\begin{aligned} \min_\theta \quad & \theta^T \Sigma\theta \\ s.t. \quad & r^T\theta = \tilde{r} \\ & \bar{1}^T\theta = w_0 \end{aligned}$$

It is solved using the Lagrangian method, which gives the solution:

$$\theta^* = \Sigma^{-1} A H^{-1} b \tag{2.3}$$

having defined the following matrices and vectors: $\bar{1} = (1, \ldots, 1)^T$ a vector of length N whose elements are equal to 1, $b = \begin{pmatrix} \tilde{r} \\ w_0 \end{pmatrix}$ is a two-dimensional column vector, A is the matrix $A = \left(r \bar{1} \right)$ and $H = A^T \Sigma^{-1} A$.

The variance of the optimal portfolio, for a fixed initial capital w_0, is a function of $\tilde{r}$ and is given by:

$$\sigma^2_{\text{opt}} = \frac{1}{\xi_1} \left(\xi_2 \tilde{r}^2 - 2\xi_3 w_0 \tilde{r} + \xi_4 w_0^2 \right)$$

with the shorthand notation:

$$\begin{aligned} \xi_4 &= r^T \Sigma^{-1} r \\ \xi_3 &= r^T \Sigma^{-1} \bar{1} \\ \xi_2 &= \bar{1}^T \Sigma^{-1} \bar{1} \\ \xi_1 &= \xi_4 \xi_3 - (\xi_3)^2 \end{aligned}$$

The graph given by the couples $\Gamma = \left\{ \left(\tilde{r}, \sigma_{\text{opt}}(r) \right) \right\}$ is called the efficient frontier; it is the curve that shows all efficient portfolios for a given expected rate $\tilde{r}$.

Markowitz's approach has more of a descriptive than a strategic scope. In fact, optimal portfolio weights depend on the level of expected return the investor is looking for.

Moreover, the minimization of portfolio's variance given the expected return (as the problem's target function) can only partially be considered as a special case of an expected utility maximization problem. In fact, in general, the specification of the utility function implies the selection of a subjective preference structure in the risk/return space.

2.4.3 Inter-temporal Asset Allocation Problems

Trading is a dynamic business. Naturally, professional investors dynamically allocate their capital in more or less risky assets, adjusting their strategy according to new information, past performance and capital constraints. It is then more realistic to consider the asset allocation problem as a dynamic problem where the overall target can be jointly related to terminal economic performance as well as to all inter-temporal capital consumption or injection plans.

The generic inter-temporal asset allocation problem can be formulated as follows:

$$\begin{aligned} \max_{\pi_t \in \mathcal{A}, c_t \geqslant 0} \quad & \mathbb{E}\left[\int_0^T e^{-\rho t} U'(c_t) dt + e^{-\rho T} U''(V_T) \right] \\ s.t. \quad & dV_t = f(V_t, \pi_t, c_t) \end{aligned}$$

where

- $U'(w)$ is the utility function connected to inter-temporal consumption;
- $U''(w)$ is the utility function connected to terminal wealth;
- π_t is the proportion of capital allocated on investment assets that lies in a suitable set $\mathcal{A}$;
- c_t is the capital consumption variable;
- V_t is the wealth variable produced by the portfolio's strategy;
- $f(V_t, \pi_t, c_t)$ is the generic inter-temporal budget constraint;
- ρ is the continuously compounded risk-free rate.

The capital consumption variable should be thought of as redundant or not significant for the typical trading investment problem. However, it may be relevant for those trading environments where deterministic capital withdrawal plans have to be matched as a fundamental part of the trading business itself. For example, this may be the case for pension funds, insurance companies and, in some cases, even hedge funds. Here, dynamic capital withdrawals are necessary for the payment of management fees, periodic coupons or dividends.

Without considering the consumption variable the problem reconfigures as follows:

$$\max_{\pi_t \in \mathcal{A}} \mathbb{E}\left[e^{-\rho T} U''(V_T)\right]$$
$$s.t. \; dV_t = f(V_t, \pi_t, c_t)$$

In traditional asset allocation strategies the so-called *self financing condition* is required. This implies that what we have called the inter-temporal budget constraint has to respect certain properties that prevent additional capital injection within the trading strategy.

Merton (1969) was the first to find a solution for the dynamic optimal investment/consumption problem analytically in continuous time under a series of simplificatory assumptions.

Traditional inter-temporal investment/consumption problems

The Merton problem is a problem in continuous time based on the fact that the investor can perform his choice not only at the beginning of a *reference period*, but also during the *life* of the problem.

Merton considers the problem of an investor who at time $t = 0$ has an initial capital w_0 and must choose, *at every instant* of a finite interval $t \in [0, T]$, how much of his wealth to consume and how much to allocate between a risk-free asset and a stock in the financial market, given that he wants to maximize the expected utility of the consumption and the terminal wealth.

The risk-free asset price is assumed to move deterministically according to the equation $\frac{dB_t}{B_t} = rdt$, while the stock follows the classic GBM dynamics:

$$\frac{dS_t}{S_t} = \mu dt + \sigma dW_t \qquad (2.4)$$

where W_t is a standard Brownian motion, μ is the drift of the asset and σ its volatility.

At every instant t the investor has the wealth V_t and he can:

i. choose his level of consumption c_t, that must satisfy the relationship: $0 \leqslant c_t \leqslant V_t$;
ii. decide how much to invest in the market;
iii. allocate in the risk-free asset the wealth not invested or consumed.

In order to satisfy the *self-financing condition* the budget constraint should have the following dynamics:

$$\begin{aligned} dV_t &= -c_t dt + \pi_t V_t(\mu dt + \sigma dW_t) + V_t(1-\pi_t)r dt \\ &= (V_t\,((\mu - r)\,\pi_t + r) - c_t)\,dt + \pi_t V_t \sigma dW_t \end{aligned} \tag{2.5}$$

where π_t is the proportion of the total wealth invested in the asset. Under the assumptions described so far, Merton solved the inter-temporal optimal investment/consumption problem presented in the previous section by assuming a power utility function ($U(\xi) = \frac{\xi^\gamma}{\gamma}$) to describe agents' preference structure.

The optimal control he obtained has the following functional form:

$$c_t^* = (\gamma - \rho)\left((\gamma - 1) - (\rho - 1)e^{\frac{(t-T)(\gamma-\rho)}{\gamma-1}}\right)^{-1} \tag{2.6}$$

$$\pi_t^* = \frac{\mu - r}{\sigma^2\,(1-\gamma)} \tag{2.7}$$

We may note that, even if it is somewhat surprising and counterintuitive, the optimal proportion π^* of the wealth invested in the stock is constant and independent of time and wealth.

Slightly surprising is the fact that if the drift μ of the asset is equal to the risk-free rate r then the optimal proportion to be invested in the market is 0: *why invest in a risky asset if the risk-free asset ensures the same expected return but without risk!?*

Merton's way of tackling the problem, that is a *stochastic optimal control problem*, is the *Hamilton-Jacobi-Bellman* approach. Due to the fact that this approach is used largely to solve this type of problem (we will see another application later), the following section briefly describes this procedure.

Mean reverting-asset: the Benth-Karlsen problem

Even if Merton's problem can be successfully applied to a large class of real problems, the weakness of the model is the statistical assumption of formula (2.4) that implies the log-normality and non-stationarity for the risky asset price dynamics.

In particular, for many energy commodities, the log-normality and non-stationarity of price dynamics is not a good assumption: statistical tests show, for example, mean-reversion, or leptokurtosis.

A good model for a mean-reverting energy price is given by the so-called *Schwartz model*:

$$\frac{dS_t}{S_t} = \alpha\left(\mu - \ln S_t\right)dt + \sigma dW_t \tag{2.8}$$

Note that $X_t = \ln S_t$ follows an Ornstein-Uhlenbeck process.

Under this framework the problem of maximizing (*only*) the utility of the terminal wealth, $U(V_T)$, was solved by Benth and Karlsen (2005).

Due to the fact that the solution is more complex than the one for Merton's problem, we will not present all the details. Here we report only the functional form of the optimal control:

$$\pi^*(t,s) = \frac{\alpha(\mu - \ln s) - r}{\sigma^2(1-\gamma)} + f_1(t) + 2f_2(t)\ln s \tag{2.9}$$

where $f_1(t)$ and $f_2(t)$ satisfy some differential equations.

It is interesting to note that in this case the optimal investment depends upon time, price level and also the distance between the price level and the attractor (long-term mean).

From a mathematical point of view it is interesting to see that small changes in the price dynamics assumptions lead to significant differences in the final solution and in the overall complexity of the problem itself. Difficult problems, in most of the cases, cannot be analytically solved. The numerical solution can be a good compromise between the exact solution and the effort required to obtain it.

2.4.4 Solution Methods – Dynamic Programming

The Hamilton Jacobi Bellmann equation

This section is not intended as a formal treatment of the Stochastic Optimal Control problems solved via the Hamilton Jacobi Bellmann equation; we are introducing this approach here without paying much attention to the mathematical details that are essential for the researcher, but superfluous for the reader. Interested readers can find a reference in Björk (2004).

Let us consider the following controlled SDE in $\mathbb{R}^n$:

$$dX_t^u = \mu(t, X_t^u, u_t)dt + \Sigma(t, X_t^u, u_t)dW_t \tag{2.10}$$

$$X_0 = x_0$$

where, in general, $\mu(t,x,u) = (\mu_1(t,x,u), \ldots, \mu_n(t,x,u))^T$ is a vector in $\mathbb{R}^n$, Σ is the variance-covariance matrix in $\mathbb{R}^{n\times n}$ and W_t is a vector of n *independent* Brownian motions.

The variable u_t is called the *control* at time t, that is the decision we have to take at time t; it does not matter what exactly this decision is about (the proportion invested, the consumption used...): here it represents the only variable we can choose to control the system. It is natural to assume that this variable has to lie in some space $\mathcal{A}$, which is useful to describe the constraints we impose on the control. The superscript u in the notation X_t^u makes explicit the fact that the decision u influences the dynamics of the system. In Merton's problem, for example, u_t is the couple $u_t = (\pi_t, c_t)$ while $\mathcal{A} = \left\{(\pi, c) \in \mathbb{R}^2 \quad s.t. \quad \pi \in [0, 1], c \geqslant 0\right\}$ and it is clear from equation (2.5) that the control affects the value of V_t.

We consider as given two utility functions $F(t, x, u)$ and $\Phi(t, s)$ and we want to solve the following problem:

$$\max_{u \in \mathcal{A}} \mathbb{E}\left[\int_0^T F(s, X_s^u, u_s)ds + \Phi\left(T, X_T^u\right)\right]$$

given the dynamics in formula (2.10) and the initial condition $X_0 = x_0$.

Define the following optimal value function:

$$V(t, x) = \sup_{u \in \mathcal{A}} \mathbb{E}_{t,x}\left[\int_t^T F(s, X_s^u, u_s)ds + \Phi\left(T, X_T^u\right)\right] \tag{2.11}$$

where $\mathbb{E}_{t,x}$ stands for the conditional expectation given the information set $\mathcal{F}_t$ at time t.

If we *assume* (and it is not trivial!) that there exists an optimal control law u_t and that the optimal value function V is regular, i.e. the first derivatives on t and the first and second derivatives on x exist, then it is possible to show that V satisfies the following Hamilton-Jacobi-Bellman equation:

$$\begin{cases} \frac{\partial V}{\partial t} + \sup\limits_{u \in \mathcal{A}} \left\{ F + \sum_{i=1}^n \mu_i \frac{\partial V}{\partial x_i} \right. \\ \qquad \left. + \frac{1}{2} \sum_{i,j=1}^n \left(\Sigma\Sigma'\right)_{i,j} \frac{\partial^2 V}{\partial x_i \partial x_j} \right\} = 0 & \forall (t, x) \in (0, T) \times \mathbb{R}^n \\ V(T, x) = \Phi(x) & \forall x \in \mathbb{R}^n \end{cases}$$

where we have used the shorthand notation V, μ_i, Σ instead of $V(t, x)$, $\mu_i\,(t, x, u)$, $\Sigma\,(t, x, u)$. Furthermore, for each $(t, x) \in [0, T] \times \mathbb{R}^n$ the supremum in the HJB equation is attained by the optimal control law.

The surprising result is that the HJB equation is not only necessary, but also sufficient for the optimal control problem; this result is contained in the so-called *Verification Theorem*.

Even if the results obtained so far are promising for finding the optimal solution, applying the Hamilton-Jacobi-Bellman equation is not always simple; schematically, the standard way to proceed is:

1. Consider an unknown, but fixed, function $V(t, x)$ and fix an arbitrary point (t, x). Solve the optimization problem:

$$u^* = \arg\sup_{u \in \mathcal{A}} \left\{ F + \sum_{i=1}^n \mu_i \frac{\partial V}{\partial x_i} + \frac{1}{2} \sum_{i,j=1}^n \left(\Sigma\Sigma'\right)_{i,j} \frac{\partial^2 V}{\partial x_i \partial x_j} \right\}$$

Note that at this point the only variable is u, all the other terms are supposed to be fixed parameters so the optimal choice u^* will depend on t, x but also on the function V and its partial derivatives.

2. Substitute the optimal control u^* and *try* to solve the PDE (partial differential equation) for $V(t,x)$:

$$\frac{\partial V}{\partial t}(t,x) + F\left(t,x,u^*\right) + \sum_{i=1}^{n} \mu_i(t,x,u)\frac{\partial V}{\partial x_l}(t,x) + \frac{1}{2}\sum_{i,j=1}^{n}\left(\Sigma\Sigma'\right)_{i,j}\left(t,x,u^*\right)\frac{\partial^2 V}{\partial x_i \partial x_j}(t,x) = 0$$

The hard work lies in solving the PDE for $V(t,x)$. In most cases one tries to *guess* at a solution: it turns out that $V(t,x)$ has often the *same form* of $F(t,x,u)$; a good idea might be to make an *ansatz* for V parametrized by a finite number of parameters hoping that the PDE leads to the identification of these parameters (very often these parameters are also functions!).

Example 1 We use Merton's problem as an example in order to show how the method works. As briefly stated above, Merton (1969) obtained results by assuming that the utility functions of the optimal investment/consumption problem have the form:

$$U'(\xi) = U''(\xi) = U(\xi) = \frac{\xi^\gamma}{\gamma}$$

for some $\gamma \in (0,1)$. Using the notation in formula (2.11), in this problem we are setting $F(t,x,u) = \Phi(t,x) = U(x)$.

The problem is:

$$\max_{\pi_t \in [0,1], c_t \geqslant 0} \mathbb{E}\left[\int_0^T e^{-\rho t}U(c_t)dt + e^{-\rho T}U(V_T)\right]$$

and the dynamics of the state is:

$$dV_t = \left(V_t\left((\mu - r)\pi_t + r\right) - c_t\right)dt + \pi_t V_t \sigma dW_t$$

so the HJB equation, for the optimal value function, termed $\mathcal{V}(t,v)$, (here $n=1$) is:

$$\frac{\partial \mathcal{V}}{\partial t} + \sup_{\pi \in [0,1], c \geqslant 0}\left\{e^{-\rho t}\frac{c^\gamma}{\gamma} + \frac{\partial \mathcal{V}}{\partial v}\left(v\left((\mu - r)\pi + r\right) - c\right) + \frac{1}{2}\frac{\partial^2 \mathcal{V}}{\partial v^2}\pi^2\sigma^2 v^2\right\} = 0 \tag{2.12}$$

The first-order conditions, using the shorthand notation $\partial_v \mathcal{V} = \frac{\partial \mathcal{V}}{\partial v}(t,v)$ for the derivatives, are:

$$c^* = \left(e^{\rho t}\partial_v \mathcal{V}\right)^{\frac{1}{\gamma - 1}} \tag{2.13}$$

$$\pi^* = \frac{(\partial_v \mathcal{V})(r-\mu)}{\left(\partial^2_{v^2}\mathcal{V}\right)\sigma^2 v} \tag{2.14}$$

These conditions are also sufficient if (second-order conditions)

$$e^{-\rho t} c^{\gamma-2}(\gamma - 1) \leqslant 0$$

that is the conditions are always satisfied due to the fact that $\gamma \in (0, 1)$ and $c \geqslant 0$, and

$$\frac{\partial^2 \mathcal{V}}{\partial v^2} v\sigma^2 \leqslant 0$$

which is satisfied if $\frac{\partial^2 \mathcal{V}}{\partial v^2} \leqslant 0$.

At this point we do the following *ansatz* for the optimal value function (as mentioned, a good class in which the value function can lie is that of the utility function):

$$\mathcal{V}(t, v) = e^{-\rho t}\frac{v^\gamma}{\gamma} b(t)$$

Here the parameter is the function $b(t)$.

Using the following derivatives of $\mathcal{V}(t, v)$:

$$\mathcal{V}_t(t, v) = \frac{v^\gamma}{\gamma} e^{-\rho t}\left(\dot{b}(t) - \rho b(t)\right)$$

$$\mathcal{V}_v(t, v) = e^{-\rho t} v^{\gamma-1} b(t)$$

$$\mathcal{V}_{vv}(t, v) = e^{-\rho t}(\gamma - 1) v^{\gamma-2} b(t)$$

in formulas (2.13) and (2.14) we obtain the optimal controls depending on $b(t)$:

$$\begin{aligned} c^* &= \left(e^{\rho t}\partial_v \mathcal{V}\right)^{\frac{1}{\gamma-1}} \\ &= \left(e^{\rho t} e^{-\rho t} v^{\gamma-1} b(t)\right)^{\frac{1}{\gamma-1}} = v b(t)^{\frac{1}{\gamma-1}} \\ \pi^* &= \frac{e^{-\rho t} v^{\gamma-1} b(t)(\mu - r)}{e^{-\rho t}(\gamma-1) v^{\gamma-2} b(t)\sigma^2 v} = \frac{(\mu - r)}{(\gamma-1)\sigma^2} \end{aligned}$$

Using the derivatives of $\mathcal{V}$ and the optimal controls obtained so far, the HJB equation in formula (2.12) reads:

$$\dot{b}(t) - \rho b(t) + b(t)^{\frac{\gamma}{\gamma-1}} + \gamma b(t)\left(\frac{(\mu - r)^2}{(\gamma-1)\sigma^2} + r - b(t)^{\frac{1}{\gamma-1}}\right) + \gamma b(t)\frac{(\mu - r)^2}{2\sigma^2} = 0$$

which is a Bernoulli partial differential equation (PDE) for the parameter (function) $b(t)$ with the final condition $V(T,v) = e^{-\rho T}\frac{v^\gamma}{\gamma}$ that leads to $b(T) = 1$. The solution of the PDE is given by:

$$b(t) = \left(\frac{1 + \left(\frac{\rho-\gamma}{1-\gamma} - 1\right) e^{\frac{\rho-\gamma}{1-\gamma}(t-T)}}{\frac{\rho-\gamma}{1-\gamma}} \right)^{1-\gamma}$$

Using the Verification Theorem we can state that we have found the optimal value function and the optimal controls, which have been obtained by substituting equations (2.13) and (2.14). The appropriate derivatives (we are supposing $\gamma \neq \rho$), are:

$$c^*(t) = (\gamma - \rho)\left((\gamma - 1) - (\rho - 1)e^{\frac{(t-T)(\gamma-\rho)}{\gamma-1}} \right)^{-1}$$

$$\pi^* = \frac{\mu - r}{\sigma^2 (1-\gamma)}$$

Recursive algorithm in discrete time: Stochastic Dynamic Programming

Dynamic programming is a method of solving complex problems by breaking them down into simpler steps. This procedure is well suited to discrete problems, i.e. problems in which decisions are taken (and the system is observed) at certain moments in time, not continuously as in the previous subsection.

In this section we will try to tackle the optimal dynamic investment problem in a numerical way, splitting it into some discrete-time problems. A simplified version of the Merton problem will initially be assumed as a reference case, then a generic framework will be introduced. We use this example in order to highlight the problems that a simple algorithmic approach would have and to introduce the principle of dynamic programming.

Let us consider the following problem. Maximize the expected utility of the final wealth without consumption, i.e. let us try to maximize

$$\max_{\pi_t \in [0,1]} \mathbb{E}\left[\frac{V_T^\gamma}{\gamma}\right]$$

given the dynamics:

$$dV_t = V_t\left[((\mu - r)\pi_t + r)\,dt + \pi_t \sigma\, dW_t\right] \quad (2.15)$$

The discretized version of (2.15) is:

$$V_{t+\Delta t} - V_t = V_t\left[((\mu - r)\pi_t + r)\,\Delta t + \pi_t \sigma \sqrt{\Delta t}\varepsilon\right] \quad (2.16)$$

being $\varepsilon \sim N(0,1)$.

The main idea is as follows. Once we have divided the interval $[0, T]$ into $N+1$ subintervals, called $\{[T_i, T_{i+1}]\}_{i=0,\dots,N}$ with $T_0 = 0$ and $T_N = T$ and such that $T_{i+1} - T_i = \Delta t$ for a choice of Δt, we can use the following backward procedure:

- when $i = N$, i.e. at time T, the utility given by a capital $V_T = v$ is $u(v) = \frac{v^\gamma}{\gamma}$;
- when $i = N-1$, if we have a capital $V_{T_{N-1}} = v$, formula (2.16) gives us the value of the capital at the next step T_N; so at this step the expected maximum utility of the final wealth is given by the function $W_{N-1}(v)$ whose formula is given by:

$$W_{N-1}(v) = \max_{\pi_{N-1}} \mathbb{E}\left[u(V_T)|\mathcal{F}_{T_{N-1}}\right] \tag{2.17}$$

$$= \max_{\pi_{N-1}} \mathbb{E}\left[u(V_T)|V_{T_{N-1}} = v\right]$$

$$= \max_{\pi_{N-1}} \mathbb{E}\left[\frac{\left(v + v\left((\mu - r)\pi + r\right)\Delta t + \pi\sigma\sqrt{\Delta t}\varepsilon\right)^\gamma}{\gamma}\right] \tag{2.18}$$

We can (numerically) maximize formula (2.18) by using some simulations $\varepsilon_j \sim N(0,1)$ from the normal distribution:

$$\max_{\pi} \mathbb{E}\left[\frac{\left(v + v\left((\mu - r)\pi + r\right)\Delta t + \pi\sigma\sqrt{\Delta t}\varepsilon\right)^\gamma}{\gamma}\right]$$

$$= \max_{\pi}\left[\frac{\left(v + v\left((\mu - r)\pi + r\right)\Delta t + \frac{1}{M}\sum_{j=1}^{M}\pi\sigma\sqrt{\Delta t}\varepsilon_j\right)^\gamma}{\gamma}\right] \tag{2.19}$$

The maximization of formula (2.19) has to be performed for some *representative* value of v in an interval $[\underline{v}, \overline{v}]$; in the next step we will consider the function $\tilde{W}_{N-1}(v)$ as a linear interpolation of (2.19) on v.

- when $i = N-2, \dots, 0$ the function we have to maximize is given recursively using both the rule of iterated expected value and the dynamic-programming principle, which states that if a control is optimal on a whole sequence of periods then it has to be optimal on every single period.

  Consider, for example, the optimal value function $W_{N-2}(v)$ at time T_{N-2} that represents the maximum expected utility of the terminal wealth. It is given by

$$W_{N-2}(v) = \max_{\pi_{N-2},\pi_{N-1}} \mathbb{E}\left[u(V_T)|\mathcal{F}_{T_{N-2}}\right]$$

$$= \max_{\pi_{N-2},\pi_{N-1}} \mathbb{E}\left[\mathbb{E}\left[u(V_T)|\mathcal{F}_{T_{N-1}}\right]|\mathcal{F}_{T_{N-2}}\right]$$

$$= \max_{\pi_{N-2},\pi_{N-1}} \mathbb{E}\left[\mathbb{E}\left[u(V_T)|\mathcal{F}_{T_{N-1}}\right]|\mathcal{F}_{T_{N-2}}\right]$$

$$= \max_{\pi_{N-2}} \mathbb{E}\left[\max_{\pi_{N-1}} \mathbb{E}\left[u(V_T)|\mathcal{F}_{T_{N-1}}\right]|\mathcal{F}_{T_{N-2}}\right]$$

$$= \max_{\pi_{N-2}} \mathbb{E}\left[W_{N-1}\left(V_{T_{N-1}}\right)|V_{T_{N-2}} = v\right]$$

$$= \max_{\pi_{N-2}} \mathbb{E}\left[W_{N-1}\left(v + v\left((\mu - r)\,\pi_{N-2} + r\right)\Delta t + \pi_{N-2}\sigma\sqrt{\Delta t}\varepsilon\right)\right] \quad (2.20)$$

having used formula (2.17). From formula (2.20) it is clear why, in the previous step, we have taken an interpolation for the function $W_{N-1}(v)$: in this step $W_{N-2}(v)$ should be evaluated on a random set of points, so in practice we can only perform the maximization:

$$\max_{\pi_{N-2}} \mathbb{E}\left[\tilde{W}_{N-1}\left(v + v\left((\mu - r)\,\pi_{N-2} + r\right)\Delta t + \pi_{N-2}\sigma\sqrt{\Delta t}\varepsilon\right)\right]$$

In the following steps the procedure will always be the same: take the maximum for some values of v in an interval $\left[\underline{v}, \overline{v}\right]$ and then take an interpolation for $W_{N-i}(v)$. And so on.

Even if the procedure described above is fairly simple, some problems can occur immediately when one tries to implement the numerical routine. First of all, the values of $\underline{v}$ and $\overline{v}$ on which we are taking the interpolant are not obvious and have to be inferred from market values and from the statistical properties of the return (i.e. one has to avoid the possibility that a few simulations lead to negative values of v). Then we have to decide on the number of subintervals in which to divide $[0, T]$, that is the length of the step Δt. The third problem is the number of simulations necessary in order to obtain accurate results: in our test a good number is (at least) 10^6; this large number of simulations leads to a very large demand of memory and to a very long maximization time (several hours). Finally, one has to take into account that due to the interpolation of the optimal value function, the accuracy of the optimization at every step rapidly slows down.

In Figures 2.14 and 2.15 we show the results obtained in the first two passages of the iteration. Looking at Figure 2.15 the problems given by the interpolation at the boundary of $\left[\overline{v}, \underline{v}\right]$ are evident.

The general case. The simplified Merton's problem addressed above can be generalized obtaining the following recursive (backward) algorithm for the dynamic programming.

Suppose that the state of the system generically evolves such that:

$$V_{k+1} = f_k(V_k, \pi_k(V_k), \varepsilon_k) \quad (2.21)$$

where $f_k(v, \pi, \varepsilon)$ is the transition function at step k, V_k the state at step k, π_k the decision taken (in general the decision is a function of the state, so we write $\pi_k(V_k)$) and ε_k a random *disturbance* of the state V_k. For example formula (2.21) can be reduced to formula (2.16) by setting $f_k(v, \pi, \varepsilon) = v + v\left[\left((\mu - r)\,\pi + r\right)\Delta t + \pi\sigma\sqrt{\Delta t}\varepsilon\right]$ for all values of k.

Now, having defined for every step $i = 0, \ldots, N$ a utility function $u_i(v, \pi)$ (in the example above we had $u_i(v, \pi) \equiv 0 \quad \forall i = 0, \ldots, N-1$ and

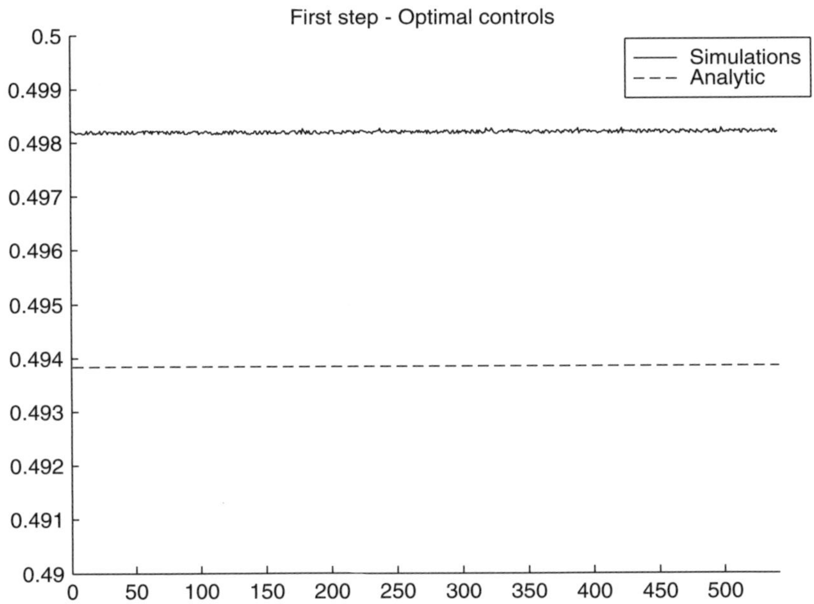

Figure 2.14 Optimal controls obtained at the first step

$u_N(v, \pi) = u(v) = \frac{v^\gamma}{\gamma}$), let $\{W_n(v)\}_{n=0,\ldots N}$ be the following function defined recursively by:

$$\begin{cases} W_N(v) = \sup_{\pi_N} u_N(v, \pi_N) \\ W_n(v) = \sup_{\pi_N} (u_n(v, \pi_n) + \mathbb{E}\left[W_{n+1}\left(f_n(v, \pi_n(v), \varepsilon_n)\right)\right] \quad n = N-1, \ldots, 0 \end{cases} \tag{2.22}$$

The main result one can obtain (see Pascucci and Runggaldier, 2009) is the relationship:

$$\sup_{\pi_n, \pi_{n+1}, \ldots, \pi_N} \mathbb{E}\left[\sum_{k=n}^{N} u_k(V_k, \pi_k(V_k)) | V_n = v\right] = W_n(v)$$

which states that the maximum expected cumulated utility from time T_n to time T is given exactly by the functions $W_n(v)$.

The Martingale method

The Martingale method, developed in the 1980s, is widely used in finance for pricing derivatives, but it can be adopted in order to solve stochastic dynamic programming: this is the aim of this section.

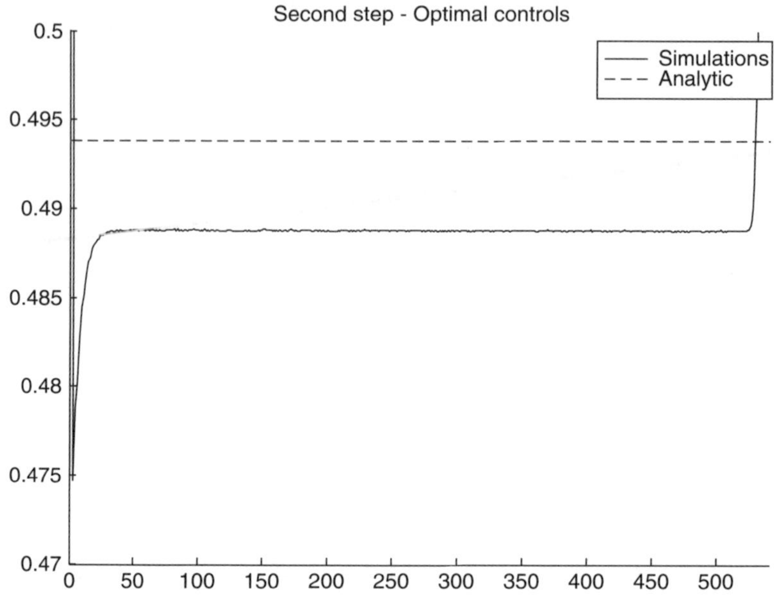

Figure 2.15 Optimal controls obtained at the second step

Consider the following problem:

$$\begin{aligned} \max_h \quad & \mathbb{E}_{\mathbb{P}}\left[u\left(V_T^h\right)\right] \\ s.t. \quad & \mathbb{E}_{\mathbb{Q}}\left[\frac{V_T^h}{B_T}\right] \leqslant v_0 \\ & V_0 = v_0 \end{aligned} \tag{2.23}$$

where $u(v)$ is a utility function, $\mathbb{E}_{\mathbb{P}}[\cdot]$ and $\mathbb{E}_{\mathbb{Q}}[\cdot]$ stand for the expectation under the real-world measure $\mathbb{P}$ and an equivalent martingale measure $\mathbb{Q}$. The notation V_t^h is used to stress the fact that at time t the wealth process V_t is obtained following the strategy h_t, that can also be characterized as a progressively measurable process[2] such that $V_t > 0$ almost certainly with respect to $\mathbb{P}$ for all time t.

The main theorem that underlies the Martingale method is the so-called *Saddle Point Theorem*, that generalizes the Lagrange multipliers. This theorem states that if we want to solve the problem

$$\begin{aligned} \max \quad & f(x) \\ s.t. \quad & q(x) \leqslant 0 \end{aligned} \tag{2.24}$$

[2] The condition of *progressively measurable* stands for the requirement that the process $h = \{h_t\}_{t\in[0,T]}$ must be continuous and adapted to the filtration $\{\mathcal{F}_t\}_{t\in[0,T]}$ (but note that the two conditions are not *equivalent*): as we saw in Chapter 1, this condition reflects the fact that our decision at time t, h_t, has to take into account only the information available at time t.

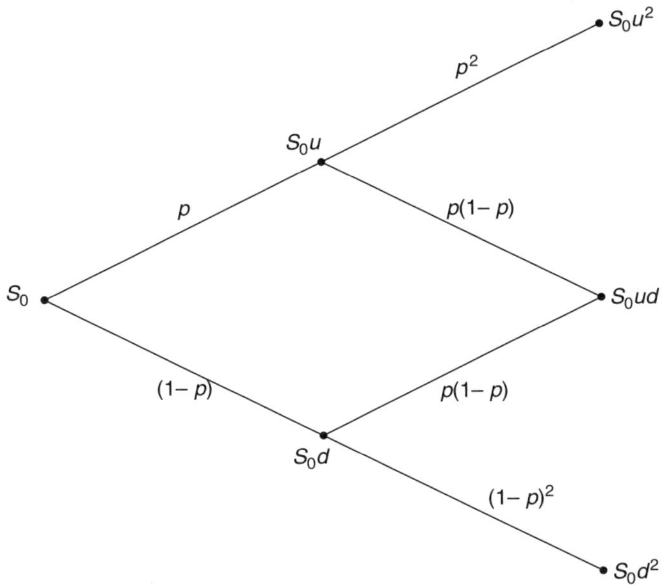

Figure 2.16 Binomial tree

having defined the following *Lagrangean* function:

$$\mathcal{L}(x, \lambda) = f(x) - \lambda q(x)$$

if (x^*, λ^*) is a *saddle point* for $\mathcal{L}(x, \lambda)$, that is if $\forall (x, \lambda) \in \mathbb{R}^n \times \mathbb{R}^+$

$$\mathcal{L}(x, \lambda^*) \leqslant \mathcal{L}(x^*, \lambda^*) \leqslant \mathcal{L}(x^*, \lambda)$$

then x^* solves problem (2.24).

We will use this theorem in order to solve problem (2.23) when the market is complete. At the end of the section we will briefly outline the case when the market is incomplete.

Let us define the Lagrangean function for problem (2.23) using the random variable (Radon-Nikodym) L_T from the Girsanov theorem to switch from the probability $\mathbb{Q}$ to $\mathbb{P}$:

$$\mathcal{L}(V_T, \lambda) = \mathbb{E}_{\mathbb{P}}\left[u\left(V_T\right)\right] - \lambda\left(\mathbb{E}_{\mathbb{Q}}\left[\frac{V_T}{B_T}\right] - v_0\right)$$

$$= \mathbb{E}_{\mathbb{P}}\left[u\left(V_T\right) - \lambda \frac{L_T}{B_T} V_T\right] + \lambda v_0$$

First of all, in order to find a saddle point, we can try to maximize the Lagrangean on the variable V_T for a fixed value of λ:

$$\begin{aligned}\max_{V_T} \mathcal{L}(V_T, \lambda) &= \max_{V_T} \left\{ \mathbb{E}_{\mathbb{P}} \left[u(V_T) - \lambda \frac{L_T}{B_T} V_T \right] + \lambda v_0 \right\} \\ &= \mathbb{E}_{\mathbb{P}} \left[\max_{V_T} \left\{ u(V_T) - \lambda \frac{L_T}{B_T} V_T \right\} \right]\end{aligned}$$

The function $w(y) = \max_x \{u(x) - yx\}$ is called the Legendre-Fenchel transform of $u(x)$.

First-order condition reads:

$$u'(V_T) = \lambda \frac{L_T}{B_T} \tag{2.25}$$

This condition is also sufficient: since $u(v)$ is a strictly concave function, its derivative $u'(v)$ is a strictly decreasing function.

If we assume also that $u'(0) = +\infty$ and $u'(+\infty) = 0$ then the inverse of u', say I: $[0, +\infty] \to [0, +\infty]$, $I(x) = (u')^{-1}(x)$, is well defined. Using I we can solve equation (2.25) finding the maximization value V_T^*, which depends on λ:

$$V_T^*(\lambda) = I\left(\lambda \frac{L_T}{B_T}\right)$$

We have just proved that $\forall \lambda \in \mathbb{R}^+$:

$$\mathcal{L}(v, \lambda) \leqslant \mathcal{L}\left(V_T^*(\lambda), \lambda\right) \tag{2.26}$$

Now we have to *minimize* on λ the function $\mathcal{L}\left(V_T^*(\lambda), \lambda\right)$. First-order conditions, in this case, become rather involved, but we can try to guess a solution: a good choice of λ may be the one that maximizes the expected terminal wealth under the martingale measure $\mathbb{Q}$. So let λ^* be such that

$$\mathbb{E}_{\mathbb{Q}}\left[V_T^*(\lambda^*)\right] = v_0$$

Such a λ^* exists and is unique, being $V_T^*(\lambda)$ a strictly decreasing function of λ.

Let us now prove that $\left(V_T^*(\lambda^*), \lambda^*\right)$ is a saddle point for $\mathcal{L}(v, \lambda)$. We have already proved (equation (2.26)) that $\mathcal{L}(v, \lambda^*) \leqslant \mathcal{L}\left(V_T^*(\lambda), \lambda^*\right)$; the second inequality needed to have a saddle point as a consequence of

$$\mathcal{L}(V_T^*(\lambda^*), \lambda) = \mathbb{E}_{\mathbb{P}}[u(V_T)] - \lambda\left(\mathbb{E}_{\mathbb{Q}}\left[\frac{V_T^*(\lambda^*)}{B_T}\right] - v_0\right) = \mathbb{E}_{\mathbb{P}}[u(V_T)]$$

which states that $\forall \lambda \in \mathbb{R}^+$ the function $\mathcal{L}(V_T^*(\lambda^*), \lambda)$ is constant and so we can write:

$$\mathbb{E}_{\mathbb{P}}[u(V_T)] = \mathcal{L}\left(V_T^*(\lambda), \lambda\right) \leqslant \mathcal{L}\left(V_T^*(\lambda^*), \lambda^*\right) = \mathbb{E}_{\mathbb{P}}[u(V_T)]$$

which is the needed inequality.

The optimal final wealth is thus $V_T^*(\lambda^*) = I\left(\lambda^* \frac{L_T}{B_T}\right)$. The optimal strategy is obtained using a martingale representation theorem and by the fact that the process $\tilde{V}_t$, i.e. the discounted wealth obtained with a self-financing strategy, is a martingale under $\mathbb{Q}$. To better show how to find the optimal strategy let us use an example. In what follows we solve Merton's problem using the Martingale method.

We solve the problem by considering one asset with the standard dynamics:

$$dS_t = S_t\left(\mu dt + \sigma dW_t\right)$$

where μ and σ can also be deterministic functions of t, but in this case they are scalar. We will use the notation $\tilde{S}_t = \frac{S_t}{B_t}$ to indicate the asset's discounted price with respect to B_t (which has the standard dynamics $dB_t = B_t r dt$); from Ito's formula it follows that the process $\tilde{S}_t$ has the dynamics:

$$d\tilde{S}_t = \tilde{S}_t\left((\mu - r)dt + \sigma dW_t\right)$$

under the probability measure $\mathbb{P}$. Switching from $\mathbb{P}$ to $\mathbb{Q}$ to obtain the martingale property for the discounted price $\tilde{S}_t$

$$d\tilde{S}_t = \tilde{S}_t \sigma d\bar{W}_t$$

leads to the following Radon-Nikodym derivative $L_T = \frac{d\mathbb{Q}}{d\mathbb{P}}$

$$\begin{aligned} L_T &= \exp\left\{-\frac{1}{2}\int_0^T \theta_u^2 du - \int_0^T \theta_u dW_u\right\} \\ &= \exp\left\{-\frac{1}{2}\int_0^T \theta_u^2 du - \int_0^T \theta_u\left(d\bar{W}_u - \theta_u du\right)\right\} \\ &= \exp\left\{\frac{1}{2}\int_0^T \theta_u^2 du - \int_0^T \theta_u d\bar{W}_u\right\} = L_t \exp\left\{\frac{1}{2}\int_t^T \theta_u^2 du - \int_t^T \theta_u d\bar{W}_u\right\} \end{aligned} \tag{2.27}$$

where we used the transformation property of the Brownian motion given by Girsanov's theorem:

$$\bar{W}_t = \int_0^t \theta_s ds + W_t$$

which states that if W_t is a Brownian motion under $\mathbb{P}$ then $\bar{W}_t$ is a Brownian motion under $\mathbb{Q}$. In this case, $\theta_t \equiv \frac{\mu - r}{\sigma}$.

Using the utility function $U(v) = \frac{v^\gamma}{\gamma}$ its derivative is $U'(v) = v^{\gamma-1}$ which has the inverse $I(v) = v^{\frac{1}{\gamma-1}}$, so the value of the final capital is given by

$$V_T^*(\lambda) = I\left(\lambda \frac{L_T}{B_T}\right) = \left(\frac{\lambda L_T}{B_T}\right)^{\frac{1}{\gamma-1}} \tag{2.28}$$

and the optimal λ is the one such that

$$v_0 = \mathbb{E}_{\mathbb{Q}}\left[V_T^*\left(\lambda^*\right)\right] = \left(\frac{\lambda}{B_T}\right)^{\frac{1}{\gamma-1}} \mathbb{E}_{\mathbb{Q}}\left[L_T^{(\gamma-1)^{-1}}\right]$$

which leads to

$$\lambda^* = B_T\left(\frac{v_0}{\mathbb{E}_{\mathbb{Q}}\left[L_T^{(\gamma-1)^{-1}}\right]}\right)^{\gamma-1}$$

and substituting in formula (2.28):

$$V_T^*\left(\lambda^*\right) = \left[\frac{B_T\left(\frac{v_0}{\mathbb{E}_{\mathbb{Q}}\left[L_T^{(\gamma-1)^{-1}}\right]}\right)^{\gamma-1} L_T}{B_T}\right]^{\frac{1}{\gamma-1}} = \frac{v_0 L_T^{(\gamma-1)^{-1}}}{\mathbb{E}_{\mathbb{Q}}\left[L_T^{(\gamma-1)^{-1}}\right]}$$

Let us introduce the notation $V_T^* = V_T(\lambda^*)$ for the optimal final wealth. Now we use the fact that under $\mathbb{Q}$ the discounted prices are martingale, so if we are able to construct a martingale M_t such that $M_T = \tilde{V}_T^*$ we can use the martingale representation theorem in order to have the optimal strategy. The construction of M_t is standard; it sufficies to take

$$M_t = \mathbb{E}_{\mathbb{Q}}\left[V_T^* | \mathcal{F}_t\right]$$

and with some analysis, using the representation of L_T obtained in formula (2.27):

$$\begin{aligned} M_t &= \mathbb{E}_{\mathbb{Q}}\left[V_T^* | \mathcal{F}_t\right] \\ &= \frac{v_0}{\mathbb{E}_{\mathbb{Q}}\left[L_T^{\frac{1}{\gamma-1}}\right]}\left(\mathbb{E}_{\mathbb{Q}}\left[L_T^{\frac{1}{\gamma-1}} | \mathcal{F}_t\right]\right) \\ &= \frac{v_0}{\mathbb{E}_{\mathbb{Q}}\left[L_T^{\frac{1}{\gamma-1}}\right]}\left(L_t^{\frac{1}{\gamma-1}} \exp\left\{\frac{1}{2(\gamma-1)}\int_t^T \theta_u^2 du\right\} \mathbb{E}_{\mathbb{Q}}\left[e^{\frac{1}{\gamma-1}\int_t^T \theta_u d\bar{W}_u}\right]\right) \\ &= \frac{v_0}{\mathbb{E}_{\mathbb{Q}}\left[L_T^{\frac{1}{\gamma-1}}\right]}\left(L_t^{\frac{1}{\gamma-1}} \exp\left\{\frac{1}{2(\gamma-1)}\int_t^T \theta_u^2 du\right\} \exp\left\{\frac{1}{2}\int_t^T \frac{\theta_u^2}{(\gamma-1)^2} du\right\}\right) \end{aligned}$$

$$
\begin{aligned}
&= v_0 \left(\mathbb{E}_{\mathbb{Q}} \left[L_T^{\frac{1}{\gamma-1}} | \mathcal{F}_0 \right] \right)^{-1} \left(L_t^{\frac{1}{\gamma-1}} \exp \left\{ \left(\frac{\gamma}{2(\gamma-1)^2} \right) \int_t^T \theta_u^2 du \right\} \right) \\
&= v_0 \left(L_0^{\frac{1}{\gamma-1}} \exp \left\{ \left(\frac{\gamma}{2(\gamma-1)^2} \right) \int_0^T \theta_u^2 du \right\} \right)^{-1} \\
&\quad \times \left(L_t^{\frac{1}{\gamma-1}} \exp \left\{ \left(\frac{\gamma}{2(\gamma-1)^2} \right) \int_t^T \theta_u^2 du \right\} \right) \\
&= v_0 L_t^{\frac{1}{\gamma-1}} \exp \left\{ -\frac{\gamma}{2(\gamma-1)^2} \int_0^t \theta_u^2 du \right\} \\
&= v_0 L_t^{\frac{1}{\gamma-1}} e^{f(t)}
\end{aligned} \tag{2.29}
$$

having used the facts that the random variable $e^{\frac{1}{\gamma-1}} \int_t^T \theta_u d\bar{W}_u$ has a log-normal distribution and $L_0 = 1$. At this point we are able to compute, using Ito's formula, the stochastic differential dM_t. Recalling that

$$
dL_t = -L_t \theta_t dW_t
$$

using the notation $f(t)$ introduced in formula (2.29) we obtain

$$
\begin{aligned}
dM_t &= v_0 L_t^{\frac{1}{\gamma-1}} e^{f(t)} f'(t) + v_0 e^{f(t)} \frac{1}{\gamma-1} L_t^{\frac{1}{\gamma-1}} \theta_t d\bar{W}_t - v_0 e^{f(t)} \frac{\gamma}{2(\gamma-1)} L_t^{\frac{1}{\gamma-1}} \theta_t^2 dt \\
&= v_0 e^{f(t)} L_t^{\frac{1}{\gamma-1}} \left[-\frac{\gamma}{2(\gamma-1)^2} \theta_t^2 dt + \frac{1}{\gamma-1} \theta_t d\bar{W}_t - \frac{\gamma}{2(\gamma-1)^2} \theta_t^2 dt \right] \\
&= M_t \frac{\theta_t}{1-\gamma} d\bar{W}_t
\end{aligned}
$$

Now we are able to find the strategy h_t. In fact, consider the dynamics of the discounted portfolio $\tilde{V}_t$ with a self-financing strategy h_t:

$$
d\tilde{V}_t = \tilde{V}_t h_t \frac{d\tilde{S}_t}{\tilde{S}_t} = \tilde{V}_t h_t \sigma d\bar{W}_t
$$

If we impose that $d\tilde{V}_t = d\tilde{M}_t$ we obtain a portfolio that has the same dynamics as the martingale M_t and then such that $V_T = M_T = V_T^*$, i.e. the portfolio replicates our claim. To do this it sufficies to take

$$
h_t = \frac{\theta_t}{\sigma(1-\gamma)} = \frac{\mu - r}{\sigma^2 (1-\gamma)}
$$

which is exactly the optimal control obtained my Merton (see equation 2.14).

Market incompleteness. If the market is incomplete then it is well-known that the martingale measure $\mathbb{Q}$ is not unique and the constraint $\mathbb{E}_{\mathbb{Q}}\left[V_T/B_T\right]$ must hold for all martingale measure $\mathbb{Q}$. The problem in this case becomes

$$\begin{aligned} &\max_h \ \mathbb{E}_{\mathbb{P}}\left[u\left(V_T^h\right)\right] \\ &s.t. \quad \sup_{\mathbb{Q}} \mathbb{E}_{\mathbb{Q}}\left[\frac{V_T^h}{B_T}\right] \leqslant v_0 \\ &\qquad\quad V_0 = v_0 \end{aligned}$$

and the Lagrangean function reads

$$\begin{aligned} \mathcal{L}(V_T, \lambda) &= \mathbb{E}_{\mathbb{P}}\left[u\left(V_T\right)\right] - \lambda\left(\sup_{\mathbb{Q}} \mathbb{E}_{\mathbb{Q}}\left[\frac{V_T^h}{B_T}\right] - v_0\right) \\ &= \mathbb{E}_{\mathbb{P}}\left[u\left(V_T\right) - \lambda \frac{V_T}{B_T} \sup_{L_T} L_T\right] - \lambda v_0 \end{aligned}$$

which has its supremum on V_T at the point:

$$V_T^*(\lambda) = I\left(\frac{\lambda}{B_T} \sup_{L_T} L_T\right)$$

It is clear that in this case the calculations are complex and are outside the scope of this book. However, one may note that the Martingale method in its general form can be useful in some situations: for example, when the control process h_t does not lie in the class of the Markovian controls, i.e. does not depend only on the present state, but also on the past.

2.4.5 Asset Allocation with Capital Constraints

The traditional asset allocation models proposed so far represent a valid framework for understanding the kind of mathematical construction that underpins the problem of strategic asset allocation within dynamic trading strategies. However, they need to be adjusted in order to work properly as a decision support tool for directional trading strategies.

A few issues need to be addressed in order to translate professional energy trading activity into the generic asset allocation scheme. First of all, as stated at the beginning of the chapter, directional trading strategies in the energy sector are typically performed by means of forward or future contracts, which imply no initial economic costs or revenues just from taking the position in the market. With respect to the standard allocation scheme described in the previous section, no initial wealth endowment is needed to perform the strategy and optimal position size and decision variable are no longer expressed as a fraction of the initial wealth but in units of the underlying asset. The second point to consider is related to capital allocation (risk capital, in particular). In traditional schemes we only require to have a positive (satisfying the self financing condition) wealth process as a unique inter-temporal budget constraint; in reality cumulative and local losses are allowed but trading position is typically limited by a VaR (Value at Risk) risk limit, which in effect represents a capital constraint. If the trading strategy is performed with futures, the VaR capital constraint translates into a cash constraint since it is usual for initial margin requirements to reflect potential daily losses.

Once risk capital constraints are respected, the trader can no longer be considered a risk-averse subject; he is at the very least risk-neutral. Hence, we can reasonably surmise that he aims to maximize the expected trading profit respecting his VaR constraint. In other words, his terminal utility is a linear function of the terminal wealth itself, simply because his personal payoff (the bonus) is a percentage of the trading profit, while his personal downside risk is simply represented by the possibility of being fired, which is at best an opportunity cost.

If we consider this framework as realistic and consistent with the professional behaviour of a directional trader, we can formalize our new asset allocation problem as follows:

$$
\begin{aligned}
& & W_0(S_0, V_0) &= \sup_{\pi_t} \mathbb{E}\left[V_T | \mathcal{F}_0\right] & & \\
s.t. & & V_t &= V_{t-1} + \pi_{t-1} \Delta S_t & \forall t \in [0, T] & \\
& & \mathrm{VaR}_{\mathrm{calculated}}(S_t, \alpha, d) &\leqslant \mathrm{VaR}_{\mathrm{limit}} + \min(0, V_{t-1}) & \forall t \in [0, T] &
\end{aligned}
\tag{2.30}
$$

where π_t is the control variable of the strategy, S_t is the price of the unique trading asset, α is the VaR's target level (e.g. 99%) and d is the VaR's holding period in fraction of years.

The problem of asset allocation optimization under risk capital constraints has already been addressed and solved in a dynamic scheme by Cuoco, He and Iasaenko (2008) and by Basak and Shapiro (2001), but in both papers risk constraints have been imposed on the percentile of the terminal wealth, more in line with a Profit at Risk limit than a Value at Risk limitation.

The common practice, as described by expression (2.30), is that of having a budgeting period (over which we would like to maximize our expected return) longer than the Value at Risk holding period. The mismatch between the time horizon in which we evaluate our trading performance and the one we use to risk control our strategy creates computational problems for the analytical and numerical solution of problem (2.30). Moreover, it can also induce logical inconsistencies between the performance we would like to attain and the risk limitation we are imposing. In other words, it may be difficult to identify clearly the overall risk capital we are effectively using over the global trading period as a function of the local VaR limit. Hence, it may be difficult to compare and benchmark the performance of our trading strategy with that of alternative investment strategies.

A numerical example, solved via backward induction on a simple two step binomial tree may help us to understand the problem's numerical complexity as well as potential business inconsistencies. Let us assume that our simplistic trading time horizon is composed of three time steps and that the time evolution of the price of the unique asset we can invest in is represented by the recombining binomial tree represented in Figure 2.16.

The inter-temporal VaR constraint expressed in (2.30) has to be modified in order to work properly over a discrete state price evolution such as the one described by the binomial tree. We will require that in every node the maximum potential loss connected to our trading strategy is bounded by an imposed amount we will call improperly the VaR limit. More formally we will have

$$|\min[\pi_t S_t(u-1), \pi_t S_t(d-1)]| \leqslant \mathrm{VaR}_{\mathrm{limit}} + \min(0, W_t) \quad \forall t \in [0, T]$$

The problem's solution, over the simple two-step binomial tree, given the risk constraint defined above, can be obtained recursively via backward induction leading to the following expression:

- if $up + d(1-p) - 1 \geqslant 0$:

$$\begin{aligned} V_0(S_0, W_0) = \sup_{\pi_0 \in C} \Bigg\{ \Bigg[& W_0 + \pi_0 S_0(u-1) \\ & - \frac{(up + d(1-p) - 1)\left(\mathrm{VaR}_{\mathrm{limit}} + \min(0, W_0 + \pi_0 S_0(u-1))\right)}{d-1} \Bigg] p \\ & + \Bigg[W_0 + \pi_0 S_0(d-1) \\ & - \frac{(up + d(1-p) - 1)(\mathrm{VaR}_{\mathrm{limit}} + \min(0, W_0 + \pi_0 S_0(d-1))}{d-1} \Bigg] \Bigg\} \end{aligned}$$

- if $up + d(1-p) - 1 < 0$:

$$\begin{aligned} V_0(S_0, W_0) = \sup_{\pi_0 \in C} \Bigg\{ \Bigg[& W_0 + \pi_0 S_0(u-1) \\ & - \frac{(up + d(1-p) - 1)(\mathrm{VaR}_{\mathrm{limit}} + \min(0, W_0 + \pi_0 S_0(u-1))}{u-1} \Bigg] p \\ & + \Bigg[W_0 + \pi_0 S_0(d-1) \\ & - \frac{(up + (d(1-p) - 1)(\mathrm{VaR}_{\mathrm{limit}} + \min(0, W_0 + \pi_0 S_0(d-1))}{u-1} \Bigg] (1-p) \Bigg\} \end{aligned}$$

with $C = \left\{ \pi_0 \quad s.t. \quad \left| \min\{\pi_0 S_0(u-1, \pi_0 S_0(d-1)\} \right| \leqslant \mathrm{VaR}_{\mathrm{limit}} + \min(0, W_0) \right\}$.

It can be shown, by means of a numerical exercise, that the value function in time zero is a linear function of the optimal control and can easily be optimized. Optimal control is itself a linear function of the VaR limit, taking positive values if the expected price increment over the tree is positive and negative otherwise. The optimal control is also a function of the price evolution uncertainty represented over the tree by the size of the difference *(u-d)*. The higher that difference, the higher the uncertainty about price evolution, the higher the risk related to the overall trading performance. Hence, the optimal control is impacted since our optimal strategy is risk bounded.

Unless the two-step binomial tree case we presented is quite unrealistic, it may be helpful to consider trading performance and risk capital allocation at this point. In fact, the proposed methodology allows us not only to calculate optimal controls step by step that can be used to benchmark ongoing directional trading performance, but also to calculate expected profits as a function of the allocated VaR limit. We will dedicate an entire chapter to the analysis of what we define as *meta-trading* and capital allocation strategies, but here it is sufficient to say that the VaR embedded leverage effect can be fully captured by the methodology proposed and, consequently, a fully comprehensive comparison with alternative investment strategies is allowed. The binomial tree description is certainly simple to understand and pedagogically useful but not sophisticated enough to allow for a full understanding of the impact of risk capital allocation rules on overall directional trading strategies. For this reason we need to go back to the original problem (2.30) and employ stochastic dynamic programming and numerical solution methods, as in previous sections, in order to probe deeper into the analysis.

With respect to the classic Merton's problem, problem (2.30) is both simpler and more complex. Simpler because the terminal utility function is imposed to be linear in the wealth variable, more complex because the inter-temporal budget constaint depends upon two stochastic variables: wealth and asset price. This complexity induces a heavier numerical procedure to reach a solution.

Here, as an example, after a discretization, we can use the stochastic dynamic programming principle and backward induction to solve backwards problem (2.30) in order to show its complexity and analyze the inner non-linear relation that in general exists between expected cumulative profits (terminal utility) and VaR limit allocation.

Taking as true the simple standard formula for the calculation of VaR for linear instruments ($\text{VaR}_{\text{calculated}}(S, \alpha, d) = \pi S \alpha \sigma \sqrt{d}$) we can make one step back, obtaining the following results:

$$V^*_{T-1}(S_{T-1} = s, W_{T-1} = v) = v + \pi^*_{T-1} \mathbb{E}_{T-1}[\Delta S_T]$$

$$\pi^*_{T-1} = \begin{cases} \frac{\text{VaR}_{\text{limit}} + \min(0,v)}{S\alpha\sigma\sqrt{d}} & \text{if } \mathbb{E}_{T-1}[\Delta S_T] \geqslant 0 \\ -\frac{\text{VaR}_{\text{limit}} + \min(0,v)}{S\alpha\sigma\sqrt{d}} & \text{if } \mathbb{E}_{T-1}[\Delta S_T] < 0 \end{cases}$$

Moving back again one step things are becoming more complicated and a closed expression for the optimal control is no longer generically available:

$$\begin{aligned} &V^*_{T-2}(S_{T-2} = s, W_{T-2} = v) \\ &\quad = \sup_{\pi_{T-2}} \mathbb{E}_{T-2}\left[V^*_{T-1}(S_{T-1}, W_{T-1}) | S_{T-2} = s, W_{T-2} = v\right] \end{aligned}$$

$$= \sup_{\pi_{T-2}} \mathbb{E}_{T-2}\left[v + \pi_{T-2}\Delta S_{T-1} + \frac{\text{VaR}_{\text{limit}} + \min(0, v + \pi_{T-2}\Delta S_{T-1})}{s + \Delta S_{T-1}\alpha\sigma\sqrt{d}} \Delta S_T \right]$$

The expression above is not very helpful from the computational point of view (further developments risk being too complex and uninformative), but it is certainly insightful with respect to the inner non-linear relationship which links trading performance and allocated risk capital.

In general, in contrast to what we saw in the binomial case example, VaR limit and optimal expected terminal payoff are not linearly related. This has strong implications for performance budgeting and capital allocation. In fact, a certain desired trading performance could not potentially be reached simply by increasing the risk capital allocation. Moreover, risk-return ratios or other risk-adjusted performance measures could be non-scalable with respect to the absolute allocated risk capital.

3 Spread Trading

In the last chapter we focused our attention on trading strategies whose rationale was based on price trends identification of one or more energy assets considered independently. This could potentially lead to taking simultaneously long positions in some assets and short ones in others but this situation would not be related to a joint view on two or more energy asset price dynamics. In the recent past market operators have dedicated ever more attention to the so-called "relative trading" strategies, those trading strategies whose rationale is based on the relative price movement of one security with respect to another one.

Relative trading strategies (sometimes called relative value trading strategies) try to capture the relative disequilibrium between two tradable financial variables by avoiding exposure to market systematic risk. They can be performed on different types of financial variables such as prices, volatilities or correlations and consequently different financial products such as options or futures/forwards should be employed. In all those cases where the object of the relative disequilibrium is a price differential between two different securities, we may talk of spread trading strategies. We will devote a section to the analysis of the nature and behaviour of price spreads. The reason for the particular attention paid to the definition and analysis of the concept of price spread is that a spread is not simply a price differential, but a price differential that displays certain characteristics: in particular, the dynamics of the price spread should be "more predictable" than that of its components (or legs) and its volatility should be lower than that of its legs. These features, as we will see in this chapter, are essential in order to achieve a better risk adjusted performance with spread trading strategies than with directional ones.

Obviously, the fact that spread trading is based on a relative disequilibrium between two different securities implies that between the two there should exist some source of strong financial, economic or physical interdependence. The typical case in traditional stock markets is that of the price spreads between two listed stocks belonging to the same industrial sector or between the single stock and the sector index. In the commodities sector, energy commodities in particular, we can list different types of relevant price spreads such as cross-commodity spreads, location spreads or time spreads. In the energy sector, typical cross-commodity spreads are crack spreads[1] and spark spreads.[2] Location spreads between neighbouring

[1] The spread created in commodity markets by purchasing oil futures and offsetting the position by selling gasoline and heating oil futures. The name of this strategy is derived from the fact that "cracking" oil produces gasoline and heating oil.

[2] The spark spread is the theoretical gross margin of a gas-fired power plant from selling a unit of electricity, having bought the fuel required to produce this unit of electricity.

countries are widely employed both in power and gas while time spread trading strategies are typical of oil, gas and environmental markets. The theoretical and substantial base of all three types of spread trading strategies is the strong physical linkage that connects different segments of the energy sector both from the physical and the financial point of view. Sometimes, indeed more and more often, the interconnection is significant also between energy and other more financial sectors like forex, stocks or fixed income but also with other commodity sectors like freight, metals or softs, allowing for a more extended version of the traditional spread trading activity. In this case, the underlying linkage between sectors can have more of a financial than a physical meaning or it can be more local than global. Certainly, traditional energy spreads are more robust through time.

In the remainder of the chapter we will examine in detail a spread definition, identification and analysis and describe why and under which conditions a spread trading strategy, based on energy commodities, should be more profitable than other strategies.

3.1 SPREAD DEFINITION AND IDENTIFICATION

We noted above that the two main characteristics a price differential needs to display in order to be defined as a spread are a higher level of predictability compared with that of its legs and a lower variability. Further, in the definition of relative trading we said that, adopting relative trading strategies, market operators aim to reach a better performance by eliminating the systematic risk component embedded in primary assets. If two financial assets somehow share a systematic stochastic trend, there will naturally be a linear combination of the two assets basically depurated by the influence of the stochastic trend itself, and for this reason more predictable and less variable. In Chapter 1, analyzing EMH, we came to understand that the more mature and liquid a certain market, the more transaction prices are informative and, consequently, the market itself efficient. In an efficient market, price predictability based on public available information is a chimera and consequently trading strategies based on individual assets are destined to fail in over-performing the market, at least in expected terms. Nevertheless, in the same situation a relative trading strategy based on a properly identified spread may result in success. In support of this statement in Chapter 2 (Section 2.4.3) we saw that in the case of a mean reverting (stationary) price dynamics, classical optimal strategic asset allocation techniques allow for a potential excess return, while in the case of a zero drift martingale (coherent with EMH) this cannot be expected.

Also without the need for sophisticated mathematical argumentation, it can easily be intuited that dealing with a mean reverting price dynamics extra money can be earned simply by selecting optimal buying and selling decisions looking at price deviations with respect to the long-term attractor (equilibrium level). Figure 3.1 provides an example of how the mean reversion works. Obviously, this is not possible if the price dynamics is characterized by an embedded stochastic trend without any plausible (and predictable) equilibrium level.

To assert that two financial variables share a common stochastic trend is, for most people, a generic statement that needs to be qualified from the business,

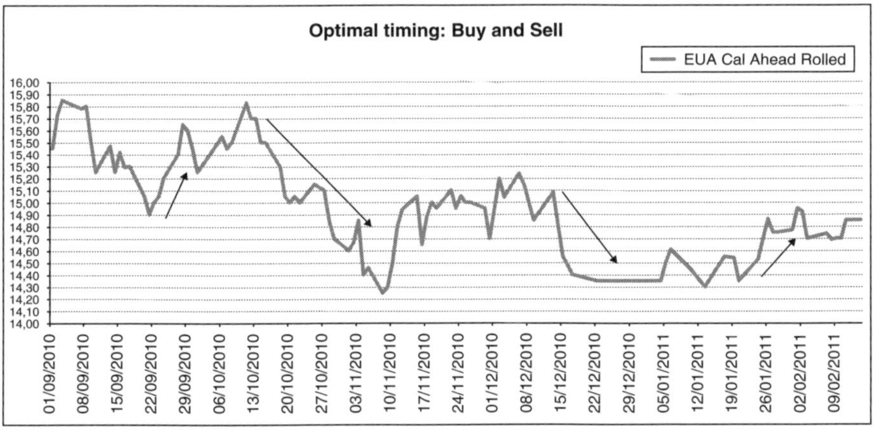

Figure 3.1 Optimal buy and sell with mean reversion

economic and statistical points of view. The fundamental linkage among variables is the basic prerequisite for the existence of a strong economic relationship between them. The aforementioned crack spread is actually the differential between the crude oil price and certain refined products (heating oil, gas oil) or a basket of them. The fundamental linkage between the legs of this spread is clearly related to the industrial process used to obtain refined products out of crude oil. The path of a spread like this is range bounded and completely different from the price path of its components, since the stochastic trend has been cancelled out.

The spark spread (power to gas spread) has the same fundamental basis for being considered a spread as crack, but other circumstances need to be taken into consideration. In fact, in countries like Italy and the UK where power production is largely obtained through gas this may be true, as shown in Figure 3.2; in other countries like Germany or Norway the economic relationship between power and gas prices is weaker since power production is not primarily based on natural gas. The result is that in this last case the power to gas differential doesn't seem to show the graphical properties of a spread, and consequently a relative trading strategy based on its risk to be unprofitable. Similar examples can be retrieved from outside the energy or commodities sectors even if the presence of strong industrial interconnections facilitates the persistence of long-term equilibrium relationships. Even from such a cursory discussion, it is already clear that the advantage of spread trading with respect to directional trading is significant when an individual spread's price legs are characterized by an unpredictable stochastic trend component. Under this condition, directional trading won't allow for excess returns while spread trading will. Nevertheless, in some situations spread trading strategies can be used to perceive directional purposes or, in other cases, directional and spread strategies can be combined to optimize overall performance. Later in the chapter we will dedicate a specific section to this issue and show how, in energy-related commodity markets, such situations are not infrequent.

In conclusion, we can say that the presence of the necessary economic conditions for the determination of a spread is related to fundamental basements which,

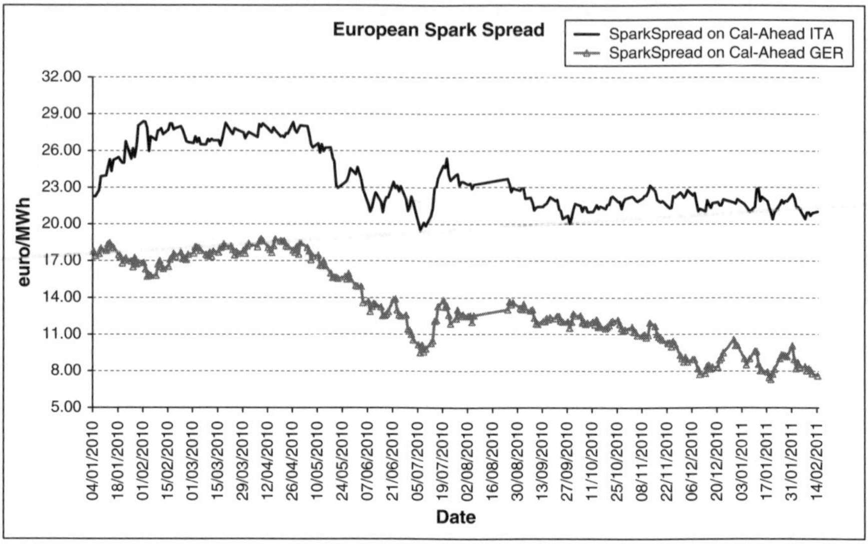

Figure 3.2 European spark spread

nevertheless, need to be tested and verified analytically before implementing the corresponding trading strategy. Moreover, spread trading is not necessarily an alternative to directional trading but in some situations they can be complementary and useful for overall trading performance optimization.

3.2 NON-STATIONARITY AND COINTEGRATION

Correlation is a crucial quantity in the valuation of many energy derivatives and assets, but without a considerable knowledge of what *correlation* really is, this well-known statement is essentially useless. Correlation is the proper measure of *linear dependence* between two variables. If there exists some non-linear dependence between the variables, correlation can lead to wrong results.

Let $\{x_n\}_{n=1,\dots,N}$ and $\{y_n\}_{n=1,\dots,N}$ be two realizations of some i.i.d. random variable. The two series are completely independent. This implies that the correlation ρ between them is 0. Now consider the new series $y_n = x_{n-k}$ for some $k > 0$ and $n = k+1, \dots, N$. It is clear that the value y_l is completely known at time $l - k$ if we have seen the value of x_{l-k}, so the series y_n is strongly dependent on x_n, but the correlation between them is 0, being $\{x_n\}_{n=1,\dots,N}$ i.i.d. If we suppose that x_n and y_n represent, for example, the returns of two assets, the correlation index $\rho = 0$ suggests to us that we cannot use the first series to predict the second, but we know this is false. A correct analysis should take into account *any* leg-ahead correlation; this clearly shows how ρ, the correlation, is a measure of *short time* co-movements.

Assuming there exists some correlation between two stocks implies that if one variable moves up the second will do the same, if $\rho > 0$, or move down, if $\rho < 0$. Confirmed also by the theoretical result which states that the volatility of the

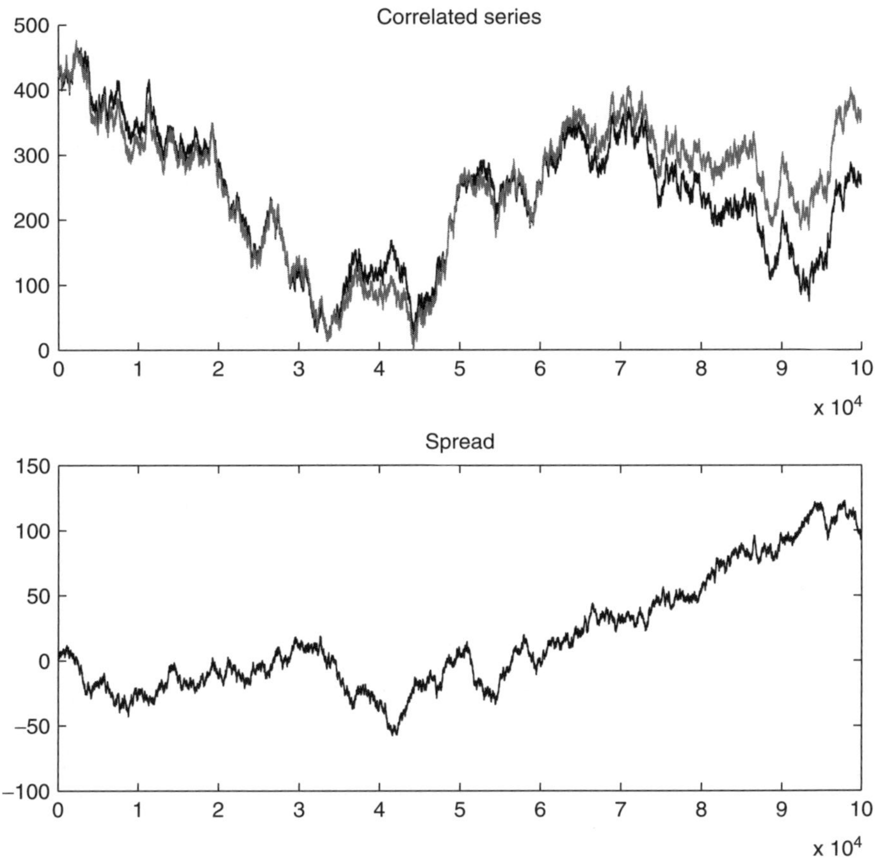

Figure 3.3 Two strongly correlated series and their spread, which is clearly non-stationary

spread between two stocks X and Y is given by $\sigma_X^2 + \sigma_Y^2 - 2\rho\sigma_X\sigma_Y$ that should be less than the volatility of a spread between two uncorrelated commodities, a non-zero correlation ρ may be a good clue to start a pair trading between two stocks. However, we have to take into account that two correlated series do not necessarily lead to a stationary spread. Figure 3.3 provides an example: the two series are strongly correlated, but their spread shows a trend, i.e. it is not stationary. A pairs trading on these two series can be a good choice if the aim of trading is to deliberately remain exposed to certain variables we cannot access directly (see next section), but having in mind the description of an *efficient market*, if the spread shows a drift greater than the risk-free rate r then the market is not efficient (see Section 1.3) and the pairs trading can lead to unexpected results.

Although correlation has become the ubiquitous tool for measuring co-movements in asset returns, its limitations are substantial: correlations are used to reflect co-movements in returns, which are liable to great instabilities over time; correlation is a *short time* measure: trading strategies based on correlations commonly require frequent rebalancing; we have also shown that there can exist other dependencies between two series which correlation does not capture and that can be more useful.

In what follows we introduce the notion of *cointegration*. Granger and Engle jointly developed the theory of cointegration in their classic paper (1987).

Two series, x_n and y_n that are non-stationary are cointegrated (of order 1) if there exists a linear combination of them that is stationary. Generally speaking, when spread is stationary the variables are cointegrated. Correlations between the two series may be low at times, but if they are cointegrated then they are tied together by a long-term common trend because of the mean-reversion in the spread. Recall that a stationary process always has some mean-reversion.

Suppose, for example, that the two series $\{x_n\}_{n=1,\dots,N}$ and $\{y_n\}_{n=1,\dots,N}$ are integrated of order 1, $x_n, y_n \sim I(1)$, that is their first difference is stationary (see Section 1.3.1) and that the following relation holds:

$$y_n = \beta x_n + \varepsilon_n$$

where ε_n are the residuals of the regression. The linear combination $(y_n - \beta x_n)$ should be $I(1)$, being $\varepsilon_n \sim I(1)$. In the special case when $\varepsilon_n \sim I(0)$ we say the two series x_n and y_n are *cointegrated of order one*.

In general, if two series x_n and y_n are both $I(d)$, integrated of order d, but there exists a linear combination of them $\varepsilon_n = \beta_1 y_n + \beta_2 x_n$ that is $I(d-b)$, integrated of order $d-b$, then we say the two series are *cointegrated of order* (d, b) and we write $xn, y_n \sim CI(d, b)$, with $d \leqslant b > 0$. Extended to more than two series, the definition in general is: the N series $x_n^1, x_n^2, \dots, x_n^N$ are $CI(d, b)$, cointegrated of order (d, b), if

- $x_n^j \sim I(d), \forall j = 1, \dots, N$
- there exists a vector $(\beta^1, \dots, \beta^N) = \boldsymbol{\beta} \in \mathbb{R}^N$ such that the linear combination is integrated of order $d-b$, i.e.

$$\boldsymbol{\varepsilon}_n = \boldsymbol{\beta}\boldsymbol{x}_n = \sum_{i=1}^{N} \beta_i x_n^i \sim I(d-b)$$

having used the notation $\boldsymbol{x}_n = \begin{pmatrix} x_n^1 \\ x_n^2 \\ \vdots \\ x_n^N \end{pmatrix}$

Notice that when $d = b = 1$, the case presented at the beginning of this section, the two $I(1)$ series x_n and y_n are both dominated by a *long wave* component (the stochastic trend), but the new series ε_n has no such component. This new series can be termed an *equilibrium error*: if it is $I(0)$, it rarely drifts far from 0 and will often cross the zero line. If the two series are not cointegrated, the equilibrium error will wander widely and zero-crossing will be rare. Thus, the idea of cointegration mimics the economic concept of *long-run equilibrium*: two cointegrated variables

x_n and y_n cannot diverge indefinitely from the equilibrium state; at some point in time they will be re-attracted towards it.

The two-step method proposed by Engle and Granger to estimate cointegration between two series is based on OLS (ordinary least square) regression and a Dickey-Fuller test on the residuals. As stated, the first step is to find β via an OLS regression between the series x and y. It is well known that such a β is the value which minimizes the quantity $\sum_{i=1}^{N}(y_i - \beta x_i)^2$, and it is given by

$$\beta = \frac{\mathrm{Cov}\left[x, y\right]}{\mathrm{Var}\left[x\right]} = \rho\frac{\sigma_y}{\sigma_x} \tag{3.1}$$

having denoted ρ as the correlation coefficient, σ_Y and σ_X as the standard deviations of the two series. Notice that on the one hand, formula (3.1) shows that two uncorrelated series cannot be cointegrated (since $\rho = 0$), on the other it shows that even for small values of ρ there may exist such a β, so even when the two series have a small correlation there may exist a chance that the spread between x_n and y_n could be a stationary series.

Once we have estimated β the second step is to determine whether or not the residuals of the regression

$$\varepsilon_n = y_n - \beta x_n$$

have a unit root or not. This can be done using the Dickey-Fuller test. To do this, consider the autoregression of the residuals:

$$\Delta\varepsilon_n = \gamma\varepsilon_{n-1} + \eta_n$$

If we can reject the hypothesis $\gamma = 0$ then we can conclude that x_n and y_n are cointegrated.

Another methodology which became the reference point in the literature to estimate cointegration is the approach proposed by Johansen (1991) and Nobel Prize Committee (2003) based on the ECM representation of a VAR (vector auto regressive) system. This test permits more than one cointegrating relationship so it is more generally applicable than the Engle-Granger test, which is based on a single cointegrating relationship. Cointegrated variables are characterized by having an ECM (error correction model) representation that takes into account the dynamics of both the short and long term. Before introducing the Johansen test as the general case, we present a two-dimensional example, which we will then extend. In the bi-dimensional case, i.e. when $\boldsymbol{x}_n = (x_n, y_n)$ with $\boldsymbol{x} \sim CI(1, 1)$, we have the following relationship:

$$y_n - \beta x_n = \varepsilon_n \sim I(0) \tag{3.2}$$

$$y_n - y_{n-1} = \beta x_n + (-\beta x_{n-1} + \beta x_{n-1}) - y_{n-1} + \varepsilon_n$$

$$\begin{aligned}\Delta y_n &= \beta\Delta x_n - (y_{n-1} - \beta x_{n-1}) \\ &= \beta\Delta x_n - \varepsilon_n\end{aligned} \tag{3.3}$$

It is a model which links both levels and variations: it takes into account both short relationships and, thanks to the cointegrated term $(y_{n-1} - \beta x_{n-1})$, also the long period relationship between x_n and y_n. The form of equation (3.3) is called the *ECM representation* of the cointegration formula (3.2).

Now suppose that the following relationship holds for the vector $\boldsymbol{x}_n$:

$$\boldsymbol{x}_n = A_1 \boldsymbol{x}_{n-1} + \boldsymbol{\varepsilon}_n \tag{3.4}$$

where $A_1 = \begin{bmatrix} a_{1,1} & a_{1,2} \\ a_{2,1} & a_{2,2} \end{bmatrix}$. The system in (3.4) is called a VAR (vector auto regressive) system: it represents general relationships among economic variables and does not impose any a priori restrictions (levels of all variables could be linked together). By subtracting the term $\boldsymbol{x}_{n-1}$ on both sides of (3.4) we obtain:

$$\Delta \boldsymbol{x}_n = \Pi \boldsymbol{x}_{n-1} + \boldsymbol{\varepsilon}_n \tag{3.5}$$

where $\Pi = A_1 - \mathbb{I}_2$ and $\mathbb{I}_2$ is the identity matrix of size 2 and it is such that its rank is $\text{Rk}(\Pi) \in \{0, 1, 2\}$. Engle and Granger (1987) have proved that under mild hypothesis the following holds:

- $\text{Rk}(\Pi) = 0$, that is the trivial case when $\Pi = \mathbb{O}_2 \Rightarrow A_1 = \mathbb{I}_2$. In this case the two series are $I(1)$, but they are not cointegrated;
- $\text{Rk}(\Pi) = 1$. In this case the two series are $I(1)$ and they are cointegrated. There exists a long period relation between them. In this case there also exist two vectors $\boldsymbol{\alpha}$ and $\boldsymbol{\beta}$ such that $\Pi = \boldsymbol{\alpha}\boldsymbol{\beta}'$ and $\boldsymbol{\beta}\boldsymbol{x}_n \sim I(0)$, so $\boldsymbol{\beta}$ is the long period multiplicator which makes the linear combination $\beta^1 x_n^1 + \beta^2 x_n^2$ stationary. In particular, we obtain from (3.5) the system $\Delta \boldsymbol{x}_n = \boldsymbol{\alpha}\boldsymbol{\beta}' \boldsymbol{x}_{n-1} + \boldsymbol{\varepsilon}_n$:

$$\left\{ \begin{array}{l} \Delta x_n^1 = \alpha^1 \left(\beta^1 x_{n-1}^1 \beta^2 x_{n-1}^2 \right) + \boldsymbol{\varepsilon}_n^1 \\ \Delta x_n^2 = \alpha^2 \left(\beta^1 x_{n-1}^1 \beta^2 x_{n-1}^2 \right) + \boldsymbol{\varepsilon}_n^2 \end{array} \right\} \tag{3.6}$$

- $\text{Rk}(\Pi) = 2$. In this case both x_n^1 and x_n^2 are $I(0)$, but they are not cointegrated.

Notice that, while for the ECM representation in (3.3) we started from cointegration in formula (3.2), the equations in (3.6) are the end point of a special case of the VAR representation (the case $\text{Rk}(\Pi) = 1$).

Switching to N dimensions, in general Johansen's test is a test on the rank of the matrix Π. We have what follows: starting from a VAR system, which can be written in general as

$$\boldsymbol{x}_n = \boldsymbol{\mu} + A_1 \boldsymbol{x}_{n-1} + \ldots A_k \boldsymbol{x}_{n-k} + \Psi \boldsymbol{\delta}_n + \boldsymbol{\varepsilon}_n$$

with $\boldsymbol{x}_n$ vector of endogenous $I(1)$ variables, $\boldsymbol{\delta}_n$ vector of dummy variables, A_i and Ψ matrixes of parameters, one can derive the error correction form:

$$\Delta \boldsymbol{x}_n = \boldsymbol{\mu} + \Pi \boldsymbol{x}_{n-1} + \Gamma_1 \Delta \boldsymbol{x}_{n-1} + \ldots \Gamma_{k-1} \Delta \boldsymbol{x}_{n-k+1} + \Psi \boldsymbol{\delta}_n + \boldsymbol{\varepsilon}_n$$

where $\Pi = A_1 + A_2 + \ldots + A_k - \mathbb{O}_N$ and $\Gamma_i = -(A_{i+1} + \ldots A_k)$. The Johansen test on $\mathrm{Rk}(\Pi)$ states that

- $\mathrm{Rk}(\Pi) = 0$: the variables are $I(1)$ and are not cointegrated, hence there are no linear combinations of them which are stationary.
- $\mathrm{Rk}(\Pi) = N$: the variables are stationary and any linear combination of them would also be stationary.
- $1 \leqslant \mathrm{Rk}(\Pi) \leqslant N - 1$: the variables are $I(1)$, but there exist $r = \mathrm{Rk}(\Pi)$ linear combinations of them which are stationary. In such a case the factorization $\Pi = AB'$ holds, where A and B are $N \times r$ matrixes such that $r = \mathrm{Rk}(A) = \mathrm{Rk}(B)$. The cointegration matrix B is such that every one of the r vectors $B\boldsymbol{x}_n$ is stationary. Every row of B is a cointegrating vector.

Cointegrated series lead to a completely different approach in pairs trading. If we suppose that the stationary spread follows the dynamics in formula (2.8) (this is a bit restrictive, since the spread is not always a positive variable), we can use the results illustrated in Chapter 2, formula 2.9, to observe how the optimal control of a spread trading varies with the speed of mean-reversion (parameter α) and stock price.

Going deeper into the mathematics, we can use numerical integration in order to plot the two functions $f_1(t)$ and $f_2(t)$ obtained in Benth and Karlsen, reproposed here:

$$a(t) = \frac{\alpha}{1-\gamma} - 2\sigma^2 f_2(t)$$

$$b(t) = \frac{\alpha(\alpha\mu\gamma - r)}{\sigma^2(1-\gamma)^2} + \left(\sigma^2 - 2r - \frac{2(\alpha\mu - r)}{1-\gamma}\right)$$

$$f_2(t) = \frac{\alpha\gamma \sinh\left(\frac{\alpha}{\sqrt{1-\gamma}}(T-t)\right)}{2\sigma^2(1-\gamma)\sinh\left(\frac{\alpha}{\sqrt{1-\gamma}}(T-t)\right) + \sqrt{1-\gamma}\cosh\left(\frac{\alpha}{\sqrt{1-\gamma}}(T-t)\right)}$$

$$f_1(t) = -\int_t^T b(s)e^{-\int_t^s a(u)du}ds$$

Figure 3.4 shows the optimal control obtained with a numerical integration: every line represents the value of $\pi^*(0, s)$ for some values of α. We note that when $\alpha = 0$ we have no drift and no mean-reversion: in this case the optimal control is constant, as in Merton's problem; on the contrary, stronger values of α lead to a longer or shorter position on the spread: longer when the present value of the spread, s_0, is less than the attractor, shorter when it is greater.

3.3 EMPIRICAL ANALYSIS OF ENERGY SPREAD TRADING STRATEGIES

In the energy and more generally in the financial markets a typical strategy is the so-called "spread trading", a strategy that aims to make a profit by trading the price

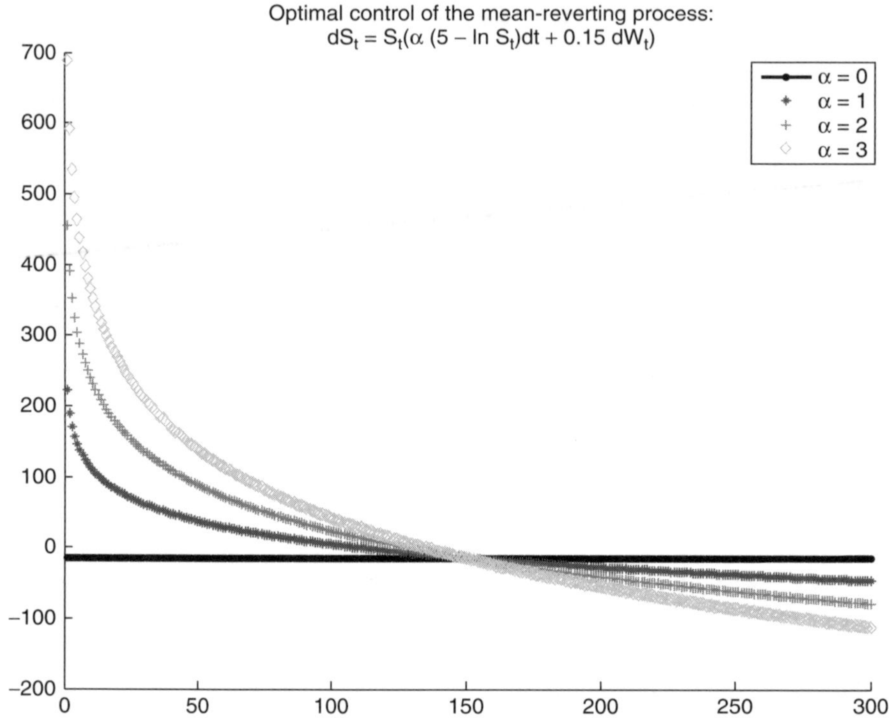

Figure 3.4 Optimal control of a mean-reverting asset as a function of price and speed of mean-reversion

differential (spread) between two different assets. Spreads may be represented by the differential of two assets that are supposed to share the same economic driver, spread on the term structure slope of the same asset (time spread), or spread on the same commodities price traded in different markets (location spread). Basically, this kind of trading strategy bets on the fact that the spread series considered is stationary and mean-reverting along an "attractor": the long-run "true" value of the spread itself. Operators usually try to identify economic relationships between different assets based on industrial or pure financial relations. Obviously, in the energy market, for example, it is reasonable to expect an economic relationship to exist between a certain basket of fuels and power prices (almost in the short term, if no improvements on the dominant technology are expected), and so the generation spread is traded both for the hedging and for pure trading purposes, in an attempt to profit from temporal deviations from the equilibrium level.

From a statistical point of view, when dealing with economic time series and spread it is common to face some consistency and estimation problems. In approaching the modelling of time series in finance we often deal with

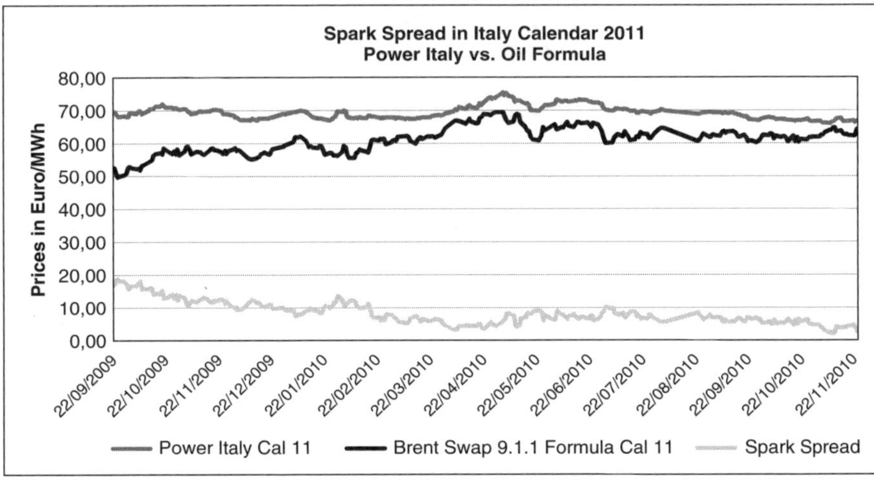

Figure 3.5 Spark spread in Italy calendar 2011

estimation consistency problems. The so-called "OLS" estimators, the well-known properties of convergences and the related statistical tests built upon Gauss Markov assumptions, are misleading when used on non-stationary series. In particular, the consistency property of the OLS estimator is no longer valid when dealing with non-stationary series, because proof of the convergence of variances and covariances of the sample to the population's variances and covariances is no longer valid. These considerations obviously have serious implications for many common statistical hypotheses that are no longer valid when dealing with non-stationary series. For these reasons the study of a spread requires us to check the nature of the series on which the spread is built in order to avoid the common problem related to a possible spurious regression.

When speaking of "spread trading" we need to identify the statistical feature of the series we are dealing with. As stated, in order to be recognized as a "spread" a series needs to be stationary in a statistical sense; in fact, the economic idea of a spread means reverting towards a long-run equilibrium level which is linked to the concept of a stationary series (statistically speaking) i.e. a series without time-dependent moments. So in order to have a stationary spread, we need to take a spread built as a difference of two stationary financial series, or a spread built as the difference of two non-stationary series with a common stochastic trend (cointegration), as the one shown in Figure 3.5. In both cases the main feature we need to check in the series, before building any trading strategy, is the stationarity that implies a mean reversion dynamic of the series allowing us to build a trading strategy around the idea of a long-run average level. In what follows we will present three different case studies mainly dealing with spreads traded in energy markets: spark spread strategy, time spread strategy and location spread strategy.

3.4 EMPIRICAL ANALYSIS OF ENERGY SPREADS AND SPREAD TRADING STRATEGIES

3.4.1 Cross Commodities Spread Trading (Spark Spread)

One of the most important spreads traded in the energy sector is the so-called "Spark Spread". This is defined as the gross generation margin that is the differential between the prices of power and the cost of fuel net of an average efficiency factor between different production technologies. Other definitions of the generation spread should be possible, also taking into consideration the cost of emission certificates or other variable components. However, the general hypothesis on how to approach this trading strategy will obviously still be valid.

Considering the Italian energy market, the most common strategy is to trade the prices differential between power and an oil-linked formula. The dominant technology in Italy is the CCGT,[3] which means that the most important fuel to be taken as the price reference for the cost side is the gas price. In Italy as in most European countries, gas is indexed to an oil-linked formula. This formula typically depends upon a basket of crude and refined oil products, which is averaged through time in order to smooth undesired volatility effects. The averaging rule is labelled by triplet of numbers (i, j, k) denoting respectively the number of months composing the backward looking average of prices, the number of months prior to delivery that should not be included in the averaging process and the number of months between one index calculation and the next (almost always equal to one). As an example, the price at a generic month n of a formula calculated every month with label $(i, j, 1)$ is given by

$$F_n = \frac{1}{i}\sum_{\xi=1}^{i} B_{n-(\xi+j)}$$

where B_n is the price of the basket at time n. Traders typically consider these formulas as a proxy of generation variable cost. A lot of different crude and distillates are usually taken as components of the basket to which the formulas are linked, leading to different strike cost for any operator. The most used formula in Italy is a simple Brent Oil (9.1.1). This is due to the fact that the hedging costs on this basket are really low (the swap on ICE Brent is the only fuel cost component of the formula). In the following we are going to analyze the time series on forward contracts on the Italian power price against the forward swap level on a 9.1.1 Brent Oil Formula, in order to implement an algorithmic trading strategy on the spread between these products. The case study will cover the period between 22 September 2009 and 24 November 2010; in particular we consider the closing prices of the Calendar 2011 forward for Italy power and the closing prices of the Calendar 2011 for the Brent Oil 9.1.1 formula.

The first step in the analysis, before proceeding with the implementation of any trading strategy, is to check the statistical nature of the spread series, and thus to

[3] Combined Cycle Gas Turbine.

Table 3.1 ADF on Italian spark spread level

	t-statistics	
Augmented Dickey-Fuller test statistic		−3.789257
Test critical values:	1% level	−3.991292
	5% level	−3.426014
	10% level	−3.136196

check for the presence of a unitary root through the ADF test on the series level. Results are shown in Table 3.1.

The results of the ADF test are over the critical level, at least at the 5% confidence level, so we reject the null hypothesis that is unit root presence, accepting instead the stationary hypothesis. We may now proceed with the implementation of a spread trading strategy based on the idea of a mean-reversion dynamic.

A basic and well-known mean-reverting process mostly used in finance is the so-called Ornstein-Uhlenbeck process with constant coefficients that in continuous time is described by the following equation:

$$dx_t = \alpha(\theta - x_t)dt + \sigma dW_t \tag{3.7}$$

with α, θ and σ positive and dW_t the differential of a standard Wiener process. This kind of model implies a non-null probability of negative price, which is an unrealistic property for an economic quantity such as a credit spread or an interest rate, but is realistic for an energy commodity spread like a spark spread. In order to carry out a spread trading strategy based on a mean-reversion idea, we will implement an algorithmic strategy that will take decisions based on a price signal provided by a mean-reverting model fitted on a specific data set. In order to do so we are going to fit the discrete version of an Ornstein-Uhlenbeck process on the Italian spark spread series, calculated as above. The explicit solution of the SDE reported in equation (3.7), is given by the following equation:

$$x_t = \theta(1 - e^{-\alpha(t-s)}) + x_s e^{-\alpha(t-s)} + \sigma e^{-\alpha(t-s)} + \sigma e^{-\alpha t} \int_s^t e^{\alpha u} dW_u \tag{3.8}$$

The discrete version of equation (3.8), given a time grid $0 = t_0, t_1, t_2, \ldots, T$ with constant time step, is

$$x(t_i) = c + bx(t_{i-1}) + \delta\varepsilon(t_i) \tag{3.9}$$

where the constant coefficients are defined as

$$c = \theta(1 - e^{-\alpha\Delta t})$$

$$b = e^{-\alpha\Delta t}$$

$$\delta = \sigma\sqrt{\frac{(1 - e^{-2\alpha\Delta t})}{2\alpha}}$$

and with $\varepsilon(t)$ defined as a Gaussian white noise. Equation (3.9) corresponds exactly to the formulation of an AR(1) process described as

$$x_{t+1} = \mu + ax_t + \sigma\varepsilon_{t+1}$$

where, having tested that $0 < b < 1$ through the ADF test, and in the presence of a coefficient $\alpha > 0$, we have an AR(1) process stationary and mean-reverting towards the long-run level θ. So, based on this discretized version of the process, we can estimate the model coefficients on the given data set and test a trading model that will take, for each time step t_i, a trading decision based on the price signal for t_{i+1}. The price signal will be delivered strictly by a comparison between the spread price level observed in t_i and the price level forecast for t_{i+1} that is computed as the conditional expectation on the observable price at time t_i:

$$\mathbb{E}_{t_i}\left[x_{t_{i+1}}\right] = \theta + (x_{t_i} - \theta)e^{-\alpha(t_{i+1}-t_i)}$$

The model's parameters have been estimated through an OLS procedure, fitting the model such that mean and variance of the process match those of the historical data set. Then we have back tested a trading strategy that, comparing the spark spread value for the step-ahead with the price observable today, will give a trading signal: if the forecast value is greater than the current observable level we get a "BUY" signal; if the forecast value is below the current value we get a "SELL" signal. In formulas, defining with s_t the price level of the spark spread at time t, we obtain an algorithm that operates according to the following rules:

- if $s_t < \hat{s}_{t+1}$ we get a BUY signal for time t, assuming the model is predicting a move up by the spread level for the step-ahead.
- if $s_t > \hat{s}_{t+1}$ we get a SELL signal for time t, assuming the model is predicting a move down by the spread level for the step-ahead.

Models like this can be improved by adding statistical confidence levels as was done for the previous case study in Chapter 2, giving the option of adjusting the trading strategy, and so also the performance of the model, according to the trader's risk appetite. As seen earlier, the more we request in terms of statistical performance, setting the statistical confidence level at a higher value, the less aggressive the model in terms of numbers of trades taken. As seen in the previous chapter, the model is valid if a trader operates coherently with the statistical hypothesis of the model itself.

Applying this algorithmic strategy to the Italian spark spread series over the time period under consideration we obtained the results presented in Table 3.2.

As shown by the numbers reported in Table 3.2, over a total of 213 trading operations the strategy reports a profit in 56% of cases. Basically, this means that "mean-reversion" hypothesis on the spread is valid and gives positive results even if taken as an absolute and unique driver (a simple price expectation) to take trading decisions on a spread strategy. The performance obviously improves if we add confidence level around the step-ahead forecast, but the basic idea of a mean-reversion dynamic, around which decisions are taken, is still valid.

Table 3.2 Italian spark spread strategy

Statistical performance	Position taken
56%	213

3.4.2 Time Spreads on Brent

Looking at the oil market, another typical strategy is to trade the differential between futures with different maturity, the so-called "time spread". This kind of strategy aims to make a profit by trading the price differential of contracts written on the same commodity but with different delivery dates. The economic idea of a time spread, on oil and in general in the commodity market, is linked to other economic quantities like interest rate level, and normally also with market participants' expectations. A market term-structure characterized by a positive time spread, the so-called "contango", is a common situation in the past few years for oil markets. Basically, a situation of positive time spread represents a market incentive in drilling activities because it allows producers to hedge their future outputs at higher level than spot prices, and means the market is pricing an expected scarcity of supply. That means that the slope of a commodity term structure, such as that for oil, is determined by a series of economic relations and is not supposed to change day on day, but is relatively stable according to a specific economic scenario. For these reasons, almost in the short-term, operators and traders may expect stable time spread level. In what follows we test the validity of a mean-reversion assumption for a liquid and traded time spread on Brent, taking the difference between the futures price for delivery in 12 months ahead and the futures price for delivery in 6 months ahead.

The case study will cover the period between April 2009 and 31 March 2010; the spread is calculated as the difference between the closing prices of the rolled futures on Brent as quoted by the ICE exchange; historical series for three calendar

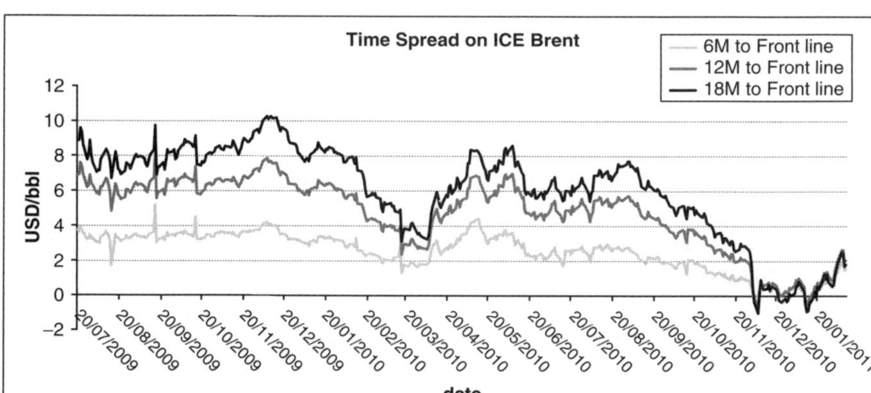

Figure 3.6 Time spread on ICE Brent

Table 3.3 ADF on oil time spread level

		t-statistics
Augmented Dickey-Fuller test statistic		−3.683619
Test critical values:	1% level	−3.977251
	5% level	−3.419191
	10% level	−3.132165

Table 3.4 Oil time spread strategy

Statistical performance	Position taken
57%	213

spreads are shown in Figure 3.6. As stated, futures for delivery in 12 and 6 months have been considered. Before proceeding with the implementation of the strategy we test the stationary hypothesis using an ADF test; the results are given in Table 3.3.

Again, as we observed for the spark spread series, the results of the ADF test are over the critical level, at least at the 5% confidence level, so we reject the null hypothesis that is unit root presence, but accept the stationary hypothesis. We may now proceed with the implementation of a spread trading strategy based on the idea of a mean reversion dynamic. The algorithm follows the same rules presented for the spark spread case study and shows similar results as those in Table 3.4.

As shown by the numbers given in Table 3.4, over a total of 213 trading operations the strategy reports a profit in 57% of cases. Again, the mean-reversion idea seems to perform well and gives positive results. Obviously we ought to consider this approach carefully when dealing with time spread because in the short term the cost of a cash and carry strategy, which represents the replicating strategy of a barrel for a generic delivery date in the futures, should be considered stable, but consistent change in interest rate levels, due to changes in the economic cycle, will deeply impact the time spread level and so the validity of a stationary series hypothesis.

3.4.3 Location Spread: Italy vs. Germany

Now let us consider the power market. A spread commonly traded by the operator is the price differential between electricity futures of various countries, the so-called "location spread". Electricity is traded at a different price level in each country; this price differential arises from the fact that the supply structure differs both in terms of cost and of installed generation capacity. From the supply point of view the different mix of technologies and fuel sources obviously characterizes the cost structure resulting in a higher or lower generation cost. Moreover, even the rate of efficiency of transmission lines, the way ancillary services are managed and the depth of the supply will determine a price differential. These economic factors

Table 3.5 ADF on location spread level

		t-statistics
Augmented Dickey-Fuller test statistic		−2.995333
Test critical values:	1% level	−3.460313
	5% level	−2.874617
	10% level	−2.573817

justify the existence of a price differential for different countries that is supposed to remain stable around an equilibrium level almost in the short to medium term, under the realistic assumption that changes in the dominant technologies take time to be implemented. Deviations from the average equilibrium level are possible and may be due to outages, transmission line interruptions, particular weather conditions and other risk factors but are supposed to virtually disappear in the short term (and so for the nearest quarter and calendar products).

In the following case study we will test the effectiveness of the mean-reversion assumption for location spread between prices of two electricity markets in Europe: Germany and Italy. Time series of the quarter forwards Q1 2011 are shown in Figure 3.7. As for the other case study we will test statistically the mean-reversion assumption considering an ADF test on the price spread series before implementing any algorithmic strategy.

As we observed for the other spread series, the results of the ADF test, shown in Table 3.5, are above the critical level, at least at the 5% confidence level, so we reject the null hypothesis that is unit root presence, but accept the stationary hypothesis.

In order to be consistent and get positive results when implementing a location spread strategy it is essential to pay due attention to the seasonal effect that deals with a power term-structure. Products for a delivery period characterized by demand peak and products for a short delivery period (monthly product) may be more unstable due to the greater effects of weather risk factors or temporary capacity

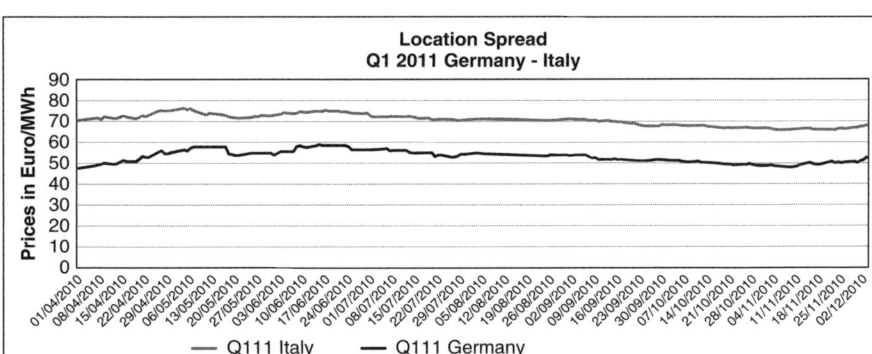

Figure 3.7 Location spread Germany-Italy Q1 2011

Table 3.6 Location spread strategy

Statistical performance	Position taken
59%	155

reduction, and so may exhibit different features year on year. For this reason it is better to consider price differential for a specific quarter or for calendar products smoothing any possible temporary effects. For this particular case study we have considered a Germany-Italy location spread on a quarter product: price differential of the 2011 1st quarter has been considered on a time window 01/04/2010 up to 30/11/2010, for a total of 155 trading dates, as reported in Table 3.6.

The mean-reversion trading strategy implemented, governed by the same rules as presented in the previous case study, seems to perform well and gives positive results. As shown by the numbers given in Table 3.6, over a total of 155 trading operations the strategy reports a profit in 579% of cases. As noted for the other case studies, confidence level boundaries will improve the trading performance of an algorithmic trading strategy; at the same time these results confirm that a basic strategy that simply aims to bet on the idea of a mean reversion dynamic performs well in the presence of stationary series.

3.5 COMBINING DIRECTIONAL AND SPREAD TRADING STRATEGIES

As outlined briefly in the introductory section, spread and directional trading strategies can also be used to achieve goals other than those analyzed so far, either separately or in combination. The first example in this field is the use of spread trading to pursue a directional objective. Up to now, when analyzing spread strategies we have focused on the identification of two assets sharing the same stochastic trend so that their spread could potentially display stationary and less erratic behaviour:

$$S(t) = Y(t) + A(t)$$

$$P(t) = Y(t) + B(t)$$

$$S(t) - P(t) = A(t) - B(t) = C(t)$$

with $Y(t)$ denoting stochastic trend and $A(t)$ and $B(t)$ independent stationary components such that $A(t) - B(t)$ is itself a stationary process.

In other situations, spreads can be used to deliberately remain exposed to certain variables we cannot access directly:

$$S(t) = Y(t) + X(t)$$

$$P(t) = Y(t)$$

$$S(t) - P(t) = X(t)$$

This situation is quite typical for commodity trading. Many different commodity sectors display a wide degree of interconnection related to their industrial use or involvement in production or consumption processes. This may be the case for energy and environmental commodities, metals and freight as also for precious metals and currencies. Not all the traders can access at the same conditions all the different commodities or financial asset sectors (simply because it is not directly their market and so the credit lines and liquidity premiums they will incur are bigger) and for these reasons sometimes some synergies are left unexploited. Playing around with spreads it is possible to recreate synthetically the movement of the variables we cannot access. A typical example in the energy sector is represented by the implied freight rates embedded in API2/API4 spread. Freight, as, for example, represented in Figure 3.8, is an illiquid market dominated by only a few players; typically, energy traders do not have direct access to it but use coal or fuel oil spreads to synthetically replicate freight market exposure.

Spread and directional trading can be combined together to exploit particular market conditions especially when absolute risk or capital constraints limit the implementation of aggressive directional trading strategies. Let's consider this simplistic example. Let us assume we have a primary asset whose price can move up €8 or down €6, in a given time horizon. Over the same time horizon we have that the spread between the primary asset and a derived one (we may recall the case of gas and power or crude and refined products) is moving in the same direction but with a compressed size. In particular, if the case asset price moves up €8, the spread moves up €4, while in the opposite situation the spread moves down only €2. A summary of the situation is given in Table 3.7. This situation is quite frequent in the energy sector when the spread is in some way representative of the production margin implied in an industrial process (e.g. power production or refining). In such cases, the asymmetric distribution of margin distribution reflects the production flexibility. Actually, margins can be compressed by competition up to the point where the convenience of the production process itself is compromised and suggests the shut off. The shut off of some production capacity pushes margins up again.

Going back to our example, we may assume a directional view of the primary asset (for example we may be bullish on it), but at the same time we may be worried

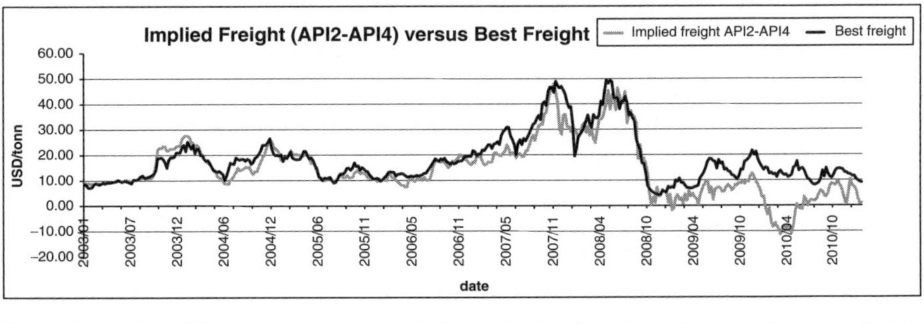

Figure 3.8 API2/API4 spread vs Best Freight, obtained as the minimum between freights Panama Bolivar, Cape Bolivar, Panamax Indonesia, Cape Rich Bay, Panamax Rich Bay

Table 3.7 Target function computed as the strategy result in case of success (scenario up) minus 10 times (e.g. generically n) the risk limit overused (risk limit €5)

	Delta asset price	Delta spread	Pure directional	Pure spread	Mixed
Scenario up	8	4	8	4	7
Scenario Down	−6	−2	−6	−2	−5
Target Function			−2	4	7

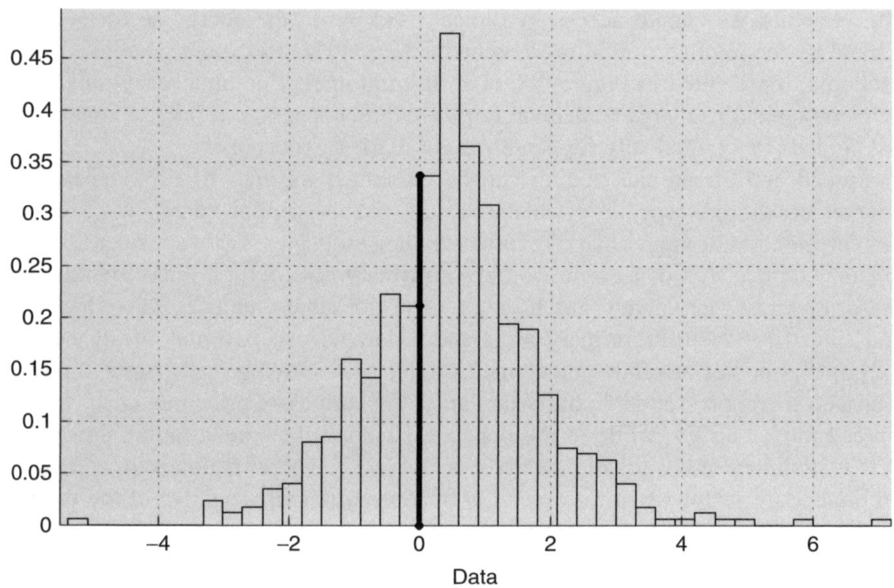

Figure 3.9 Empirical distribution of gasoil crack spread returns

about the risk that our view will turn out to be wrong. As we saw earlier often risk constraints have an absolute dimension, in the sense that we cannot risk losing more than a certain absolute amount of money and not necessarily a proportion of the expected gain. For the sake of our example, let us imagine we have a risk limit of €5 and any risk limit abuse is highly penalized. Under this framework the pure directional strategy is not attainable, while the pure spread strategy is unsufficiently remunerative. A mixed approach may be considered optimal (in this case 75% directional, 25% spread).

Irrespective of their theoretical optimality, mixed strategies are often used by traders also as moral hedges. We have seen, in fact, that psychological aspects are very important to explain the behaviour of directional traders. Hence, risk reduction strategies are often undertaken instinctively without a proper risk–reward analysis; nevertheless they may turn out to be successful.

4 Options and Non-Linear Derivatives

4.1 THE ESSENCE OF NON-LINEARITY

Options are financial instruments whose value depends upon one or more underlying variables such as traded assets (stocks, futures, interest rates, etc.), but not solely. Options are like a *bet* between the buyer and the seller on the underlying: depending upon the value at the expiry of this bet (or some other state if the underlying is not a traded asset, such as the weather), the buyer *wins* and receives some profit from the other player.

In this chapter we will describe properties and characteristics of the most used European and Asian options, their combinations and their usage for speculative purposes or positions hedging.

When used for hedging purposes the options are a sort of *insurance*: the hedger initially has to pay the option, but he maintains the privilege to benefit from positive movements of the markets. This does not happen if the hedge is done with futures or forwards: the hedger initially does not pay anything to enter into such a contract, but he will not eventually benefit from positive movements of the market, having locked his position in with the forward.

When used for speculative purposes, options permit the speculator to lock in the maximum loss he may face: this is equal to the initial payment for the option.

The peculiar characteristic of options is that profits and losses of both the buyer and the seller of an option are not linearly linked to the movements of the underlying. Since the option is an *insurance*, or a *bet*, on the underlying, either the buyer or the seller will make some profits or losses *only if* the movements of the underlying fall under some conditions fixed in the contract (i.e. a kind of *contract of wager*). We will analyze this concept in depth after presenting the two basic, and most traded, options: calls and puts.

A (European) **call** option is a financial contract which gives the buyer the right, *but not the obligation*, to buy an agreed quantity of a particular commodity or financial instrument (the underlying) from the seller at a certain time (the expiry date or maturity) and for a certain price (the strike price). On the one hand, the seller is obligated to sell the commodity or financial instrument at maturity *if* the buyer so decides; on the other hand, the buyer pays a fee (called a premium) to the seller for this right.

A (European) **put** option is a financial contract which gives the buyer the right to sell the underlying instrument to the seller of the option for a specified price at a specified date. If the option buyer exercises his right, the seller is obligated to buy the underlying instrument from him at the agreed upon strike price, regardless of the current market price. In exchange for having this option, the buyer pays the seller a fee (the option premium).

There exist also so-called *American* versions of call and put options: the only difference with European ones is that the holder of the option can exercise it not only at maturity, but at any time prior to maturity. The premium paid for American options is bigger than for European due to the greater flexibility they offer. We will analyze other types of non-European options in the next section.

From the definitions given above, three differences between forwards (or futures) and options are evident:

1. While the buyer of an option has to pay a premium to the seller, the buyer of a forward does not have to pay anything to enter a forward contract.
2. While the option gives the buyer some rights, the forward contract gives both buyer and seller obligations only.
3. While the payoff of a forward contract with delivery price equal to K is linear with respect to the underlying, given (in a long position) by $(S_T - K)$, where S_T represents the value of spot price of the traded stock at time T, the payoff of a call option is not linear: the buyer of a call will exercise his rights (i.e. he receives from the seller the quantity $S_T - K$) only when the underlying price at maturity time is greater than K; otherwise if $S_T \leqslant K$ he can buy the underlying directly from the market.

$$\begin{cases} (S_T - K) & \text{if } S_T > K \\ 0 & \text{otherwise} \end{cases} = \max(S_T - K, 0) = (S_T - K)^+ \tag{4.1}$$

The put option has an analogous non-linear payoff given by

$$\begin{cases} (K - S_T) & \text{if } S_T < K \\ 0 & \text{otherwise} \end{cases} = \max(K - S_T, 0) = (K - S_T)^+ \tag{4.2}$$

A payoff's non-linearity strongly influences not only the final value of a portfolio, but also hedging strategies. Consider the following example: a company knows that in the following month it has to buy a baseload of 1MWh of electricity; today this company has at least three choices:

1. Wait until the beginning of the next month and then buy the electricity day by day in the spot market. The price at every hour t the company pays is the spot price, denoted by S_t.
2. Lock the price today by buying a forward contract, called *month ahead*, at some price F.
3. Buy a call option today with strike K for every hour on the spot, wait until the beginning of the next month and then buy the electricity hour by hour in the spot market using the call rights every time $S_t > K$. In this way the company pays the options and the spot price $(S_t - K)^+$.

The first choice is the most risky: the company has a total exposure to spot price variations both when the price goes up (and the company loses a lot of money) and when the price falls down (in this case the company benefits greatly due to the low spot price). The second choice completely eliminates all risks by locking today the price of the furniture; in this way the company is exposed neither to the disadvantages of high prices, nor to the benefits of low prices. The third choice, on the other hand, is probably more expensive than the first two: the company has to buy the options and pays a premium for them, but in this way the risk of extreme high prices is completely eliminated by the options while the benefits of low prices are always alive due to the fact that the company is buying in the spot market.

4.1.1 Factors that Influence Option Value

We have seen that options are market instruments with non-linear payoffs; a natural consideration is that even their market value should be influenced in a non-linear way at least with respect to the underlying as also to maturity and strike and finally to other market factors such as interest rates. This section is devoted to a qualitative overview of these dependencies for calls and puts, and the results are summarized in Table 4.1.

Underlying price and strike. A call option is exercised at maturity when $S_T - K > 0$: this final value is increasing with respect to the underlying price S_T, and decreasing with respect to strike K. This behaviour must be reflected in the market price of the option: it should be increasing with respect to the spread $s_0 - K$, where s_0 is the current price of the underlying; in particular, for a fixed K it will be increasing in s_0, and for a fixed s_0 decreasing with respect to K. In contrast, a put option should have a decreasing market price with respect to the spread $S_0 - K$, decreasing wrt s_0 for a fixed K, and increasing wrt to K for a fixed s_0.

Volatility. Volatility is a measure of uncertainty: high values of volatility lead to a very fluctuating underlying price, which, at maturity, will potentially be very far from strike K. Options written on very volatile assets may well be *in the money* with high probability, and this grows their present value. Viewed thus, volatility always increases option price.

Time to maturity. If no dividends are paid, the longer the time to maturity, the higher the value of the option both for calls and puts: this is simply due to the higher uncertainty about the future price embedded in the option with longer maturity date.

Interest rate. When the interest rate goes up, the trend of the asset is expected to go up: this will influence the final payoff of a call that at maturity will more probably be *in the money* and so presents higher present value, and of a put that will more probably be *out of the money* with a lower present value. Added to this, in both the call and put case, the present value of a future cash flow is lower with a higher interest rate: this further lowers the put price, but tends to raise the call price. In this last case, this second effect is weaker than the probability of the call being *in the money*, and so the call price goes up when the interest rate increases.

Table 4.1 Factors influencing call and put values. The symbol ↗ represents an increasing value, while ↘ represents a decreasing value

	European call	European put
Underlying price	↗	↘
Strike	↘	↗
Time to maturity	↗*	↗*
Volatility	↗	↗
Interest rate	↗	↘

*This is the case when no dividends are paid.

4.1.2 Option Traders

As we mentioned earlier, we can trade options for hedging purposes or for trading ones. Hedgers select options for managing their natural risk exposure because they prefer to pay an upfront premium in order to protect their downside without losing opportunities on the upside. In any case hedgers are concerned with the aggregated payoff structure of their portfolio in a given time horizon. On the other hand, we have option traders who are linked together by their willingness to make money using non-linear derivatives. Among option traders we can identify different option trading styles according to the particular value effect the trader is trying to exploit. Basically, we can identify three different kinds of option trader: net option sellers, net option buyers and market makers. Obviously, we can also find people who use options to perform a directional trading strategy on the underlying, but as stated in Chapter 2, this approach cannot be considered as efficient with respect to the final scope of the trading strategy; moreover, it can have undesired effects that are unrelated to underlying asset price movements.

Option sellers are traders who typically like to have a small but continuous increase in their profit and loss accounts negatively exposed (as little as possible) to extreme market events. Their profits come from the premiums of the options they sell and their risk is represented by the events where options they sold finish in the money. An opposite attitude is displayed by net option buyers. Basically their profit and loss account is characterized by a slightly continuous sequence of small losses with sudden and infrequent significant profits. Their losses are due to the payment of option premiums while their profits are related to the combination of extreme market events and options' non-linear payoff structure. Obviously, net option sellers can also buy options for portfolio balancing purposes in exactly the same way as net option sellers can buy options to create complex structures, but we need to state clearly the intrinsic difference between the two categories: net option sellers bet against extreme market events and earn money selling insurance products to hedgers and net option buyers; on the other hand, net option buyers bet on extreme market events and invest money in order to be positively exposed to unpredicted and abnormal market movements.

While hedgers focus mainly on option payoff, option traders are mainly focused on option value and do not usually let the option reach maturity before closing up their position. This is particularly true for options' market makers. A market maker runs a book of options with the scope of hedging out all possible risks and gaining from trade intermediation. Obviously, and despite what financial theory teaches, since options are not completely replicable instruments and are also locally exposed to market risk, from time to time we can decide to adopt a net option seller or buyer trading attitude. For all these option trader categories it is essential to know and thoroughly understand all the instrument types they use and also how the different option combinations behave with respect to market variables movements both in terms of payoff and value.

4.1.3 Energy Option Markets

Standardized energy option trading is not as diffuse as option trading in other more traditional markets. Despite energy market liberalization processes (mainly gas and power) which began more than ten years ago and saw a significant increase in trading volumes, price transparency and liquidity almost everywhere, energy option markets (organized exchanges and OTC markets) are still niche markets more related to oil products than are power and gas markets. This phenomenon is even more evident in European markets than in the American one.

Only in a few European energy markets are standardized options regularly traded with a reasonable liquidity. In Germany, options on forward power contracts are traded OTC, while on the EEX (European Energy Exchange) options on futures are regularly quoted, again with a non-impressive liquidity level. In the Nordpool power area electricity options are more intensively traded, both OTC and on the NASDAQ OMX (formerly Nordpool ASA). Again, options exchanged are still options on forwards/futures (monthly, quarterly and yearly contracts). The UK is the only place in Europe where natural gas options are actually traded. In the ICE exchange in London options on futures on the NBP are currently quoted as well as options on oil futures (Brent, WTI and Gasoil). As we mentioned oil-based options are usually much more widely traded, and the range of options traded is also wider. On the ICE, for example, American-style future options and Asian style bullet future options are listed.

America is definitely the land of energy option trading. Just by mentioning NYMEX CME exchange we can get trading and clearing facilities for options on oil products such as WTI, Brent Heating Oil and Gasoline as well as for Henry Hub natural gas options or ethanol futures contracts.

We can reasonably expect that with energy market globalization (as is happening for natural gas after oil) and market coupling (as is occurring in European power markets) standardized energy option trading will also increase in importance.

4.2 EXOTIC OPTIONS

Classical put or call options, European or American, are considered non-exotic options, while all the other (typically specific tailor-made options OTC traded, or rights embedded on structured note or products) are considered exotic. In order to give a better specification of an "exotic" product, the more relevant features of such products are detailed below:

- Path dependency: the payoff at maturity depends not just on the value of the underlying at maturity but on the underlying's value being taken several times during the contract's life.
- Conditional events: the presence of callability and putability rights depending on spot trading within a range, or above/below a certain threshold level.
- Basket of underlying: payoff at maturity could depend on more than one underlying.
- Nature of the underlying: may not be a traded (liquid) underlying.
- Payoff currency: the payoff should be returned in a different currency from the currency of the traded underlying ("quanto" option on foreign exchange).
- Strike price structure: the strike may be indexed (and not fixed) or a basket of indexed ones.

By their specific nature these products are usually traded on OTC markets, after a negotiation and structuring phase during which traders and structures usually try to design a product's payoff in order to match the specific needs of their customers or for other financial counterparties. This kind of product is applicable when used to cover specific ad-hoc requests from industrial customers as well as when used in an option trading strategy. The advantage of this class of option has different reasons depending on the specific hedging-trading strategy. This is a class of more cost effective products since the premium is lower than a plain vanilla one, and the customer is not paying for hedging he doesn't need. They can also be used to implement specific directional views for proprietary trading strategy (bounded rise-up or specific view on trading range level) and volatility strategy.

Barrier options. A Barrier option is a kind of derivative characterized by a conditional event. The value of these products depends on the underlying's path and the value of the barrier. Differently from a standard plain vanilla, the value of a barrier option is related to the expected future value of the underlying under either, or both, of the following conditions:

- the *outstrike* has never been touched during the lifetime of the option;
- the *instrike* has been touched during the lifetime of the option.

Hence under the condition that outstrike is never reached or instrike touched, the intrinsic value of a Barrier option is exactly the same as for a standard option. In all other cases the value is different and the risk parameters (Greeks) and the management techniques may be significantly different from those of standard options.

Barrier options with *out* strikes, also called *Knock out* or *Kick out* options depending on the direction in which the barrier is placed, can be considered as a standard option at inception since the product starts active at initial time. For a *down-and-out* barrier option the barrier is set below the spot level, then the option de-activates during the lifetime if the spot price drops below the barrier. For an *up-and-out* Barrier option the barrier is set above the spot level, then the option de-activates during the lifetime if the spot price rises above the barrier.

For *in*strikes Barrier options, also called *Kick in* options, the reverse holds since the product starts inactive at the initial time. For *Down-and-in* Barrier options the barrier is set below the spot level, then the option activates only if the spot price falls below the barrier during the option lifetime. For *up-and-in* Barrier options the barrier is set above the spot level, then the option activates during the option lifetime if the spot price rises above the barrier.

The reasons for using these kinds of exotic options are related to type of trading and hedging strategy a customer is willing to adopt. The *Knocked out* options are used in active hedging strategy. If the barrier is touched the hedge is no longer in place, but we get a chance to rehedge on a better level either through a new call or by linking a spot buy order to the touch of an out strike barrier. In any event, since the premium is low the strategy allows us to save money. Monitoring and action are needed to implement hedging strategy using Knocked out options.

Kick out options are used to express mildly bullish/bearish views; the premium is really low since the holder is exchanging a lower upfront fee for a potential give up. These kinds of option benefit from low volatility levels and from a stable spot market. *Kick in* options are used to hedge strategy for the buyer: the premium is lower and the hedge appears only when needed. For the options seller they represent commercial alternatives to standard put options and allow the seller to collect their premium with no obligation if the in strike is not breached.

Payout options. A Payout option is a kind of derivative characterized again by a conditional event but the value of these products depends simply on a trigger and on a fixed "pay-out" amount. This type of option can be divided into different categories.

The *one touch* option gives the owner the right to receive a fixed payout amount if a specific trigger has been activated during the life of the product. Buyers of this option are likely to be interested to use this product to implement a strong directional view paying a low premium. Sellers have an alternative product to short a standard option in Risk Reversal strategy, and this kind of option has limited downside risk.

The *no touch* option gives the owner the exact opposite right with respect to a one touch: a fixed payout amount is given if a specific trigger has not been activated during the life of the product.

An alternative, in the class of the payout options, is represented by the *Double No Touch* option that pays a pre-specified payout amount if and only if the spot does not touch either of the two out strikes during the life of the option. Operators will benefit from range-bounded market' movements using this product: it is essentially a way to short volatility.

Asian option. For this type of option the payoff at maturity depends on the average price of the underlying asset during the whole, or at least part, of the life of the option. The payoff of an Asian option is calculated as the maximum between zero and the difference between the average value of the underlying asset calculated over a predetermined averaging period. As an example, a call's payoff could be (notice the analogy with formula (4.1)):

$$P_T = \max\left\{\frac{1}{T}\int_0^T S_t dt - K, 0\right\}$$

Products that guarantee such a payoff are particularly likely to reach hedging purposes in a particular situation. Especially when an operator needs to hedge a floating value spread over a longer time period, a product that provides an average market value of the underlying really meets their needs. Obviously, the up-front premium fee required is higher than for a plain vanilla one, but the hedging efficiency is guaranteed. Another type of Asian option is the so-called "average strike Asian"; in this case the structure is quite similar: given an asset as underlying, the strike is not a fixed term but will be determined at the end of the averaging period as the mean price of the underlying. Such a product can guarantee for the operator that the price paid to buy the asset is no greater than the average traded price over a certain time horizon, and the reverse holds for a put. A natural buyer of particular goods or stock can benefit from this kind of option.

Lookback option. Similarly to the Asian option, the Lookback option also depends on the path, on the past life of the underlying. For a Lookback option in particular the payoff depends on the maximum or minimum asset price reached during the life of the option. For a call European Lookback the payoff at maturity is calculated as the differential between the final observed price and the minimum price $S_{\min}$ reached during the option lifetime:

$$P_T = \max\{S_T - S_{\min}, 0\} = S_T - S_{\min}$$

For a put European Lookback the reverse holds, since the payoff is the amount by which the maximum price exceeds the final observed price:

$$P_T = \max\{S_{\max} - S_T, 0\} = S_{\max} - S_T$$

Lookback options are financial instruments that guarantee that the holder can buy or sell the underlying at the lowest/best price achieved during the option life. Often, with this type of product, the underlying is a commodity. As for other path-dependent options, the value of this product is highly sensitive to the frequency at which the asset price is observed in order to enter the calculation of the minimum/maximum price. As for the Asian price options, the observation period is usually intended to be a set of discrete trading times ideal for taking price observations. The frequency of these observations has a profound effect on the final value of the product.

Quanto option. A quanto option may be thought of as a "quantity adjusting option", providing currency protection on a notional not known until expiry. A quanto option, in fact, is an option where any payout at expiry is converted to a third currency at an FX rate fixed on the trade date. That means the buyer has the right to exercise the option like a vanilla product but is obligated to receive any payout in the quanto currency. This kind of product is of particular interest to a client looking to take position on an underlying movement but not wishing to have exposure on the option payout.

Another type of structure is called quanto in the weather/energy markets. In these markets, a quanto is a weather-contingent energy (or commodity) derivative. Weather contingent means that a payoff is triggered if some weather variable (typically temperature, but also precipitation or any other weather variable) crosses (from above or from below) a specified strike value. These products have higher efficiency and, in many cases, are significantly cheaper than the composition of simpler plain vanilla options. As an example within the energy market, a quanto option can take into account the volumetric impact of weather conditions on energy price. For instance, when the winter is colder than expected, the energy market suffers an increase in demand and an increase in energy price. In this case, energy producers should hedge the volume risk while also taking into account the benefits of price increase. So the quanto option's payoff depends on the product of two indices: energy price and temperature level, and permits an hedged position only in those cases where higher demand caused by the cold winter is not compensated for by higher energy price levels.

4.3 COMBINATIONS

Calls and puts are the most used type of options. They can be combined together as *building blocks* for portfolios of combinations of them or combinations of options and assets (in particular, the underlying asset). Here we present some of the most used portfolios to give an idea of how a large number of payoff functions can be created using only calls, puts and the underlying asset.

Option and asset. A portfolio composed of a long (short) position on a call and the inverse position on the underlying is used to cover the risk due to a strong upward of the underlying price. The risks of a fall of asset price are avoided by taking the same position both on a put and the underlying. As an example, Figure 4.1(a) presents the payoff of a portfolio composed of a short position on the asset and a long position on an out of the money call: it is evident that the maximum loss the holder could face is locked by the call, so the short position can be closed with a controlled maximum loss. Figure 4.1(b) presents the cases of a long position both on the asset and in the money put option: this portfolio controls the maximum loss due to low values of asset price.

Spreads. Spread strategies are useful to lock both the risk of a fall and of an increase in prices. They are obtained with a portfolio consisting of a long position on a call with strike K_1 and a short position on a call with strike K_2 with $K_1 < K_2$, both options having the same maturity. The same strategies can be obtained with a put-based portfolio, with the same position and the same relationship between

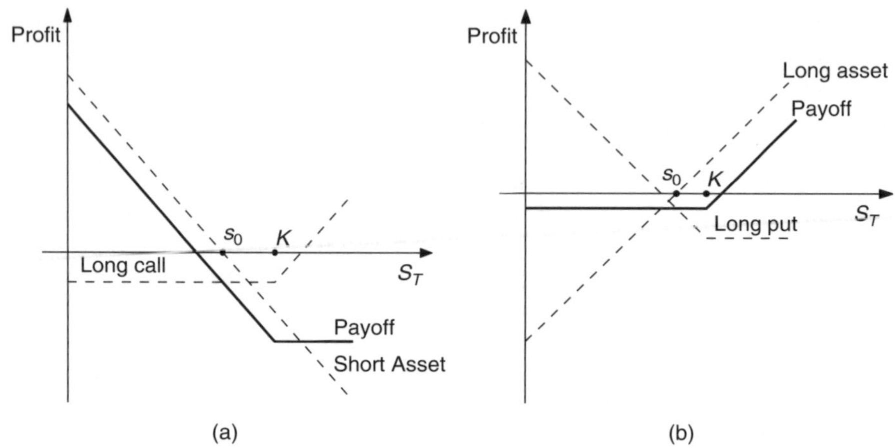

Figure 4.1 Combinations between one options and the underlying. (a) long position on a call and short on the asset; (b) long position on the asset and on a put

the strikes of a call-based portfolio. The two main differences between the two portfolios are the initial and final value of the portfolios: while in the case of a call-based portfolio the investor has to pay an initial amount to build up the strategy (the price of a call decreases wrt the strike K), in the put case the investor obtains an initial income because the price of the put is increasing wrt K; conversely, the profit at maturity when $S_T \geqslant K_2$ obtained by the call-based portfolio is higher than that obtained with the put-based one. Both strategies are built by investors who expect a rise in prices, the difference is the cash flow during portfolio lifetime. Figures 4.2(a) and 4.2(b) show the final payoff of the two strategies described.

Analogous results can be obtained for *downwards spread* strategies, which are portfolios whose final payoff is positive whenever $S_T \leqslant K_1$ and limited whenever $S_T \geqslant K_2$. The call case presents a positive initial income with possibly high but

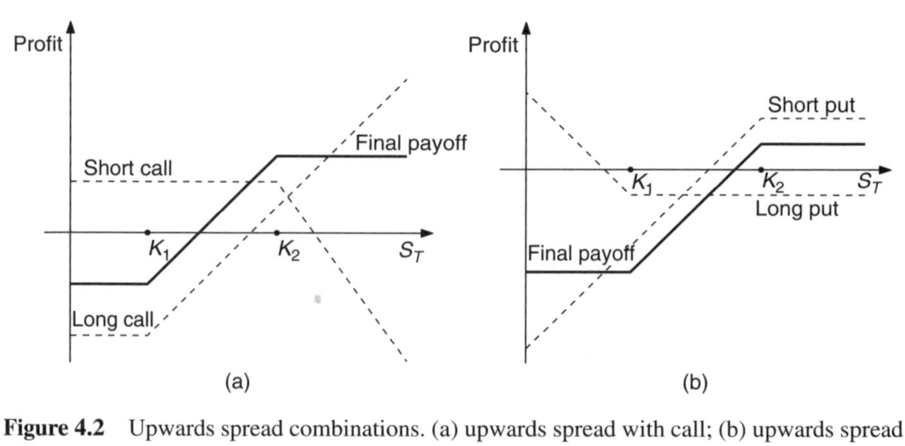

Figure 4.2 Upwards spread combinations. (a) upwards spread with call; (b) upwards spread with put

limited loss when $S_T \geqslant K_2$, while the put case has a negative initial cash flow with high profits when $S_T \leqslant K_1$.

Butterfly spreads are combinations of options with different strikes $K_1 \leqslant K_2 \leqslant K_3$ (for example, going long of one call with strike K_1, one with K_3 and going short of two call with strike K_2). These types of option are profitable whenever the final underlying price is near K_2, and limit the risk of large losses when S_T is far from K_2.

Calendar spreads are combinations of options with different maturity date. As an example, they can be obtained by selling a call with maturity T and buying a call with maturity $T + \Delta T$, both with the same strike K. They are similar to butterfly spreads, being profitable when the underlying price at maturity is near to K and unprofitable whenever S_T is far from the strike; in this case they also limit the maximum loss the investor may face.

Straddles, strips, straps and strangles. These kinds of combinations of both calls and puts, with same maturity and same strike, offer a final payoff profitable whenever the final underlying price S_T is far from the strike K and limit the maximum loss when S_T is near the strike K.

Straddles are combinations of a long call and a short put. As shown in Figure 4.3(a) a straddle permits high profits when the price S_T is far from K, but has a negative profit when $K - P_C - P_P \leqslant S_T \leqslant K + P_C + P_P$ with the lowest loss equal to $P_C + P_P$ for $S_T = K$ having denoted with P_C, P_P the prices of the call and put options. Straddles are useful for traders who anticipate large *unexpected* deviations of the underlying price both upward and downward. Those deviations have to be unexpected events in the market: on the contrary the call price or the put price will be so high as to render the straddle useless, since the interval $[K - P_C - P_P, K + P_C + P_P]$ is very large.

Strips and straps are very similar to straddles: the strip is obtained by buying one call and two put, the strap by buying two call and one put. Payoff behaviour is similar to that for straddles, but it permits higher profit than the straddle in cases when the price is lower (strips) or higher (strap) than K. On the other hand, the initial price is bigger than for straddles. So these kinds of contract reflect the expectation of the buyer of a probable downward (or upward) of final price.

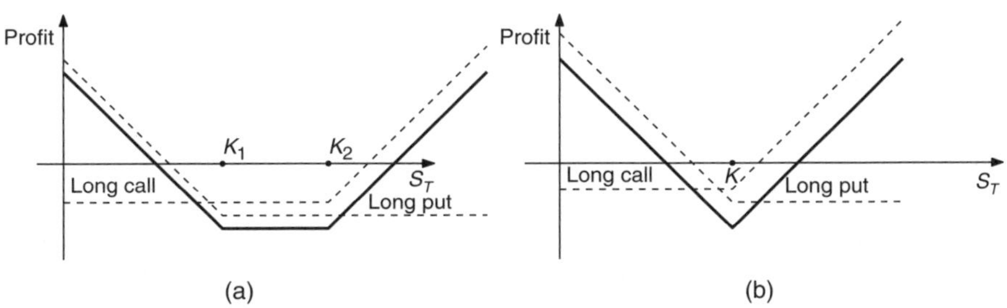

Figure 4.3 Straddle and strangle. (a) straddle; (b) strangle

Strangles are obtained, as in Figure 4.3(b), with two long positions on a call and a put both with the same maturity but different strikes: the call one, K_1, greater than the put one, K_2. These kinds of contracts have a payoff similar to straddles: they are useful when large jumps of asset price are expected, but not reflected in call and put options. In difference to the straddles, very large jumps of asset price are required to make the strangle profitable (i.e. it is profitable only when $S_T \notin [K_1 - P_C - P_P, K_2 + P_C + P_P]$), but on the plus side the maximum loss for $S_T \in [K_1 - P_C - P_P, K_2 + P_C + P_P]$, achieved for $K_1 \leqslant S_T \leqslant K_2$, is lower than the one obtained with straddles.

4.4 VALUE BOUNDS AND PARITY RELATIONSHIP

Before approaching methods for pricing options, in this section we present some properties of both call and put price. These properties, basically lower and upper bounds and parity relationship, are inferred only with economic arguments based on a *no-arbitrage* hypothesis and must be valid independently from the method used to infer the option's price. The no-arbitrage hypothesis is as follows. If two financial instruments will definitely have, at a future date, exactly the same value then these two instruments must also have the same value at current time; conversely, if one instrument will in the future have a lower value than the other, the present value of the first instrument must be lower than that of the second. In formula, if X_t and Y_t are the value of the two instruments at time t, then:

$$X_T \leqslant Y_T \Rightarrow X_t \leqslant Y_t \tag{4.3}$$

If this condition does not hold, then one (the *arbitrageur*) can make a profit without any risk. As an example, let us suppose that $X_t \leqslant Y_t$ and $X_T > Y_T$ then an arbitrageur can create a portfolio at time t by going long on X_t and short on Y_t: at time t he has the profit $Y_t - X_t \geqslant 0$ and at time T when he closes his positions: $X_T - Y_T > 0$.

Let us start with the upper bounds of a call (European or American). Call option gives the right to buy the underlying at a maximum price that is K. Now consider two portfolios. The first consists of only one share of stock S: its value is S_t; the second one consists of one call option on S: its price is C_t. At maturity date, the value of the second portfolio will always be lower than the first, being $(S_T - K)^+ \leqslant S_T$. This relationship must hold at current time as well, and so:

$$C_t \leqslant S_t$$

On the other hand, we know that the current price of a call option is decreasing with respect to strike K. A call option with strike $K = 0$ will always be exercised at maturity because in this case the call option is equal to the value of the stock. Since a call option with strictly positive strike is less valuable than a call with strike zero, the price of the call option with strike 0 is an upper bound, and at current time this upper bound is exactly equal to the value of a portfolio of one stock S, whose value is S_t. Thus we have proved again that $C_t \leqslant S_t$. Using non-arbitrage, one can also argue that if $C_t > S_t$ then an arbitrageur can easily make a riskless profit by buying S_t and selling the call option: the final value of this portfolio will be $(-S_t + C_t)\, e^{r(T-t)} + S_T - (S_T - K)^+ > 0$ which is always a positive number if $-S_t + C_t > 0$ and so an arbitrage exists.

With similar arguments one can find the upper bound for the put price P_t:

$$P_t \leqslant Ke^{-r(T-t)}$$

The rationale is the same as for a call option: $(K - S_T)^+ \leqslant K$, i.e. the portfolio consisting only of a long position on the put has a final value $(K - S_T)^+$ that is always less than the final value of a portfolio consisting of the strike price K. This relationship must also hold at current time, and so the current value of the first portfolio, P_t, should be less than or equal to the current value of the second portfolio which is $Ke^{-r(T-t)}$.

Now let us concentrate on the lower bounds. For the call option, let us consider the two portfolios, the first consisting in a long position on the asset, the other in a long position on a call and an amount equal to $Ke^{-r(T-t)}$. At maturity date the value of the first portfolio is S_T, the value of the second is $(S_T - K)^+ + K \geqslant S_T$. As usual, this relationship must hold at current time as well, and so:

$$C_t + Ke^{-r(T-t)} \geqslant S_t \quad \Rightarrow \quad C_t \geqslant S_t - Ke^{-r(T-t)}$$

The lower bound for the put option is obtained with exactly the same argument on a first portfolio consisting of an amount equal to $Ke^{-r(T-t)}$ and the second one consisting of the asset and a put on it. The final values are K for the first and $(K - S_T)^+ + S_T \geqslant K$ and so at current time the following must hold:

$$P_t + S_t \geqslant Ke^{-r(T-t)} \quad \Rightarrow \quad P_t \geqslant Ke^{-r(T-t)} - S_t$$

Taking into account that by no-arbitrage the current value of both call and put options cannot be negative (their final value is definitely positive so their present value must also be definitely positive by no-arbitrage), summing up the relationship found hitherto we obtain:

$$\left(S_t - Ke^{-r(T-t)}\right)^+ \leqslant C_t \leqslant S_t \tag{4.4}$$

$$\left(Ke^{-r(T-t)} - S_t\right)^+ \leqslant P_t \leqslant Ke^{-r(T-t)} \tag{4.5}$$

The last part of this section is devoted to the so-called *put-call parity* which is a no-arbitrage relationship between the price of a put option and a call option written on the same underlying and having the same strike and maturity. Let us consider the following two portfolios: the first one composed of a call option and an amount equal to $Ke^{-r(T-t)}$, the second consisting of a put option and one stock of the underlying. Their final value will be exactly the same, being:

$$(S_T - K)^+ + K = (K - S_T)^+ + S_T$$

Notice that this formula is simply a corollary of the mathematical relationship: $a = \max\left\{a^+, 0\right\} - \max\{-a, 0\}$. Now the no-arbitrage condition is used: having the same value at maturity date T, these two portfolios must also have the same value at current time and so the following holds:

$$C_t + Ke^{-r(T-t)} = P_t + S_t$$

This implies that the put and call current value is strictly linked by

$$C_t = P_t + S_t - Ke^{-r(T-t)} \tag{4.6}$$

As a final remark, let us note that starting from the put-call parity in (4.6), using the no-arbitrage to infer $C_t \geqslant 0$ and $P_t \geqslant 0$, we can easily get bounds in (4.4) and (4.5). For example, the call case is:

$$\begin{cases} C_t &= P_t + S_t - Ke^{-r(T-t)} \geqslant S_t - Ke^{-r(T-t)} \\ C_t &\geqslant 0 \end{cases} \Rightarrow C_t \geqslant \left(s_0 - Ke^{-rT}\right)^+$$

and being $(S_T - K)^+ < S_T$ by no-arbitrage as in formula (4.3) $C_t < S_t$ must hold. The put case is analogous.

Storage Cost and Convenience Yield. The results obtained so far are valid for options whose underlying is both a stock asset or a future (forward), taking into account the relationship between spot price S_t and the future's price $F(t, T)$:

$$F(0, T) = S_0 e^{rT} \tag{4.7}$$

For storable commodity futures such as oil, gas, corn, gold, equation (4.7) needs to be rewritten due to (the often very high) storage cost. Assuming a proportional storage cost per year of the spot product equal to h, equation (4.7) becomes:

$$F(0, T) = S_0 e^{(r+h)T} \tag{4.8}$$

In general, equation (4.8) is valid only for *investment goods*, while for *consumption goods* only the following is true:

$$F(0, T) \leqslant S_0 e^{(r+h)T}$$

This is a consequence of the utility that a *consumption good* has. The utility of the detention of the *physical* commodity is higher than that of a simple future contract: for example, the physical commodity can maintain as active a production process (such as the gas in a power plant), or benefit from local shortages. Those benefits are often called *convenience yields*. Denoting the convenience yield for a commodity with y, it is defined such that

$$F(0, T) = S_0 e^{(r+h-y)T}$$

Now we can reformulate the value bounds and the put-call parity simply by substituting in equations (4.4, 4.5, 4.6) the present value (at a generic time t) of the future, using the relationship:

$$S_t = F(t, T)e^{-(r+h-y)(T-t)}$$

4.5 BASICS ON OPTION PRICING

In this section we will describe the basic ideas underpinning the option pricing methods commonly used in finance to derive the present value of call and put options. This section is not intended as a complete description of all pricing methods and models aiming only to summarize general basic economic and mathematical concepts.

The first mathematical distinction we have to draw is between discrete time and continuous time models. In discrete time models the dynamics of asset prices evolve step by step on a discrete time scale: there exist some points $\{t_n\}_{n\in\mathcal{I}\subset\mathbb{N}}$ such that $t_n < t_{n+1}$ where the asset prices change and where decisions are taken, and nothing happens between the two; in a continuous time model asset prices change at every *instant* t, so for example between two reference points t_i and t_{i+1} the dynamics is not constant and changes countless times. On one hand, even if this assumption may seem unrealistic, it is a natural extension of high frequent data as tick-by-tick and not so distant from real life; on the other, the continuous time leads to a more advanced mathematics that, unexpectedly, may be less involved than the discrete one. Regardless of the numerosity of the flow of time, there are some basic concepts that are still valid in both continuous and discrete time: this section will focus on this giving only a brief resumé of particular models.

Let us start with basic notation. Let S_t^0 be the price of a riskless asset capitalized with the interest rate $r \geqslant 0$. In the standard literature it has the dynamics in discrete and continuous time, respectively, given by

$$S_{n+1}^0 = S_n^0(1+r)$$
$$dS_t^0 = S_t^0 r dt$$

The price at time t (or t_n in discrete time, but we will write t for the sake of notation) of the risky assets will be denoted by S_t^i, $i = 1, \ldots, M$ where M is the number of risky assets. These risky assets are *random variables*; we denoted with $\mathcal{F}_t = \sigma\left(S_u^i, 0 \leqslant u \leqslant t, i = 1, \ldots, M\right)$ the natural filtration generated by them. Here we are using the same notation and terminology as in Chapter 1.

The major assumption of every pricing model is the dynamics of the risky assets. Clearly, this dynamics will influence the price of a financial instrument as an option. Also at this stage the no-arbitrage assumption plays a fundamental role in the mathematical modelling of the markets. The link between economics and mathematics is contained in the so-called *first theorem of asset pricing* which states that *a model is arbitrage-fundamental free essentially if and only if there exists a (local) martingale measure*. The proof of this sentence underpins the scope of the present book; we invite the interested reader to refer, for example, to the proof contained in Björk (2004). However, what is remarkable here is the definition of *martingale measure* and its link with efficient market hypothesis described in Chapter 1. A martingale measure $\mathbb{Q}$ with numeraire S_t^0 is a probability measure that is *equivalent* to the real-life measure $\mathbb{P}$ but such that the discounted price of the risky asset is a martingale.

$$\tilde{S}_t^i = \frac{S_t^i}{S_t^0} \qquad i = 1, \ldots, M$$

Equivalent is the mathematical way of expressing the fact that if an event has zero probability under $\mathbb{P}$ (it is *impossible*), then it also has zero probability under $\mathbb{Q}$, and vice versa. The martingale measure $\mathbb{Q}$ is not always unique. As explained in Chapter 1, $\tilde{S}_t^i$ is a martingale if it is a random variable such that its expected (discounted) value at time $s > t$, given the information $\mathcal{F}_t$ at time t, is equal to its present (discounted) value $\tilde{S}_t^i$:

$$\mathbb{E}^{\mathbb{Q}}\left[\tilde{S}_s^i | \mathcal{F}_t\right] = \widetilde{S_t^i} \tag{4.9}$$

In Chapter 1, Section 1.3 we saw that the martingale property is associated with the weak form of an efficient market: if the market is efficient no players are supposed to have a rational chance to profit from trading activities. A necessary implication of this statement is that the expected value of any increment of an asset price, given the information at that time, must be 0. This is precisely the martingale property (even if applied to the discounted price). With $\widetilde{S_t^i}$ a $\mathcal{F}_t$-measurable random variable, formula (4.9) could be rewritten as

$$\mathbb{E}^{\mathbb{Q}}\left[\tilde{S}_s^i - \widetilde{S_t^i} | \mathcal{F}_t\right] = 0.$$

In conclusion, the first fundamental theorem of asset pricing states that if the no-arbitrage hypothesis is valid then the market is at least weakly efficient (and the discounted prices are martingales, i.e. their increment has zero mean); if the market is at least weakly efficient then no arbitrage opportunity exists. The martingale hypothesis is one of the basics of every pricing model. We always consider a weak efficient market where arbitrages are not possible.

Before going in depth into pricing models, we need to introduce some notations. A *portfolio* $V(\alpha_t, S_t, t)$ (or simply α) is a linear combination of the assets, so it is also a random variable whose value depends upon the weights at time t that we decide and the value of the assets at every step (instant):

$$V(\alpha, S, t) = V_t^\alpha = \sum_{i=0}^{M} \alpha_t^i S_t^i \qquad \alpha_t^i \in \mathbb{R}$$

Notice that with $\alpha_t^i \in \mathbb{R}$ we are allowing short selling of the assets. A portfolio is said to be *self-financing* if its value changes are due only to changes in asset prices: we are not allowed to withdraw or bank money in this portfolio, we can only *rebalance* it, i.e. by changing at every step (instant) the weights α_t^i. If this is true, in discrete and continuous time, respectively, the following relationship holds for the dynamics of the portfolios:

$$V_{t+1}^\alpha - V_t^\alpha = \sum_{i=0}^{M} \alpha_{t+1}^i \left(S_{t+1}^i - S_t^i\right)$$

$$dV_t^\alpha = \sum_{i=0}^{M} \alpha_t dS_t^i$$

both obtained by the fact that in a self-financing portfolio the only changes in the values are due to changes in asset price (in discrete time, it is equivalent to assuming that $V_{t-1} = \sum_{i=0}^{M} \alpha_t^i S_{t-1}^i$: the value of the rebalanced portfolio at time t does not change if asset prices do not change).

In discrete time the sequence of weights α_t must be *predictable*, that is *adapted* to the filtration $\mathcal{F}_{t-1}$ at time $t-1$. This property is simply the mathematical representation of the idea that the rebalancing from α_t to α_{t+1} is done at time t when the only information is given by $\mathcal{F}_t$. In continuous time α_t is assumed to be *adapted* to $\mathcal{F}_t$. One can easily prove that under the equivalent martingale measure the discounted portfolio is also a martingale:

$$\mathbb{E}^{\mathbb{Q}}\left[\tilde{V}_s^\alpha | \mathcal{F}_t\right] = \tilde{V}_t^\alpha \tag{4.10}$$

Finally, let us introduce the mathematical definition of option: a *claim* X_t with underlying S_t^i and maturity T is a random variable measurable with respect to the filtration $\mathcal{F}_t$. A claim is *path-independent* when its final value depends only upon the value of the asset at maturity: $X_T = \Phi(S_T)$ and *path-dependent* when its final value depends also upon the past values of the underlying.

A claim X is said to be *reachable* if there exists a portfolio α such that

$$V_T^\alpha = X_T \tag{4.11}$$

If *any* claim is reachable the market is said to be *complete*. Now the no-arbitrage assumption, jointly with equation (4.11), intervenes: if a claim X is reachable by replicating portfolio α then the only reasonable price process and current price by no-arbitrage is given by V_t^{α}. On the other hand thanks to formula (4.10) this is the same as using the martingale assumption:

$$\tilde{X}_t = \mathbb{E}^{\mathbb{Q}}\left[\frac{X_T}{B_T}|\mathcal{F}_t\right] = \tilde{V}_t^{\alpha} \tag{4.12}$$

In conclusion, if a claim is reachable then we can infer its current discounted price under the martingale measure by constructing a replicating portfolio and calculating its present discounted value. It is also possible to prove (see Theorem 3.19 in Pascucci, 2008) that if a claim is reachable and there exists more than one martingale measure $\mathbb{Q}$ then *for every* martingale measure formula (4.12) holds. When a claim is not reachable we cannot find $\tilde{V}_t^{\alpha}$, but the market is free of arbitrage and so at least one martingale measure exists; we can still define the discounted price $\tilde{X}_t = \mathbb{E}^{\mathbb{Q}}\left[\tilde{X}_T|\mathcal{F}_t\right]$ even if it will be dependent on the martingale measure $\mathbb{Q}$.

With these assumptions we can move on to option pricing. Let's start with the discrete time *binomial* model with one asset. In this model the dynamics of asset price is given by

$$S_{t+1} = (1 + \xi_{t+1})$$
$$(1 + \xi_t) = \begin{cases} u & \text{with probability } p \\ d & \text{with probability } 1 - p \end{cases}$$

with $p \in]0, 1[$ and $0 < d < u$. This problem could easily be drawn with binomial trees where the branch represents the two possibilities u or d. In this model:

$$\mathbb{P}\left(S_n = S_0 u^m d^{n-m}\right) = \binom{n}{m} p^m (1 - p)^m, \quad 0 \leqslant k \leqslant n \leqslant N$$

One may prove that if $d < 1 + r < u$ the equivalent martingale measure exists and is unique. The uniqueness is important: now using the second *fundamental theorem of asset price* which states that *a market free of arbitrage is complete if and only if there exists only one martingale measure* the completeness follows and so every claim with maturity T is reachable. Its present discounted value is given by formula (4.12) and when it is path-independent, that is $X_T = \Phi(S_T)$, we can calculate it with the formula:

$$\tilde{H}_0 = \frac{1}{(1+r)^T}\mathbb{E}^{\mathbb{Q}}[X] = \frac{1}{(1+r)^T}\sum_{k=0}^{N}\binom{T}{k} q^k (1-q)^{T-k}\Phi\left(S_0 u^k d^{T-k}\right)$$

where the transformation from probability $\mathbb{P}$ and $\mathbb{Q}$ is given by: $q = \frac{1+r-d}{u-d}$. The interested reader may find all the details in Björk (2004), chapter 2. Another example of a discrete time model is the trinomial model, where the stochastic factor $(1 + \xi_t)$ may assume three values. For this model too one may find the equivalent martingale measure, but it turns out that it is not unique and so the market is incomplete: there exists an infinite martingale measure and the risk-neutral price of a claim depends on it.

In continuous time the most popular model is the so-called *Black-Scholes* model. The dynamics of an asset is given by:

$$dS_t = \mu dt + \sigma dW_t$$

with W_t the Brownian motion. Many extensions of this model are possible: one is the multidimensional case, where there are many assets driven by many Brownian motions (possibly correlated); another is when the volatility σ is itself a stochastic process; one may model both drift and volatility as general functions of time and price value; and, finally, one may also add some jumps by adding, for example, a point process. There is a lot of literature on these models and a description of every one is outside the scope of this book. The main ideas we have presented are still valid: the no-arbitrage assumption, the existence of one or infinite martingale measures and the two theorems of asset pricing are the basics of all those models; what changes are the complexity of the mathematics (which is not always, but often, more difficult) and also the way all those models describe the real world. Every one has its positive and negative aspects: the hard work is often in the choice of the right model for the problem one is facing.

4.6 THE GREEKS

The previous section was devoted to analyzing how the value of an option can be derived using no-arbitrage arguments and then some mathematical assumptions and models.

Once an option has been sold, the seller is exposed to considerable uncertainity such as the underlying movements or the changes of its volatility. Even if not all possible movements are risk factors for the seller, a trader must have a tool to control these kinds of risk and hedge the position taken. This tool could be given by the so-called *Greeks of the option*.

The Greeks are the quantities representing the movements of the price of options with respect to the movements of the underlying parameters such as its price, volatility, time to expiry. They are vital tools in risk management, but only if their meaning is completely clear to the risk manager. Mathematically speaking, the Greeks are defined as the mathematical derivative of the option price P_t with respect to the underlying price S_t, its volatility σ_t and so on. From this mathematical definition it is clear that these kinds of measures are only useful to control the changes in the option's price stemming from infinitely *small* changes in the underlying's parameters. Such a mathematical derivative is, in fact, defined as the *limit of the difference quotients* when the changes in the x scales are very small. In practice, such infinitely small movements in underlying parameters are not observable or not relevant for a trader's purposes. So, even if a general understanding of what exactly the Greeks are from a mathematical point of view is useful, some *modified* notion of Greeks is necessary to manage options' embedded risk. In the first part of this section we will briefly present the formal definition of the most used Greeks, while in the second part we will analyze the discrete version of those Greeks that are useful in practice.

4.6.1 Delta and Delta Hedging

The Delta, Δ, is probably the most famous Greek. It is defined as the derivative of the option price with respect to the underlying price:

$$\Delta = \frac{\partial P_t}{\partial S_t}$$

Its meaning is: if the underlying price moves by x then the price of the option moves by $x \cdot \Delta$. A portfolio consisting of a short position of one option and long of Δ stocks:

$$\Pi_t = -P_t + \Delta S_t$$

is Delta-neutral. This means that small changes in the stock price do not affect the value of the portfolio, being:

$$\frac{\partial \Pi_t}{\partial S_t} = -\frac{\partial P_t}{\partial S_t} + \Delta = 0$$

so this portfolio is not exposed to underlying movements. Notice that the Δ can change very frequently, so a continuous rebalancing is needed. Hedging schemes that have to be changed very frequently are called *dynamic* hedging.

4.6.2 Gamma

We stated that a Delta-neutral portfolio needs to be rebalanced very often. In most cases, rebalancing leads to transaction costs, so a good question might be: how often do we have to rebalance the portfolio? That is, how often and how much does the Δ change its value depending on the underlying asset price movements? The Greek Γ (Gamma) is a first answer to this question. This Greek is defined as the movements of the Δ with respect to the movements of the underlying price:

$$\Gamma = \frac{\partial \Delta}{\partial S_t} = \frac{\partial^2 P_t}{\partial S_t^2}$$

it is the second derivative of the option price with respect to the underlying price. If Γ is small then Δ does not change much when S_t changes, and so the rebalancing should not be very frequent. On the other hand, if Γ is big then very frequent rebalancing is needed.

One can try to construct a portfolio that is both Δ-neutral and Γ-neutral. This portfolio would not need very frequent rebalancing and it is such that its value does not change with small changes in asset price. In order to have a Γ-neutral portfolio we need to add to our portfolio another option (let us call this the *auxiliary option*) on the underlying. Suppose that this auxiliary option has a Gamma equal to $\hat{\Gamma}$ and a Delta $\hat{\Delta}$, while the Gamma of the original Δ-neutral portfolio is $\tilde{\Gamma}$ (while $\tilde{\Delta} = 0$). If we take a position on this auxiliary option equal to a quantity $-\frac{\tilde{\Gamma}}{\hat{\Gamma}}$ we obtain a new portfolio that is Γ-neutral, being the total Gamma given by $\tilde{\Gamma} - \frac{\tilde{\Gamma}}{\hat{\Gamma}}\hat{\Gamma} = 0$, but that is not Δ-neutral. So we need to readjust the position on the underlying of a quantity $\hat{\Delta}$. Now we have a Δ-neutral and Γ-neutral portfolio so the portfolio is completely hedged to small changes in S_t and does not require frequent rebalancing at every small fluctuation of the underlying.

Notice that on the whole the Δ can also depend on other underlying and option parameters such as volatility and maturity so there exist the Greeks for these two derivatives: they are, respectively, Vanna $\left(\frac{\partial \Delta}{\partial \sigma}\right)$ and Charm $\left(\frac{\partial \Delta}{\partial T}\right)$ which should both be taken into account when hedging the Delta.

4.6.3 Theta

Theta is the Greek representing the derivative of the option price with respect to time:

$$\Theta = \frac{\partial P_t}{\partial t}$$

It represents the *time decay* of the option value. It is often negative, because in most cases the price drops when the lifetime of the option shortens.

4.6.4 Vega

This "Greek" (Vega ($\mathcal{V}$) is not a letter in the Greek alphabet) represents the changes in the option price related to small changes in the volatility of the underlying. Formally:

$$\mathcal{V} = \frac{\partial P_t}{\partial \sigma}$$

In practice, the volatility of a traded stock can change and so the option trader should also take into account this variable affecting the portfolio. A lot of mathematical models model the volatility such that it is not constant: it can be both a deterministic function of time and price ($\sigma(t, S_t)$) or a stochastic variable itself.

As for the Delta and Gamma cases, a Δ-Γ-$\mathcal{V}$-neutral portfolio can be constructed by using *two auxiliary options on the underlying*. Suppose that the original portfolio is Δ-neutral, but has a positive $\tilde{\Gamma}$ and $\tilde{\mathcal{V}}$, and that there exist two tradable options with their own $\left(\hat{\Delta}_1, \hat{\Gamma}_1, \hat{\mathcal{V}}_1\right)$ and $\left(\hat{\Delta}_2, \hat{\Gamma}_2, \hat{\mathcal{V}}_2\right)$. To have a neutral portfolio we have to invest the amounts w_1 and w_2 on these two auxiliaries such that

$$\begin{cases} \tilde{\Gamma} + w_1\hat{\Gamma}_1 + w_2\hat{\Gamma}_2 = 0 \\ \tilde{\mathcal{V}} + w_1\hat{\mathcal{V}}_1 + w_2\hat{\mathcal{V}}_2 = 0 \end{cases}$$

Once we have taken our positions the rebalanced portfolio is no longer Δ-neutral, so a final step is to also adjust the Δ of this new portfolio by assuming a position on the underlying equal to $-\left(w_1\hat{\Delta}_1 + w_2\hat{\Delta}_2\right)$.

4.7 ADJUSTING THE CONTINUOUS TIME DYNAMIC HEDGING FRAMEWORK

The paradigm of options' dynamic hedging is based on the assumption that continuous trading is feasible and that asset prices move smoothly through time. But the reality of financial and commodity markets is different. Transaction number and size are not homogeneous in time since new incoming information is a discontinuous process, hence significant price moves behave more like a jump than a diffusion. Moreover, trading activity is not free of charge. Liquidity premiums (measured by bid-ask spreads), which are rather significant in energy commodities markets, and transaction costs will penalize an extremely intense and frequent portfolio rebalancing strategy. As a consequence, theoretical derivatives portfolio management tools, developed so far, need corrections to work properly in real option markets.

4.7.1 Discrete Δ and Extreme Market Moves

Since price movements are in practice discrete and not continuous the concept of option's Δ and Δ-hedging should be revised accordingly. We should ask ourselves what the sensitivity of our portfolio Π is with respect to different levels of changes in the underlying relevant assets by computing a discrete Delta, which we will continue to indicate as Δ:

$$\Delta = \frac{\Delta\Pi}{\Delta S} = \frac{1}{2}\left(\frac{\Delta\Pi}{\Delta S^{+}} + \frac{\Delta\Pi}{\Delta S^{-}}\right)$$

where $\Delta S^{\pm}$ indicates respectively a positive or negative shift in the asset value. In the discrete Delta calculation a Gamma effect is also embedded since a portfolio's value changes are related to Gamma and Delta (ignoring higher order effects) by the following relationship:

$$\Delta\Pi = \Delta \cdot \Delta S + \frac{1}{2}\Gamma\,(\Delta S)^2$$

Hence, the higher the price jump, even in a very short discrete interval of time, the poorer the effectiveness of the traditional delta hedging strategy. Moreover, for a portfolio of different options it is not infrequent to observe situations of

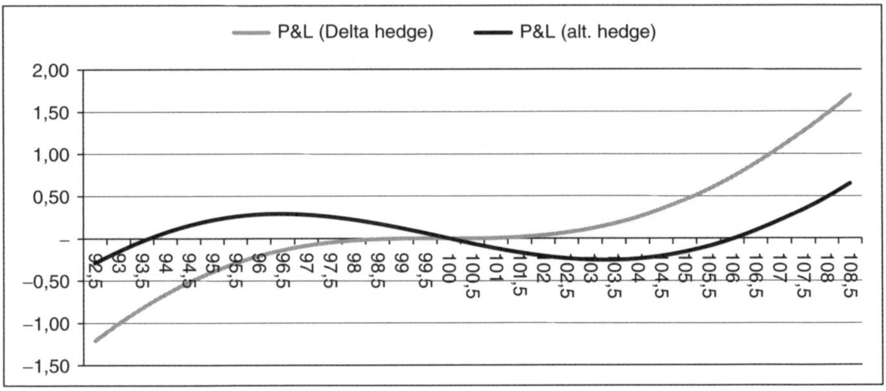

Figure 4.4 Short call (96), long call (104), long asset

local Delta neutrality (the portfolio is Delta immunized by small underlying price changes) which turn into quasi-directional positions enlarging the size of the price change. Pretty typical is the example proposed by Taleb (1997), and represented in Figure 4.4, of a portfolio composed of a short call position at 96 and long call symmetric position at 104 Delta hedged with the theoretical BS Delta, the underlying being at 100. This simple portfolio is only locally Delta flat, becoming similar to a long asset strategy (always Delta positive) everywhere that is far from the starting point. Adjusting (in this case by reducing) the Delta hedging ratio will compromise local Delta neutrality, but will improve hedging effectiveness for large price movements.

We may conclude that since the market does not move smoothly, market view on volatility matters greatly in the determination of the proper Delta hedge. Moreover, as already stated, price moves are often simultaneously accompanied by changes to other market parameters (volatility, correlations) which have their own joint effect on a portfolio's value, hence scenario analysis is always a very useful tool for the option portfolio manager.

4.7.2 Gamma and Shadow Gamma

Even more than for the Delta, the Gamma measure is extremely local and for that reason extremely dependent upon volatility and time (the reader should remember that time and volatility are the two main ingredients of price variance within diffusive price models). Most traders, then, monitor the behaviour of a portfolio's Gamma not only locally (at today's market conditions) but also at different time, price and volatility buckets paying attention to its stability. Proper Gamma bucketing visualization (Gamma surface, an example is provided in Figure 4.5) is the necessary instrument in order to understand how Gamma can evolve with sudden evolutions of market scenario. In this regard, the reader should note that the model used to calculate Gamma will inject into Gamma analysis and bucketing its own bias and assumptions that must be properly considered and eventually adjusted.

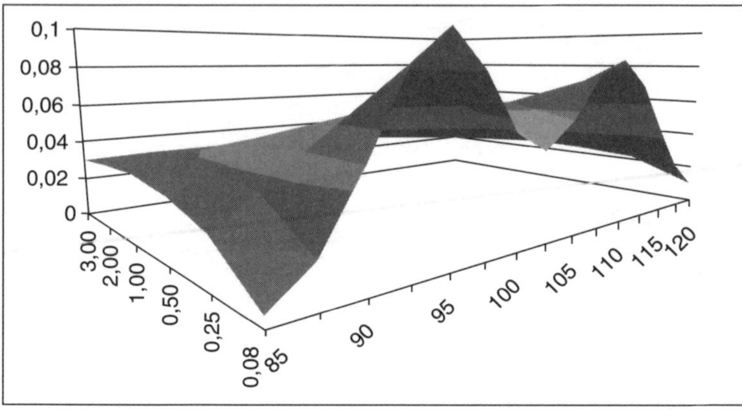

Figure 4.5 Gamma surface (time & price) of a 95–110 strangle

Just as the Delta, Gamma measures the change in a portfolio's value due to an *isolated* market price movement without taking into consideration that in real markets price movements, especially big shocks, come hand in hand with volatility and correlation changes. Mathematically speaking, this is exactly the difference between only one partial derivative, which takes into account the changes of a function in one direction only, and the gradient of a function, which takes into account all the partial derivatives. Gamma standard measure can then be corrected to also take care of other market joint events, such as both price and volatility movements. In particular *Shadow Gamma* takes into account changes in both underlying levels and volatility values, and can be thought of as a surface as in Figure 4.5, but where the time axes are replaced with the volatility axis.

4.7.3 Vega and Volatility Surface Movements

As previously defined, Vega is the Greek indicating the sensitivity of an option's portfolio with respect to underlying implied volatility changes. It is usually expressed as the value change corresponding to a 1% change of the implied volatility. Just as the Gamma, so the Vega also has the bell shape flattening and decreasing with maturity. Vega and Gamma are strongly related not only by their shape. In fact, at least in a BS world, Vega can be thought of as the integral of Gamma profits over the duration of the option, calculated at a certain volatility level, minus the same integral calculated at a different one.

A portfolio of options, different per strike and per maturity, is exposed to the movement of the so-called implied volatility surface that is the matrix of volatility parameters that when inputted into the BS (or Black76) formula will give exactly observed market prices of traded options with different strikes and maturities. Volatility surface shape and dynamics indicate how real option markets deviate from BSM theoretical assumptions mostly in terms of underlying distributional and stochastic behaviour. The more convex and inclined the surface, the more price behaviour differs from log-normal assumption in skewness and excess kurtosis (as opposed to traditional assumptions in financial economics and option pricing).

Again, the movements of the volatility surface are not completely random even if they are usually very sharp and discontinuous. Typical configurations and movements can be identified market by market and for this and in-depth scenario analysis aimed at verifying the robustness of our portfolio with respect to significant volatility changes it is an essential activity for any option trader.

4.7.4 Theta, and the Greek's Importance for Exotic Option Traders

An option's value is also not linearly related to time decay. The shorter the remaining lifetime of the option, the lower its value. Theta, the Greek that measures precisely this effect, goes hand in hand with the Gamma. In fact, the ratio $\frac{\Theta}{\Gamma}$ of the Theta and Gamma (also know as Alpha) will remain constant (at least in a BSM world) irrespective of the remaining option's lifetime.

The more complex and diversified the structure of a portfolio of options, the more the portfolio's value will become extremely sensitive to even very small changes in standard Greek parameters. This is particularly true for portfolios of exotic options. In such situations options' traders watch and manage higher order Greeks such as Vanna (dvega/dvol) or Volga (dgamma/dvol). Obviously, particular types of option will require specific management tools and practical adjustments. Due to space constraints we cannot cover the analysis of exotic option trading techniques here with the proper precision (we refer the reader to N. Taleb (1997) and Gatheral (2006)). As stated, energy option markets are relatively immature compared to other sectors but nonetheless they are in continuous expansion. Hence we may imagine that in a few years energy exotic options will also be extensively traded. At the moment in the energy field it is more common to trade asset-based structured products, which will be the subject of the next chapter.

4.7.5 Futures and Forwards to Hedge the Risk: Structured Products

There is a class of instruments, in particular in the energy market, for which the concept of Delta hedging as defined above loses its significance or becomes extremely difficult to calculate by either analytical or discrete means. We prefer to speak of *optimal hedging ratio*, in particular when forwards and futures are the only available instruments one has to hedge one's position.

Structured products, which will be the subject of the next chapter, such as swing or VPP are the main examples for which one cannot trust in the liquidity of the spot underlying while calculation of the Delta (when this mathematical derivative has sense) is also very challenging with numerical schemes. This is because these types of contract are not simply European or Asian options on one or more underlying, but always integrate additional constraints, for instance on the *physical* underlying asset (as a min/max quantity covered by the option), or other inter-temporal constraints which emulate the *real world* those contracts are imitating. (For example, if the option is exercised at a certain hour of a certain day, then it has to be exercised also in some other consecutive hours.)

If the pricing of this type of option is not simple, the hedging (and the calculus of the Delta) may be even more difficult. For such contracts it turns out that the pricing problem is often a *stochastic optimal control problem*, as described in Chapter 2 (see equation (2.22)), so it may prove effective to embed the hedging problem into the general pricing problem, without calculating any (analytical or numerical) derivatives.

The idea behind this method is similar to that used in delta hedging: to try to find the optimal long or short position on the forward (or future) one has to lock (and then rebalance) in a portfolio a given measure of the risk associated with the exposition given by the option. For instance, if we have an option which gives the right to buy a certain quantity of gas in the range $[m, M]$ at a predetermined price, but forces the purchase of the minimal quantity m, then when we build up the position we face the problem of having to choose if we want to fix today the price of a certain amount of gas (the amount m for instance, but higher or lower quantities would also be good choices) with a forward contract or if we prefer not to fix any price, leaving the entire quantity exposed to the spot price. A more technical description of this type of hedge will be presented in the next chapter, Section 5.3.1.

4.8 CASE STUDY

This section seeks to analyze how Delta hedging, and some other Greeks, work. The case is performed using historical market data. The portfolio we consider is very simple, consisting (initially) only of a long position on a call with strike \$120 and underlying the ICE Brent futures with delivery in July 2011. The reference period is the month of April 2011, so we are considering a call on the 3-months ahead future. The maturity of the call is 10 June 2011. For simplicity, we assume the interest rate to be zero.

Table 4.2 presents, in the first three columns, the trading date, the closing price of the futures for that date and the closing price of the European call option with strike 120.[1] All those prices are referred to as a barrel, while the standard contract both for futures and options is often 1,000 barrels, but we need pay no attention to this and suppose we can trade only one barrel (and its fraction).

In order to appreciate the day-by-day changes in a portfolio's profit and loss, in the rest of this section and in Table 4.2, the so-called *portfolio value* is calculated as follows: the long position on the call is added to a portfolio's value by using

[1] Brent call options traded on ICE are American type, so the prices used in Table 4.2 are of the American options. The price of this type of option should not be calculated using the standard Black76 formula. Here we consider those prices as the price of a European call and we derive the implicit volatility with the Black76 formula. This simplification does not affect the results we wish to show. We could also get the European prices by starting from market volatility and using Black76 to calculate new prices.

Table 4.2 Value of a portfolio composed of a long position on a call (with underlying futures ICE Brent 3 months, strike \$120) and the underlying. For every trading date the value of the portfolio, calculated as described, is shown, both before and after the rebalancing

DATE	BRENT	CALL 120	IMPL. VOLA	DELTA CALL	PORT. VALUE (post)	PORT. VALUE (pre)	$\frac{\Delta\Pi}{\Pi}$% Hedged	$\frac{\Delta\Pi}{\Pi}$ % Naked
01/04/2011	\$ 118.12	\$ 5.35	29.833%	0.478	\$ 51.11			
04/04/2011	\$ 120.27	\$ 6.41	30.351%	0.533	\$ 57.69	\$ 51.08	−0.06%	19.81%
05/04/2011	\$ 121.57	\$ 6.98	29.874%	0.566	\$ 61.83	\$ 57.82	0.21%	8.89%
06/04/2011	\$ 121.59	\$ 6.92	29.749%	0.566	\$ 61.90	\$ 61.90	0.12%	−0.86%
07/04/2011	\$ 121.90	\$ 7.07	29.844%	0.574	\$ 62.90	\$ 61.93	0.04%	2.17%
08/04/2011	\$ 125.64	\$ 9.50	30.641%	0.664	\$ 73.92	\$ 62.62	−0.45%	34.37%
11/04/2011	\$ 122.94	\$ 7.68	30.801%	0.601	\$ 66.21	\$ 73.95	0.04%	−19.16%
12/04/2011	\$ 120.06	\$ 6.09	31.234%	0.527	\$ 57.18	\$ 66.07	−0.21%	−20.70%
13/04/2011	\$ 121.92	\$ 6.91	30.432%	0.576	\$ 63.32	\$ 57.34	0.28%	13.46%
14/04/2011	\$ 121.64	\$ 6.55	29.644%	0.569	\$ 62.66	\$ 63.51	0.31%	−5.21%
15/04/2011	\$ 122.78	\$ 7.32	30.456%	0.599	\$ 66.23	\$ 62.54	−0.19%	11.76%
18/04/2011	\$ 120.97	\$ 5.93	29.393%	0.551	\$ 60.72	\$ 66.53	0.46%	−18.99%
19/04/2011	\$ 120.70	\$ 5.65	28.943%	0.543	\$ 59.89	\$ 60.86	0.22%	−4.72%
20/04/2011	\$ 123.14	\$ 6.91	28.364%	0.616	\$ 68.94	\$ 59.96	0.11%	22.30%
21/04/2011	\$ 123.30	\$ 6.94	28.248%	0.622	\$ 69.75	\$ 69.01	0.10%	0.43%
25/04/2011	\$ 122.97	\$ 6.75	29.505%	0.612	\$ 68.51	\$ 69.74	−0.02%	−2.74%
26/04/2011	\$ 123.45	\$ 6.91	28.998%	0.628	\$ 70.62	\$ 68.64	0.20%	2.37%
27/04/2011	\$ 124.56	\$ 7.39	27.845%	0.667	\$ 75.69	\$ 70.83	0.31%	6.95%
28/04/2011	\$ 124.41	\$ 7.21	27.650%	0.664	\$ 75.40	\$ 75.77	0.11%	−2.44%
29/04/2011	\$ 125.30	\$ 7.78	27.751%	0.692	\$ 78.93	\$ 75.42	0.03%	7.91%

the minus sign and the market price of the call; the short position on the future is added as a positive amount using the market value of the future. For instance, if at a certain date the call price is c and we go long of a quantity q_c, the future price is f and if we go short of a quantity q_f, the so-called *portfolio's value* will be given by $-q_c \cdot c + q_f \cdot f$. Even though this notation may not be consistent with reality, it becomes very useful for evaluating the Δ of the portfolio, i.e. the day-by-day differences in its value when market prices change and on which this example is focused (because they really represent the profit and loss we face).

Naked position. Relative differences (in percentages) of the day-by-day changes in portfolio value, with the naked position, are shown in the last column. They are obtained as $\left(100 \cdot \frac{\Pi_t - P_{t-1}}{\Pi_{t-1}}\right)$ where in this case the portfolio is given by a naked long position on the call. For example, the value for the date 04/04/2011 is obtained in this way: $100 \cdot \frac{6.41-5.35}{6.41} = 19.81$. This value shows a huge increment in portfolio values due to a relatively small change in the underlying, being $100 \cdot \frac{120.27-118.12}{118.12} =$ 1.82% . Moreover, big drops are evident, such as the one observed on 12/04/2011. We can conclude that this naked position is also very sensitive to small changes in the underlying value.

Δ-neutral position. Now let us analyze the case of a Δ-hedged portfolio. In theory, a Δ-neutral portfolio is such that small changes in the underlying do not affect portfolio values.

At the beginning of the reference period, i.e. the first day of April 2011, we build the Δ-neutral in this way. First we buy the call option at price \$5.35. Then we need to estimate the Δ of this portfolio. Using the Black76 model for a call option written on a future, we first derive the implied volatility of the future from the model. It turns out that this volatility is 29.833%, as shown in the column "impl. vola" of the table. With this (implied) volatility we can use the same model to calculate the Δ, obtaining $\Delta = 0.478$. The portfolio becomes Δ-neutral if we take a short position on the future by selling 0.478 barrels. In conclusion, the value of the portfolio the first day is:

$$-5.35 + 0.478 \cdot 118.12 = \$51.11$$

At the beginning of the second day, at 04/04/2011, Brent's price changes, reaching \$120.27, as does the option's price, to \$6.41. These two new prices lead to a different implied volatility and to a new Δ for the call, and so the portfolio needs to be rebalanced by changing the short position on the future to the new Δ that is now equal to 0.533 (in other words, we sell $0.533 - 0.478 = 0.055$ barrels of futures). The value of the portfolio obtained *after* the rebalancing is shown in the column headed "port.value (post)".

But the interesting point is something else: what is the portfolio value *before* the rebalancing? If the theory holds, i.e. the portfolio is Δ-neutral, the changes in the underlying price did not affect the portfolio's value, which however prior to rebalancing, was:

$$-6.41 + 0.478 \cdot 120.27 = \$51.08$$

In practice, the portfolio's value dropped only by about -0.06%, a very small value compared to the 19.81% in the naked position. The Δ-hedging has worked *pretty* well. Comparing the last two columns of Table 4.2 we can see that the Δ-hedging works by significantly reducing the changes in our portfolio's value. Figure 4.6 shows the graphs of these two columns giving an idea of how the Δ-hedging can improve the stability of the value.

On the other hand, we note that even with a Δ-neutral position, the portfolio *always* changes its value, in contrast to the fact that a Δ-neutral portfolio is not affected by changes in the underlying. This is exactly the effect of the difference between the theory and the practice. The mathematical derivatives are built considering *infinitely small* changes. In practice, such small changes do not exist, so a Γ effect is present on our portfolio. In addition, a look at the column "imp. vola" shows that the volatility σ of the underlying changes every day and so a $\mathcal{V}$ effect is also present on the portfolio's value. This is the same as stating that this portfolio is not *shadow* Γ-neutral.

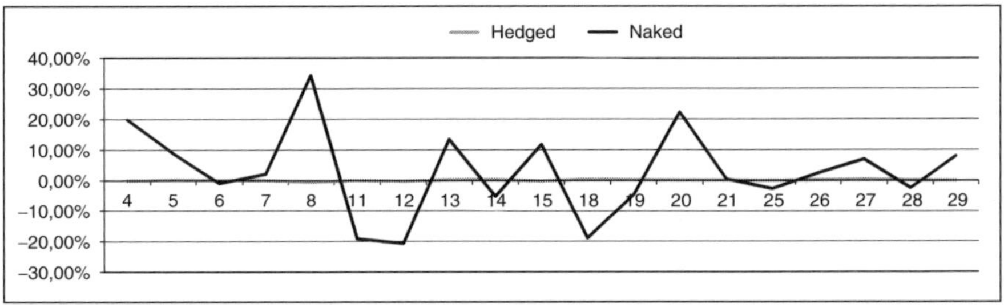

Figure 4.6 Historical relative percentage changes in a portfolio's value from 01/04/2011 to 29/04/2011 for the naked and hedged position on a call with strike 120, maturity at 11/06/2011 and as underlying the future on Brent for July 2011

Finally, we note that this example has also illustrated the practical use of the so-called *adopted stochastic process*. This property of a stochastic process was introduced in Section 4.5 and in Chapter 1, Section 1.3. It describes exactly the fact that we perform the rebalancing of our portfolio with the information given the time t, which we have called $\mathcal{F}_t$ and that in this example is represented by the new future's price observed day by day. This new price allows us to calculate our *adopted stochastic control*: the quantity Δ at time t, which is decided only by using the future's price on the day we perform the rebalancing.

5 Structured Products on Energy

5.1 STRUCTURED PRODUCTS ON ENERGY: MAIN TYPOLOGY

In financial markets and also energy markets, operators need to face the complexity embedded in the management of exposure and risk from structured products. The identification of a structured product varies from market to market, but a simple definition terms "structured' any non-standard financial product. Hence each product is not a plain vanilla derivative (excluding standard forward, futures, swap and plain vanilla options) and needs to be classified in this category. Since this general definition does not help us address the issue in rigorous way, we will attempt to specify the peculiar features of these kind of product and, in particular, provide an answer to the question in relation to power and gas markets. This should help provide a better framework for a more articulated and detailed discussion of energy structured products. The first element characterizing a non-standard product is related to its complexity. A structured product is a product that implies a higher degree of complexity in its pricing and management. In traditional financial markets, such as fixed income or foreign exchange markets, a structured product is usually classified as an exotic derivative, with respect to its payoff, which implies a higher complexity level. Commonly accepted features of what constitutes a structured product are described in Table 5.1.

According to previous definitions, forwards on really illiquid parts of the term structure, or forwards written on illiquid underlyings, must be considered as simple structured. Hence simple outright written on non-tradable assets, or written on illiquid products, requires the use of non-standard techniques for hedging and pricing activities. The dependence upon multiple risk factors implies the use of proper modelling techniques in order to take into consideration all the embedded risks. In financial and energy markets risk factors are often not separately tractable as individual sources of randomness, so a correct approach requires the joint modelling of their behaviour in order to address pricing and hedging issues correctly. This task may be especially complicated when risk drivers display a strange dependence structure or some of them are extremely illiquid or not traded.

The majority of energy structured products we are going to describe in what follows cannot be simply decomposed into a strip of plain vanilla call/put options and forwards. When possible, an effective decomposition in basic traded products allows a replication and a full, or partial, offsetting of the risk. On the other hand, theoretical decomposition allows us to use standard pricing techniques and

Table 5.1 Main features of structured products

Main features of structured products
– Non-standard maturity compared with the liquid part of the forward curve
– Multiple risk factors
– Product decomposable in standard plain vanilla products
– Non-perfect "hedgability"
– Inter-temporal constraints that imply co-dependency in exercising rights

to determine the whole value of the contract as a combination of different standard products. As stated, where building block products are available, risks can be potentially cancelled out by taking positions on market products (which is not the standard situation in energy and gas markets). The decomposition is often only theoretical because standard option pricing techniques may just be partially used. The use of a standard pricing approach should be only partially adopted for the majority of structured products, since we are observing inter-temporal constraints that imply co-dependency in respect of exercising rights. That means the exercise of an option right on any date should result in a future obligation to exercise, or not, on a future date; in all these cases the valuation problem may be highly related to an optimization one. In general, given that energy markets are extremely dynamic, the range of structured products traded varies continuously. Any additional complexity in the structure is usually accompanied by an additional complexity in pricing techniques. The capability to optimally manage this increased level of complexity is the key factor to success in energy structured products trading.

Power and gas industries are based on physical assets and infrastructures which are intrinsically complex in their physical and operational constraints. The liberalization of energy markets has introduced competitive access to market products and infrastructures; this implies a complex risk exposure for market actors. New complexity needs ad-hoc instruments to manage and hedge portfolios of assets and customers, to protect market values or to profit from market movements. Actually, energy trading covers much more than just proprietary energy trading. Merchant trading (also known as asset backed trading) is an activity that every integrated energy company has to do in order to optimize its portfolio (see Table 5.2).

The use of complex structured products in energy markets is related to the intrinsic complexity of the business which, in order to replicate financial cash

Table 5.2 Merchant vs proprietary perspective on structured products

Proprietary trading	Merchant trading
Profit making purpose	Optimization of asset
Take advantage of fluctuations	Optimization according to market fluctuations
Independence from industrial activities	Connection with industrial activities
Position only on liquid product	Use of structured products
Small/medium size position: "stop-loss" strategy	Medium/big size position
Liquid part of term-structures	Long time horizon

flows and payoff of a physical portfolio, requires the trader to virtually replicate assets and their operational constraints. With the liberalization process operators have come to realize the importance of the risk embedded in the trading of these products, and so benchmark pricing and hedging techniques have been developed. Nowadays energy structured products are traded all along the value creation chain of an integrated company: in the upstream (production and asset management side), to stabilize inter-company production cash flows (e.g. tolling contracts for power and gas swing); and in the downstream for retail customers. The same product can be used and valued differently according to whether it is dedicated to a wholesale/trading counterpart or to a retail customer. A trading counterparty exercises product flexibility in order to maximize its return while a retail customer, for example, trades it to satisfy its consumption needs. All the previous issues need to be carefully considered when approaching the pricing and hedging of a structured deal.

5.2 RETAIL STRUCTURED PRODUCTS

Retail structured products are structures created in order to match needs from industrial or domestic final consumers. These are called "structured" in relation to the tailoring needed to fit the specific requirements of the customer, which entails a low level of standardization and non-standard volume profiles. Regarding price structure there are a lot of possible choices depending on the floating index to which each contract will be linked. For their specific features this kind of product is bilaterally closed between parties and not directly exchanged in OTC or deregulated markets.

5.2.1 Profiled Forward Contracts

In this type of contract a specific loading profile is provided to the buyer and no volume flexibility is allowed. The seller has only the obligation to serve the hourly agreed profile of energy or gas while other unexpected deviations from the contract profile will be managed by the buyer. These contracts are also called "take or pay" which means the customer has the obligation to take the agreed hourly profile; otherwise the customer is anyway forced to pay for the energy or gas not consumed. The consumption profile is very peculiar and strongly dependent on the kind of customer served. In fact, domestic usage of gas and power is different from industrial usage and, among different industrial sectors, typical profiles may change drastically. The payoff of a profile forward contract may be related to a fixed price or to an indexed one, and is generally described as follows. For a fixed price profile forward contract the final payoff is given by:

$$\text{Payoff fixed} = \sum_{t=0}^{T} L_t[F - E_t]$$

where $[0, T]$ is a fixed time horizon, L_t denotes the load value at time t, E_t denotes the power price at time t and F denotes the fixed price to be paid. For an indexed price profile forward contract the final payoff is given by:

$$\text{Payoff fixed} = \sum_{t=0}^{T} L_t[I_t - E_t]$$

where I_t denotes the indexed value to be paid at time t. The indexes usually chosen by operators are oil, coal or gas linked formulas that better replicate individual generation cost or are the most representative proxy for a country's generation park.

5.2.2 Full Requirements Contracts

In other types of retail contract, known as Full Requirements, the seller is called to fully satisfy the consumer's hourly consumption with the commitment to fully serve the customer's load. This kind of product is used to serve customers not able to foresee their loading needs over a long time period and unable to manage eventual misalignment from the initial prevision. In these cases the seller is called to fully provide the customer's load fully taking the price and volume risk. The management of the risk is remunerated through a fee that is charged on top of the normal price for a profiled load contract. The fee depends on the total final amount of served load or should be computed as a fixed fee for a unit of served volume. Hence the payoff of Full Requirements can be functionally represented as

$$\text{Full Requirements Payoff} = \sum_{t=0}^{T} [C - (L_t E_t)]$$

where $[0, T]$ is a fixed time horizon, L_t is a random variable denoting the load value at time t, E_t is the power price at time t and C the corresponding monetary fee for serving the load. If the fee is intended as fixed for unit of served volume, the payoff is described as

$$\text{Full Requirements Payoff} = \sum_{t=0}^{T} [L_t(C - E_t)]$$

where the fee now depends on the unit volume. In this kind of contract the load in not known in advance and hence, in contrast to profiled contracts, the seller needs to fully satisfy the customer's consumption facing this risk. As noted above, risks related to this kind of contract are really significant and a correct pricing and management of the exposure are fundamental to determine a fair price and a correct risk management policy. In power markets buyers of Full Requirements are typically local distributors serving a portfolio of small customers, and they are basically swapping volume and price risk they are not able to manage with power traders. Sellers are typically power producers willing to sell their own production on the market without developing a commercial network necessary to reach domestic consumers. Even if a simple structure to understand, this kind of contract effectively implies an idiosyncratic risk source, a volumetric one, that heavily impacts the risk associated with the product. The profile is not determined a priori, is not easy to forecast and is mostly subject to changes unrelated to price movements. Further, the price's variable is difficult to hedge: energy spot prices are highly volatile and standard forward products can be insufficient to hedge non-standard profiles (intraday, hourly, block or even with higher granularity are needed). In the following we are coming closer to the hedging approach of non-standard products in incomplete markets, and examples will be presented of how to tackle this kind of problem in order to mitigate risks.

5.3 WHOLESALE STRUCTURED PRODUCTS

5.3.1 General Pricing Issues on Structured Products

Wholesale structured products are typically thought of and built up to replicate the characteristics of physical assets in order to work properly as hedging instruments or direct substitutes to direct asset investment.

Virtual asset is a generic term to indicate a class of structured products. In the different branches of the energy sector, different products belonging to this class are often observed. *Virtual Power Plants* (VPP) in the power sector, *Virtual Gas Storages* (VGS) in the gas sector and *Virtual Refineries* in the oil sector, to mention just a few examples.

As stated, the introduction of such a contract is strictly related to the need of energy producers to hedge their risk exposure in a more effective way compared to the effectiveness attainable through standard products like forwards or options. In fact, real energy production assets are characterized by operational flexibilities and constraints. Energy producers try to maximize their margins by managing optimally an asset's flexibility within the allowed physical constraints. Obviously, a contract that replicates virtually all the financial flexibilities and constraints of the real asset is an optimal hedging instrument for the producers. Virtual assets are not only good hedging instruments for energy producers, but also capital saving alternatives to real asset investments. In dynamic and extremely volatile markets, like energy markets, investment decisions are often made on the basis of market conditions or scenarios which are rapidly obsolete. Under these conditions, virtual asset contracts, for their short/mid term maturity, are interesting tools for a dynamic portfolio management policy. As a capital saving alternative to traditional investments, virtual assets can also be used as limited risk instruments for new markets exploration. Operational flexibilities represent options that have to be fully exploited and optimized with respect to physical constraints which may convert options into obligations. Among all the physical constraints, inter-temporal constraints (those physical limitations in the inter-temporal exercise of the asset's flexibilities) have a particular importance. If an inter-temporal constraint affects the free exercise of an asset's flexibility, the option to exercise it turns into an obligation to exercise, reducing, as a consequence, the value of the contract. The additional complexity embedded in virtual assets is also reflected in the increased complexity of their valuation and optimization techniques. In fact, their payoff is not only a straightforward function of a bunch of underlying variables, but is also the consequence of an operational policy the owner decided to execute. The way options embedded into the product are managed has a tremendous impact on the final payoff. A consistent pricing technique has necessarily to take this complication into account. American options are simple examples where the pricing technique has to take account not only of the payoff structure at maturity but also of the eventual early exercise. The early exercise decision is taken in order to maximize the value of the option itself, hence the solution of the pricing problem is de facto the solution of an optimization problem (optimal stopping time). In general, the decision strategy associated with the exercise rule of a particular asset-based structured product is represented by a particular choice of a set of *control variables* $a(t)$ which we can manipulate to achieve our optimization. On the other hand, the payoff of the instrument (which is the function we try to maximize) is affected by another set of variables which the optimization agent cannot control. Those variables are "stochastic variables" $(S(t))$ (e.g. electricity price, fuel price, etc). The last group of variables, which are important for our problem definition, is the set of "state variables" $(x(t))$ that determines the exact state of our system as a function of time. State variables are important because the operational constraints of the system can be imposed on them. The combination of the three aforementioned groups of variables generates a certain economic flow function $f(t) = f(x(t), a(t), S(t))$. Our objective is that of determining the set of control variables (strategy), which maximizes a certain function (the straightforward maximization of cumulated profits may not be enough for a risk-averse subject) of the cumulated economic flows over a certain time horizon, subject to some operational constraints. The expression for the value function V may be written as

$$V(t, x_t, S_t) = \max_{a_t, a_{t+1}, \ldots, a_T} \mathbb{E}_t \left[\sum_{m=t}^{T} \beta^{m-t} K(f(x_m, a_m, S_m)) \right] \tag{5.1}$$

where K can be thought of as the pricing utility function, β is the discount factor and $\mathbb{E}_t$ is the expectation operator conditioned to the information available at time t. Thanks to Bellman's optimality principle, using the iterated law of expected value of formula (1.2), our expression for the value function V may be rewritten as follows:

$$V(t, x_t, S_t) = \max_{a_t} \left[K\left(f(x_t, a_t, S_t)\right) + \beta \mathbb{E}_t (V(t+1, x_{t+1}, S_{t+1})) \right] \tag{5.2}$$

This principle is exactly the same as that described in Chapter 2, equation (2.22), when we presented the general algorithm.

This kind of stochastic optimization problem can be solved by means of backward induction. Unfortunately, easy solutions are not always attainable with reasonable effort. For that reason, in the industry feasible approximations to the true solutions have been proposed with some pros and cons that the final user should at least be aware of before choosing a method. Let us summarize briefly some solution methods moving from the simplest to the more complicated.

Perfect foresight

The most naïve approximation we can do to simplify the nature of the problem is to forget about the stochastic nature of the optimization problem. We can solve it in a deterministic environment where stochastic variables are replaced by their expectations.

$$V(t, x_t, S_t) = \max_{a_t, a_{t+1}, \ldots, a_T} \left[\sum_{m=t}^{T} \beta^{m-t} K(f(x_m, a_m, \mathbb{E}[S_m])) \right] \tag{5.3}$$

Deterministic problems are much easier to solve with traditional optimization algorithms. The perfect foresight assumption has important impacts on the pricing and optimal hedging we get as a result of the optimization. In fact, ignoring uncertainty, product flexibilities are sensibly undervalued and, moreover, the optimal hedge can be biased by the assumption.

Naïve Monte Carlo

The simplest – and also incorrect – way of considering the stochastic nature of the optimization problem stated above is that of repeating the deterministic optimization problem above, considering more than one scenario for the involved set of stochastic variables and then calculating the asset's value, and all the other interesting outputs, as an average according to the following scheme:

- Simulate N paths of the stochastic vector $S(t)$ for every t belonging to $[0, T]$
- Use the deterministic algorithm to determine $V^i\,(0, x_0, S_0)$
- Determine the asset's value as the average value over the N simulated paths

$$V(0, x_0, S_0) = \frac{1}{N} \sum_{i=1}^{N} V^i\,(0, x_0, S_0) \tag{5.4}$$

where $V^i(\cdot)$ is the value obtained at the i-th simulation.

This straightforward application of the Monte Carlo simulation to solve sequential choice problems in a stochastic environment is, of course, simple to understand and computationally fast, but unfortunately displays serious problems which act as a disincentive to its application. In particular, the method presented overestimates the true asset value since it assumes that, for every price path, the decision maker knows future prices in advance and consequently takes unit commitment decisions ignoring all the uncertainties. In a certain sense, the excess of information set that is assumed by this method implies that commitment policy is optimal in every price scenario.

If we want to get closer to the true solution, and so to the most correct evaluation of our product, it is necessary to solve the stochastic optimization problem by considering the dynamic nature of the decision process, as is suggested by

Bellman's representation of the problem. The crucial point is the evaluation of the so-called *continuation value* $\mathbb{E}_t\left[V(t+1, x_{t+1}, S_{t+1})\right]$.

Lattice approach

The first solution is represented by the *lattice approach method*. Traditionally, both in financial and decision sciences applications, binomial and trinomial trees represent the most appropriate environment in which it is possible to solve backward induction problems, or when optimal exercise policies have to be found. The classical approach of American option pricing proposed by Cox, Ross and Rubinstein (1979) is the most famous example of such a method. According to this method, the evolution of the stochastic vector $S(t)$ for every t belonging to $[0, T]$ can be fully discretized and represented by a lattice, that is a combination of trees. Also, the state space $x(t)$ should be discretized. The most important feature of a lattice representation is the reduction of the feasible transition for the stochastic vector $S(t)$. In fact, for every single node of the lattice, only a discrete and finite number of nodes of the successive time step can be reached with a positive probability and consequently conditional expectations of continuation value can easily be computed for every single system state $x(t)$. This leads to the following representation of the continuation value:

$$\mathbb{E}_t\left[V(t+1, x_{t+1}, S_{t+1})\right] = \sum_{i \varepsilon I} p_i \left(V(t+1, x_{t+1}, S^i_{t+1})\right) \tag{5.5}$$

Unfortunately, lattice schemes present some bad features, which can be summarized as follows:

- Lattice methods become impractical when the number of stochastic factors we want to represent increases and also when the frequency of simulations is very high (such as hourly simulations for power prices).
- Only a few types of continuous time stochastic processes can be discretized within a lattice scheme and essentially most of them are inappropriate to represent energy price dynamics.

Least square Monte Carlo

The main intuition behind this method is that continuation values can be estimated from cross-sectional information contained in Monte Carlo simulations of the relevant stochastic variables by using the least squares regression method. In particular, we can estimate conditional expectation regressing ex-post product values on functions of the state variables. By means of this estimation process, repeated for every decision time t, we are able to determine the optimal exercise strategy and hence the power plant value. This method was originally developed by Longstaff and Schwartz (2001) for valuing American-style options. The hypothesis on which this approach is based can be theoretically justified in all those situations where the conditional expectation operator is an element of the space $\mathcal{L}^2$ of square-integrable functions relative to some measure. In fact, since $\mathcal{L}^2$ is a Hilbert space it is provided with a countable orthonormal basis and the conditional expectation operator can be represented as a linear function of the elements of the basis. For example, if we assume that S is the one-dimensional Markovian process describing relevant stochastic variables, then we can write:

$$\mathbb{E}_t\left[V(t+1, x_{t+1}, S_{t+1})\right] = \sum_{j=0}^{\infty} \gamma_j f_j(S_t) \tag{5.6}$$

where the type of basis functions f_j could be Leguerre polynomials, Hermite polynomials, Chebyshev polynomials and many others. Empirical tests emphasize how Fourier, trigonometric or even simple power series of the state variables can also provide accurate results. In practice, the infinite series is approximated using only the first M basis functions. Using this method and moving backwards in time from terminal conditions it is possible to estimate continuation values for every time step t and system state x_t, and then by recursive substitutions to obtain the asset's value at the initial time. An obscure part of the LSMC method is represented by the choice of the class of basis functions. In fact, it is not clear how to select the class according to the kind of problem we have to solve and how big the impact of one choice is as opposed to another. The suspicion is that the impact may be significant in some cases. More details on these issues are to be found in Rodrigues and Rocha Armada (2006). Also the choice of the number M of the basis one has to use is not standard.

Including the hedging with forwards

As stated in Section 4.7.5, the decision of the position on the forward contracts one can take when the strategy is built up can be embedded in the pricing problem. Denoting with $F(t, T)$ the price at time t of a forward contract with delivery T, with $\theta(t, T)$ the position taken at time t on $F(t, T)$ we can modify equation (5.1) including the hedging strategy with forwards, obtaining a value contract given by:

$$\begin{aligned} &V(t, x_t, S_t, F(t, T)) \\ &= \max_{\{a_n, \theta(n,\xi)\}_{n=t,\dots,T}^{\xi=t,\dots,T}} \mathbb{E}_t\left[\sum_{m=t}^{T} \left(\beta^{m-t} K\left(f(x_m, a_m, S_m) + \theta(t, m)\left(F(t, m) - S_m\right)\right)\right)\right] \end{aligned}$$

When solved, the equation above gives the strategy $\theta(t, T)$ which has to be used to hedge the position. Notice that, as usual in dynamic control theory, the sequence $\theta(t, T)$ is a stochastic process which depends on time (as well as states and prices), so it requires a rebalancing of the position through time. If this behaviour is not desired, a simpler problem should be considered, where the hedging position is taken only at time 0 and then maintained during all the life of the contract without rebalancing. In this static hedge (also called myopic hedge without any type of rebalancing) θ_m does not depend on time and we can write θ_T instead of $\theta(t, T)$ and solve the problem:

$$V(t, x_t, S_t) = \max_{\{a_n,\theta_\xi\}_{n=t,\dots,T}^{\xi=t,\dots,T}} \mathbb{E}_t\left[\sum_{m=t}^{T}\left(\beta^{m-t}K\left(f\left(x_m, a_m, S_m\right)+\theta_m\left(F(0,m)-S_m\right)\right)\right)\right]$$

Unfortunately, not all the term structure $F(t, T)$ for all T is available, in particular in illiquid markets, so one should only take into account the tradable forwards, which in practice are less than the number of all the possible maturities. In addition, considering market liquidity and mainly transaction costs one has to choose between the static (myopic) and dynamic strategy as to which is the best. In theory, in a completely liquid and frictionless market, dynamic hedging produces the better (or equal) results compared to static hedging, simply because it gives more control over the state variables. In practice, markets are always incomplete and so neither hedging strategy leads to a perfect hedge where all risk is covered, but rather to an *hedging error*. The main reasons for this error are, as stated, the incompleteness of the market given by the limited number of forwards available (we don't have a forward for every possible maturity) and the so-called *market risk premium* which could be summarized as the difference between the forward price and the expectation of the spot price $F(t, m) - \mathbb{E}_t[S_m] \neq 0$.

Finally, from a computational point of view the dynamic hedging problem is very intensive and it cannot be disentangled from the asset valuation one. In a static hedging scheme optimal hedging (risk reduction) and asset value maximization can theoretically be separated: the optimization goal should be that of maximizing cumulated profit while hedging should minimize the risk.

5.3.2 Virtual Power Plants: Structure and Pricing Techniques

Virtual power plants are energy structured contracts built up to replicate the characteristics, in terms of financial payoff, of a power generation facility. This product finds great application in energy markets because of the need of power producers to hedge their risk exposure in a more effective way compared with that reachable through standard products like forwards or plain vanilla options. VPPs are characterized by some or all of those features (flexibility and constraints) that typically affect the operational way of working of real power generating assets. They can be grouped into five generic categories as shown in Table 5.3.

All of the physical constraints presented above complicate the optimal commitment decision-making problem, and all of these constraints are usually present in VPP or Tolling contracts. The standard payoff structure, the constraints and the

Table 5.3 Virtual power plant's operational constraints

Virtual power plant	
– Commitment/de-commitment lead times	Non zero response time of the unit from the time a commitment decision is taken
– Inter-temporal constraints (min/max time on/time off)	The unit commitment decision cannot be modified in real time. Once the plant is on it has to stay on for a minimum time (minimum time on) and the same when it is switched off (minimum time off)
– Min/max generation capacity and ramp	The operating regime of a power plant is characterized by a minimum (non zero) capacity regime and by a maximum one. The capacity gradient that a certain plant can perform (increasing or reducing operating capacity) is called ramp
– Variable heat rate (efficiency level)	Efficiency is a function (usually quadratic) of the generation level
– Other costs	Non fuel costs like start-up costs, shut down costs, variable operating and maintenance costs (VOM)

optimization problem related to a VPP product can be mathematically described as follows. Defining the time horizon of the optimization problem as T, let us introduce the commitment variable:

$$c_t = \begin{cases} 1 & \text{if unit is turn-up at time } t \\ 0 & \text{if plant is switch-off at time } t \end{cases} \tag{5.7}$$

That is a zero-one variable that determines whether the generation is turned up or shut down at each time. Then let us introduce the duration state variable d_t that indicates, for each time, the length of time the power plant has been up or down in time t. Defining with t^{on} and t^{off} the minimum time a power plant is forced to stay on or off when a change of state occurs, the variable d_t should be defined as follows:

$$d_{t+1} = \begin{cases} \min\big(t^{\text{on}}, \max(d_t, 0) + 1\big) > 0 & \text{if } c_t = 1 \\ \max\big(-t^{\text{cold}}, \min(d_t, 0) - 1\big) < 0 & \text{if } c_t = 0 \end{cases} \tag{5.8}$$

Hence it is now possible to describe the inter-temporal constraints on the commitment decisions for each time t as stated below:

$$c_t = \begin{cases} 1 & \text{if } d_t < t^{\text{on}} \\ 0 & \text{if } -1 \geqslant d_t > t^{\text{off}} \\ 0 \text{ or } 1 & \text{if } d_t = t^{\text{on}} \text{ or } -t^{\text{off}} \geqslant d_t > t^{\text{cold}} \end{cases} \tag{5.9}$$

Let us next define respectively q^{min} and q^{max} as the hourly minimum and maximum quantity of energy a power plant is allowed to produce. Then it is possible to describe the capacity constraint defining an interval of allowed output quantities:

$$q^{\min} \leqslant q_t \leqslant q^{\max}$$

The previous equations describe mathematically the relations between the commitment decision variable and the state variable (which indicates the duration, in time unit, of the state). With respect to the value of the state variable, d_t, the operator needs to take a decision on the unit commitment or, if the minimum uptime or downtime constraints are not yet satisfied, he has no commitment decision to take. Once the commitment decision is taken the generation unit needs to fulfil the minimum up-down time limits before changing the state.

On the cost side, given the heat rate function $H(q)$ that is the function which describes the heat required to generate an amount q (MW) of power, and defining with P_t^{Fuel} the fuel price at time t, the final fuel cost is defined as stated below:

$$C(q_t,\ P_t^{\text{Fuel}}) = H(q_t)P_t^{\text{Fuel}}$$

In addition to the fuel cost other variable costs are represented by $S^u(d_t)$ (start-up costs) and $S^d(d_t)$ (shut down costs). It is also possible to account for variable start-up costs that depend on the temperature of the boiler: that means the longer a generator has been off line the more time it should take to warm up. In the function defining the start-up costs we can also account for labour costs plus fixed operating and maintenance expenses of the plant adding a constant. Shut-down costs are simply defined as a constant for the labour and maintenance costs.

Finally we can describe the target of a VPP holder (or a unit generation operator) as the maximization of the total expected profit of a unit generation subject to the inter-temporal and quantities constraints described above. Hence, defining with P_t^{Power} the electricity price at time t, assuming the interest rate equal to 0, the objective function of the optimization problem is stated in the following equation:

$$\max_{u_t, q_t} \mathbb{E}\left[\sum_{t=0}^{T} \left(P_t^{\text{Power}} q_t - C(q_t,\ P_t^{\text{Fuel}})c_t - S^u(d_t)c_t - S^d(1 - c_t)\right)\right] \tag{5.10}$$

5.3.3 Virtual Refinery: Structure and Pricing Techniques

A refinery asset can be represented as a string of crack spread call options and evaluated within the traditional Black-Scholes framework. In particular, the well-known Margrabe formula can be used to calculate refinery production value and risk exposure. However, while the straightforward "option approach" is useful conceptually, it fails to account for some important operating characteristics that may affect refinery production value and the optimal operating policy. Consequently, an accurate description of refinery operational flexibilities and constraints is essential in order to understand to what extent option-pricing techniques can be used and why a real-option framing is often preferred. In the following we describe the structure of a Virtual Refinery.

Timing flexibilities. Given the availability of a spot crude oil market or the possibility of stocking the crude, a refinery faces many economic alternatives such as: transforming a barrel of crude to obtain a basket of products, or selling the barrel of crude in the spot market. The refinery could also store it in order to sell it or refine it at a more profitable moment in the future. Obviously, the refinery will take the optimal decision in order to maximize its profit.

Timing constraints. The refining process has minimum times required to transform crude oil into refined products. In fact, a particular time frame is required from the moment the decision to refine has been taken to the moment the refined products can be sold in the market. Moreover, it could be the case that a minimum time is necessary after a shut down of the process and before a new start. These facts introduce a series of time-dependent constraints into the decision-making process and in practice affect the possibility of the refinery capturing profitable market opportunities.

Input flexibilities. The refining process can be quite flexible in the terms of choice of the most appropriate production input. Usually, the production input (the type of crude oil) is selected for its relative price spread with respect to the attainable basket of refined products, obviously taking into consideration the economic fixed and variable costs of the transformation process.

Input constraints. Once the refining process has begun with a certain production input, technical constraints will not allow swapping to a more "convenient" production input before a minimum time has passed. This represents yet another inter-temporal constraint on the decision-making process.

Output flexibilities. The proportion of refined products obtained as output of the standard refining process can be partially modified in order to exploit modifications in standard price ratio between low-valued products and higher-valued ones. Obviously, the additional processing has associated costs, which have to be considered in the optimization problem.

Output constraints. As in the case of input constraints, when a certain process has been initiated for the production of a certain basket of intermediate products, even in the presence of production flexibilities, it takes a minimum time to modify the proportion of products in the final basket. Again, we are dealing with an inter-temporal type constraint.

Minimum/maximum production regimes. Once the refinery process has been committed it can produce a variable quantity of the final output bounded by a minimum and a maximum level. Since some variable costs are associated with the level of production selected, those costs have to be considered in the optimization process. Minimum/maximum production regimes represent simultaneously a technical flexibility and a constraint. In fact, they determine the range of variation of the production regime (operational flexibility) within certain limits represented by the minimum and maximum thresholds (operational constraints). These operational features apply without imposing any time dependence on the decision-making process.

Generally speaking, as stated for other virtual asset presentations, when valuing an asset it is extremely important to understand whether a certain operational flexibility or constraint induces co-dependence in the operational policy (sequence of operational decisions). The absence of co-dependence in the operational policy would allow for a straightforward option representation of the virtual asset, since every operational decision is independent of the previous one, exactly like the exercise decision policy of a string of European financial options. Unfortunately, even in a simplistic representation of the refinery asset some operational constraints, such as output and input constraints, induce co-dependence in the refinery's operational policy. For this reason traditional option pricing techniques cannot be used for a realistic valuation of the refinery production value and optimal operating policy; stochastic optimization techniques are needed.

5.3.4 Virtual Gas Storage: Structure and Pricing Techniques

In deregulated energy markets physical storage facilities have changed their role. From a purely physical function in the ancillary services for simply balancing customer demand between winter–summer fluctuations, they become strategic products to add flexibility to gas markets. Since gas demand has grown in Europe, and is growing again due to the intended decommissioning of some nuclear power plants, on the supply side the system also needs to add flexibility. The presence of spot and forward markets for gas allows operators to buy and optimize gas storage contracts against the market, adding flexibility to their physical portfolio in order to better hedge the value or to try to take profit from market volatility from a proprietary trading perspective. A physical gas storage facility gives the owner the option to capture market opportunities by transforming the availability of a physical gas flow over time. The possibility of carrying gas over time is performed by injecting and withdrawing gas to/from the storage over the contract's life.

From a financial point of view gas storage can be represented as a stream of co-dependent options on time-spread between summer and winter. For every decision time t the owner of such a product has the right to inject or withdraw gas into or from the storage. As seen for our Virtual Power Plant, even in this case the structure of the product implies that each decision should impact the following one. In order to replicate the physical constraints of the storage in the injection/withdrawal capacity and on the maximum/minimum inventory level, the product has a series of financial constraints that link each other to decisions taken at different times. In a Virtual Gas Storage the owner has the right, during the whole life of the product, to withdraw gas previously injected (and yet paid at injection time) from the storage, or to inject (paying it at the spot price) gas into the storage. That means the value of a Virtual Gas Storage is related both to the time-spread between summer and winter forward level, the so-called intrinsic value observable on the market at the inception date, and to the future evolution of this time-spread level together with the overall gas price daily volatility, the extrinsic (flexibility) value. Obviously, changes in the time-spread level will be determined by changes in the expected demand and offer level, such as by pure price factor movements given by other related commodities markets. The main variables that determine the product's features are given in Table 5.4.

Table 5.4 Parameters of a Virtual Gas Storage

Parameters of a Virtual Gas Storage
– Maximum storage capacity (minimum working gas and maximum inventory level)
– Withdrawal rate as a function of the inventory level
– Injection rate as a function of the inventory level
– Costs associated with injection/withdrawal operations

As for all time-spread products the time-value and the dimension of the committed "working capital" also play an important role in the exercising policy of these kinds of product. In contrast to a Virtual Power Plant, which initially requires just the payment of an up-front fee for the buyer, a Virtual Gas Storage also implies negative cash flows during the exercising period. In fact, each time we decide to inject gas into the facility we are paying at the spot price for the quantity stored. Hence thin time-spread levels, which are profitable in theory, will bring financial losses if the impact of negative interest rates on the capital used in the injection phase is not compensated for by the margin realized in the withdrawal phase. Obviously, contract duration and frequency of decision making are also important features of the Virtual Gas Storage contract. Injection and withdrawal quantities are typically functions of time and of the inventory level, since the injection rate is usually lower when the facility is near to the maximum storage level, and the reverse holds for withdrawal rate. Injection and withdrawal daily quantities are also constrained between a minimum and maximum level, as given below:

$$q_{\min}^{\text{inj}}(t, \text{inv}(t)) \leqslant q^{\text{inj}}(t) \leqslant q_{\max}^{\text{inj}}(t, \text{inv}(t))$$

$$q_{\min}^{\text{with}}(t, inv(t)) \leqslant q^{\text{with}}(t) \leqslant q_{\max}^{\text{with}}(t, inv(t))$$

Operational costs of storage are usually a function of the injected or taken quantity according to a linear relationship of the following kind:

$$\text{InjCost}(t) = q^{\text{inj}}(t) \cdot C_{\text{inj}}$$

$$\text{WithCost}(t) = q^{\text{with}}(t) \cdot C_{\text{with}}$$

Maximum and minimum inventory levels represent constraints to the global volume that can be stored in any time. Those values can be functions of time as well.

$$\text{inv}_{\min}(t) \leqslant \text{inv}(t) \leqslant \text{inv}_{\max}(t)$$

Usually in Virtual Gas Storage initial and final inventory levels are imposed; terminal inventory level, in particular, is important since it represents a constraint for the contractor. If the constraint is not respected penalties may apply. Obviously, an injection will imply an increase in the inventory level and a spot cost for the Virtual Storage owner, while a withdrawal will imply a decrease in the inventory level and a spot profit for the Virtual Storage owner. Formally, we will have the following equations to define inventory levels' dynamics and storage's payoff:

$$\Delta \text{inv}(t) = \begin{cases} q^{\text{inj}}(t) & \text{if injection at time } t \\ q^{\text{with}}(t) & \text{if withdrawal at time } t \\ 0, & \text{if nothing is done at time } t \end{cases}$$

$$\text{Payoff}(t) = \Pi(t) = \begin{cases} -S(t)q^{\text{inj}}(t) - \text{InjCost}(t)q^{\text{inj}}(t) & \text{if injection} \\ S(t)q^{\text{with}}(t) - \text{WithCost}(t)q^{\text{with}}(t) & \text{if withdrawal} \\ 0 & \text{otherwise} \end{cases}$$

5.3.5 The Structure of Swing Contracts and *Make-up* Clause

Swing contracts are typical contractual structures in physical gas and electricity wholesale markets; they are typically used in the gas market for long-term supply agreement. Structures like these imply embedded options where the buyer has the possibility to exercise the right to buy gas at a discrete time during the life of the product paying a certain price (floating or fixed), the strike. The flexibility typically embedded in the contract can be exercised under some physical inter-temporal constraints that make this kind of product particularly complicated to evaluate and manage. Swings are usually characterized by maximal and minimal daily and yearly withdrawal quantities. The annual global minimum and maximum level of gas callable during a year is usually not simply the sum of the maximal and minimal daily quantities (not trivial constraints), but is settled to different levels. If constraints are not respected penalty payments are imposed; penalty amounts are usually calculated as a percentage of the strike price for the extra volume over or under the contractual threshold. Long-term forward gas contracts are often structured with such volumetric flexibilities in order to inter-temporally manage gas demand fluctuations year by year. Among those flexibilities options the so-called *make-up* and *carry forward* clauses have particular importance since they allow the buyer to delay or anticipate, respectively, the withdrawal of contractual gas from one year to another without full exposure to annual volume constraints. The *make-up* clause allows the buyer to go under the minimal yearly quantity for a certain year, without paying penalties, and then call back the gas in a future year before the maturity of the contract. In other words, this is an option that allows the buyer to locally modify the global annual minimum quantity. The reverse holds for the *carry forward* clause that allows the buyer to anticipate the gas consumption going over the yearly maximal annual quantity, and then reducing the withdrawal in the following years. Modelling of the *make-up* clause has recently become a very important topic for holders of European long-term forward contracts due to the recent decoupling observed in oil and gas markets. Gas and oil markets are extremely volatile and so contracts optimization and hedging need to be continuously rebalanced during the whole business life of the contract in order to protect the contract's value or at least contain financial losses. The optimization/valuation problem of the swing contracts described is certainly not a trivial problem. The sub-period decisions to withdraw the maximum possible quantity will impact the possibility of exercising this option somewhere in the future due to annual volume constraints. It is axiomatic that the sequential decisions process has to be tackled in an uncertain environment where relevant costs and revenues related to the contract have to be modelled as stochastic processes.

The details of a generic swing structure are described as follows. Ordinary swing contract schemes are normally defined dividing each of the $\boldsymbol{D}$ yearly delivery periods $\{[T_{j-1}, T_j)\}_{j=1,\dots\boldsymbol{D}}$, into N sub-periods $\{[t_{j,i-1}, t_{j,i})\}_{i=1,\dots,N}^{j=1,\dots,\boldsymbol{D}}$ obtaining the sequence $\{t_{j,i}\}$ such that

$$
\begin{aligned}
0 = T_0 = t_{1,0} < t_{1,2} < \dots < t_{1,N} = T_1 = t_{2,0} < t_{2,1} < \dots \\
\dots < t_{j,i} < \dots < t_{j,N} = T_j = t_{j+1,0} < \dots < t_{\boldsymbol{D},N} = T_{\boldsymbol{D}}
\end{aligned}
$$

In particular in every year $[T_{j-1}, T_j]$ we have the $N+1$ points $t_{j,i}$ such that $i \in \{0, \dots, N\}$ and $t_{j,N} = T_{j+1}, t_{j,0} = T_j$.

Let us suppose that N is also the number of exercise swing rights the holder has in every year and that he can exercise these rights exactly at the points $t_{j,i}$, for $i = 0, \dots, N-1$ i.e. at the beginning of every sub-period. At the end of the last sub-period, in $t_{j,N}$, he cannot take any decision. For example, if the decisions are taken month by month, at the beginning of every month, $N = 12$, if day by day, $N = 365$.

Over each one of the N sub-periods, minimum (mDQ) and maximum (MDQ) delivery quantities are established; these capacity constraints usually reflect effective transportation capacity limitations. For every contractual year, minimum and maximum quantities are also established, called respectively minimum annual quantity (mAQ) and annual contract quantity (ACQ): often we have non-trivial volume constraints, in the sense that

$$
\mathsf{mAQ} \geqslant N \cdot \mathsf{mDQ}, \qquad \mathsf{ACQ} \leqslant N \cdot \mathsf{MDQ}
$$

Finally, we denote by $u_{j,i}$ the quantity of gas we decide to buy in the sub-period $[t_{j,i}, t_{j,i+1})$, $i = 0, \dots, (N-1)$ which is the decision we have to take at time $t_{j,i}$.

In the light of the above discussion, we have the constraints

$$
\mathsf{mDQ} \leqslant u_{j,i} \leqslant \mathsf{MDQ} \qquad \forall i = 0, \dots, (N-1), \quad \forall j = 1, \dots, \boldsymbol{D} \tag{5.11}
$$

and, without any additional clause,

$$
\mathsf{mAQ} \leqslant \sum_{i=1}^{N} u_{j,i-1} \leqslant \mathsf{ACQ} \qquad \forall j = 1, \dots, \boldsymbol{D}
$$

Penalty payments can be imposed if the volume constraints are exceeded in order to stimulate the buyer to respect the volumetric limits imposed; these are additional costs which the algorithm should be easily extended to include. In what follows, as in general, we are not considering penalties but concentrating more on the optimal exercise of the swing quantity and make up in a stochastic price framework. The difference between swing contracts with trivial and non-trivial volume constraints is extremely important in the pricing and hedging of the contract. The aim of a contractual clause such as *make-up* is to guarantee the buyer a certain degree of flexibility in the volume which can be taken since, typically, the gas and electricity consumer is not always in a situation to know exactly, *ex-ante*, the quantity he is going to consume period by period and in total during the year. To introduce a formal definition of the *make-up* clause and its "rules", according to the previous notation, we need to give some definitions. Let $P_{j,i}$ and $I_{j,i}$ be respectively the prices of gas and index in the sub-period $\left[t_{j,i}, t_{j,i+1}\right) \quad \forall i = 1, \ldots, N$. The contract holder has to buy the gas at the price $I_{j,i}$ and can sell it at the price $P_{j,i}$. Let $z_{j,j}$ be the cumulated quantity at time $t_{j,i}$. At the beginning of every year $j = 1, \ldots, \boldsymbol{D}$ we have $z_{j,0} = 0$ while at the end of every sub-period i of year j, $z_{j,i}$ is given by

$$z_{j,i} = \sum_{k=0}^{i-1} u_{j,k} \quad \forall i \in \{1, \ldots, N\} \tag{5.12}$$

An analytical and formal representation of the make up clause and its constraints is now given.

Let M_j be the make up quantity nominated in the year j. It is worth remarking that this quantity is known only at the end of each year and is defined as

$$M_j = \left(\mathsf{mAQ} - z_{j,N}\right)^+ \quad \forall j = 1, \ldots, \boldsymbol{D} \tag{5.13}$$

that is the quantity less than mAQ we have not taken at the end of each year.

Moreover let $\boldsymbol{M}_j$ be the remaining make up not called back at the end of year j:

$$\boldsymbol{M}_j = \sum_{k=1}^{j} M_k - \sum_{k=2}^{j} (z_{k,N} - \mathsf{ACQ})^+ = \sum_{k=1}^{j} \left(M_k - (z_{k,N} - \mathsf{ACQ})^+\right) \geqslant 0 \tag{5.14}$$

where the last equality is obtained noting that $z_{1,N} \leqslant \mathsf{ACQ}$.

The make up quantity M_j has to satisfy the following constraints:

i. since the quantity mDQ will be taken in every sub-period, in general

$$M_j \in \left[0, \mathsf{mAQ} - \mathsf{mDQ} \cdot N\right] \quad \forall j = 1, \ldots, \boldsymbol{D}$$

ii. the make up M_j nominated in year j can be *called back* in *one or more* subsequent years (the quantity M_j can be split and called back in more than one year)
iii. at the end of the contract all the nominated make up must have been called back
iv. from the second year onwards some previous make up quantity can be called back *only if* ACQ quantity has been reached in that year. This implies that the

maximum possible quantity $\bar{\mathcal{M}}$ of make up we can physically call back in any year is given by

$$\bar{\mathcal{M}} = N \cdot \mathsf{MDQ} - \mathsf{ACQ} \tag{5.15}$$

Notice that conditions (iii) and (iv) imply, for example, that if at the beginning of the last contract year we have some make up not called back, i.e. $\boldsymbol{M_D} > 0$, in year $\boldsymbol{D}$ we necessarily have to reach the quantity $\mathsf{ACQ} + \boldsymbol{M_D}$.

v. the price of the make up quantity nominated in year j and called back in year k, sub-period i, is defined as the weighted sum of two components respectively paid at two different times:
   a) at time $t_{j,N}$ (i.e. at the end of year j when M_j becomes known) the buyer pays $\alpha\overline{\Gamma}_j$ where $\overline{\Gamma}_j$ is the average index price observed in year j;
   b) at time $t_{k,i}$ of withdrawal the price paid is $(1-\alpha)I_{k,i}$

   for some $0 \leqslant \alpha \leqslant 1$ defined in the contract.

The make up price, as defined above, is associated with the gas volume $u_{k,i}$ physically delivered at time $t_{k,i}$. This means that the part $\alpha\overline{\Gamma}_j$ in (a) of the price needs to be capitalized from time $T_j = t_{j,N}$ up to time $t_{k,i}$ and this leads, at time $t_{k,i}$, to the following price, $\mathcal{I}_{j,k,i}$ of the make up nominated in year j and called back in year k, sub-period i:

$$\mathcal{I}_{j,k,i} = \alpha\overline{\Gamma}_j e^{r\left(t_{k,i}-t_{j,N}\right)} + (1-\alpha)I_{k,i} \tag{5.16}$$

Actualizing at time $T_0 = 0$ the make up price we have in $t_{k,i}$ leads to

$$\begin{aligned} e^{-rt_{k,i}}\mathcal{I}_{j,k,i} &= e^{-rt_{k,i}}\left(\alpha\overline{\Gamma}_j e^{r\left(t_{k,i}-t_{j,N}\right)} + (1-\alpha)I_{k,i}\right) \\ &= \left(\alpha\overline{\Gamma}_j e^{-rt_{j,N}} + (1-\alpha)I_{k,i}e^{-rt_{k,i}}\right) \end{aligned}$$

Having defined all the essential elements for a formal representation of a swing contract structure we could coherently define the objective function of a contract holder, which is to maximize the discounted global margin of the contract defined as

$$\begin{aligned} V(T_0, p_{1,0}, \iota_{1,0}, 0) = \max_{u\in\mathcal{A}} \mathbb{E}\Bigg[\sum_{j=1}^{\boldsymbol{D}}\Bigg(\sum_{i=1}^{N} e^{-rt_{j,i}}u_{j,i-1}\Big(P_{j,i} - I_{j,i}\Big(\mathbf{1}_{\{z_{j,i}<\mathsf{ACQ}\}} \\ + (1-\alpha)\mathbf{1}_{\{z_{j,i}\geqslant\mathsf{ACQ}\}}\Big)\Big) - e^{-rt_{j,N}}\alpha\overline{\Gamma}_j M_j\Bigg)\Bigg] \end{aligned}$$

where the space $\mathcal{A}$ designates *admissible* controls.

5.4 HEDGE IN INCOMPLETE MARKETS

Hedging is a risk management activity that aims to eliminate completely, where possible, the price risk of a portfolio. In theory when operating in a complete and frictionless market perfect hedges are possible via dynamic trading using standard no-arbitrage methods that allow, through a continuous rebalancing of the positions (see, for instance, the last example in Chapter 4), the trader to locally immunize the profit and loss associated with a certain position. In reality, however, perfect hedges are extremely rare. Market operators are predominantly asked to reduce the risk of non-tradable or illiquid assets. Main examples of such assets include various commodities, human capital, financial liabilities and credit risk.

A market is defined as *incomplete* when some contingent claims which cannot be replicated exist, that is when a hedger will not be able to completely hedge such claims using the available securities. In incomplete markets the traditional dynamic hedge is no longer efficient because there no longer exists the possibility to dynamically offset the risk associated to a contingent claim because there are too many random sources we cannot control, or because the underlying is non-tradable (for instance, the temperature), or not liquid.

One approach developed while searching for solutions to pricing and hedging in incomplete markets involves picking a specific martingale measure (the definition of martingale measure has been given in Chapter 4), for pricing according to some optimal criterion. The incompleteness of the market usually gives rise to an infinite number of martingale measures, each of which produces a no-arbitrage price. Market data (for example, prices of vanilla options) are often used to calibrate those parameters of the underlying probability market model which determine a probability measure picked by the market.

Because not every contingent claim can be replicated by self-financing portfolios, in general we can only construct a self-financing portfolio of tradable assets such that at maturity the portfolio's value is *near to* the claim. This leads to a shortfall, the risk of which, measured by a suitable risk measure, should be minimized. This *proxy hedge* is done using assets correlated (in some way) assets to the non tradable one: a static hedging policy is found according to some criterion that determines the quality of this hedging. Finally this static hedge is repeated over time, at discrete dates, leading to the so-called *myopic hedge*.

As stated, the static hedge involves minimization of the *hedging error*, calculated according to some mathematical criterion. In order to better introduce these hedging criteria and techniques let us give some definitions. Consider a continuous-time incomplete-market setting and let us define X_T as the payoff at time T of a non-tradable asset a hedger is committed to hold over the finite horizon $[0, T]$. The risky tradable asset F_t considered can be a forward, future or any other derivative whose price is related in some way to the non-tradable asset. Both the assets we are committed to hold and the risky tradable assets are characterized by different price dynamics with proper drift and volatility. We could manage the risk of the position by continuously trading in the available tradable risky securities (and eventually at the risk-free rate). The hedging policy of the hedger is denoted by θ_t, representing the number of risky tradable assets held at time t, leading to the following cumulated gain for the dynamic trading strategy θ:

$$C_t^\theta = \int_0^t \theta_s dF_s$$

Given such definitions and the general set-up described and since, as stated, the economy is incomplete, it is impossible for the trader to hedge the fluctuation of the non-tradable asset to reach a perfect hedge (i.e. $C_T^{\theta} = X_T$ almost certainly for some strategy θ), so the hedging policy is determined via the minimization of the *mean* squared hedging error, in an attempt find the trading strategy which best matches the final payoff:

$$\min_{\theta} \mathbb{E}\left[\left(L + X_T - C_T^{\theta}\right)^2\right]$$

where L is any given target level for the final wealth.

Duffie and Richardson (1991) provide an explicit solution for the case when both non-tradable and tradable asset prices move according to:

$$\begin{aligned} dX_t &= X(t)\left(\mu_X(t)dt + \sigma_X(t)dW_X(t)\right) \\ dF_t &= F(t)\left(\mu_F(t)dt + \sigma_F(t)dW_F(t)\right) \end{aligned}$$

where $W_X(t)$ and $W_F(t)$ are two correlated Brownian motions.

Another related criterion for determining the hedging policy and assessing its quality is the *minimum variance of hedging error*:

$$\min_{\theta} \operatorname{Var}\left[X_T - C_T^{\theta}\right]$$

employed in static and myopic hedging schemes. Notice that this criterion does not imply that the replicating portfolio reaches a level near to the payoff:

$$\mathbb{E}\left[X_T - C_T^{\theta}\right] \simeq 0 \tag{5.17}$$

so the minimum variance criterion should be integrated with the constraint

$$\mathbb{E}\left[X_T - C_T^{\theta}\right] = M$$

for some (small) quantity M. This approach is very similar to finding the efficient frontier in Markowitz's approach given above in Chapter 2.

Another class of approach steadily growing in popularity and presented in the current literature investigates optimal dynamic hedges consistent with the hedger's utility maximization in continuous-time incomplete market settings. To obtain an explicit solution authors focus on constant relative risk aversion (CARA) (Svensson and Werner, 1993; Tepla, 2000; and Henderson, 2005), modelling a traded asset as GBM or additionally adding a mean-reversion term.

In this chapter we are going to employ the minimum-variance criterion in order to obtain a practical solution for the hedging problem of complex payoff structures in the incomplete settings of energy markets, according to the minimization target function in formula (5.17). In the presentation of different business cases, only the implementation of static hedging schemes has been considered.

5.5 CASE STUDY: STRUCTURED PRODUCTS

5.5.1 Virtual Power Plants

Consider the valuation of a 20-MW capacity Virtual Power Plant with minimum time-off and minimum time-on of 10 hours, ramp-up time and fixed start-up costs. All the relevant parameters for the VPP structure considered are given in Table 5.5.

We consider a VPP written for the German market and indexed to a classical oil-linked formula. Hence payoff of this financial structure is given by the hourly difference between spot power prices on the German power exchange and the monthly level of the oil formula, net of an efficiency factor, minus start-up, shut-down and other fixed costs as described in the previous section. As stated, we consider a strike indexed to an oil formula as proxy of a gas price. The hourly nomination is intended to be ex-ante, hence with the spot prices unknown at nomination time.

The forward price curve for German power and the oil-linked formula have been taken as of close of business on 3 December 2011. For a realistic business case the oil formula will consider seasonal fixed parameters, which means that the fix terms for months falling respectively in the winter or summer season are different, and are settled such that the strike levels recalibrate on the observed gas forward term-structure. This allows the structure to be "at the money" almost at the inception date, for a non-trivial business case, as shown in Figure 5.1.

On the pricing side, as described in the theoretical section, the literature presents different approaches in order to determine intrinsic and extrinsic value of a VPP. As noted, naive Monte Carlo optimization suffers from the well-known problem of "perfect foresight" due to the uncertainty not being taken into account in the path-by-path deterministic solution. To overcome this problem a VPP product can be priced using a "multi-stage" stochastic model, the LSMC (Least Squared Monte Carlo), presented earlier. Using these two different pricing methods it is possible

Table 5.5 VPP parameters

VPP parameters	value
Ramp up time (h)	8
Ramp down time (h)	8
Hot start-up time (h)	6
Max number of start-up	50
Minimum time-on (h)	10
Minimum time-off (h)	10
Max global volume (MWh)	NA
Min global volume (MWh)	0
Min hourly capacity(MW)	0
Max hourly capacity(MW)	20
Shut-down cost (euros)	0
Start-up cost (euros)	9000

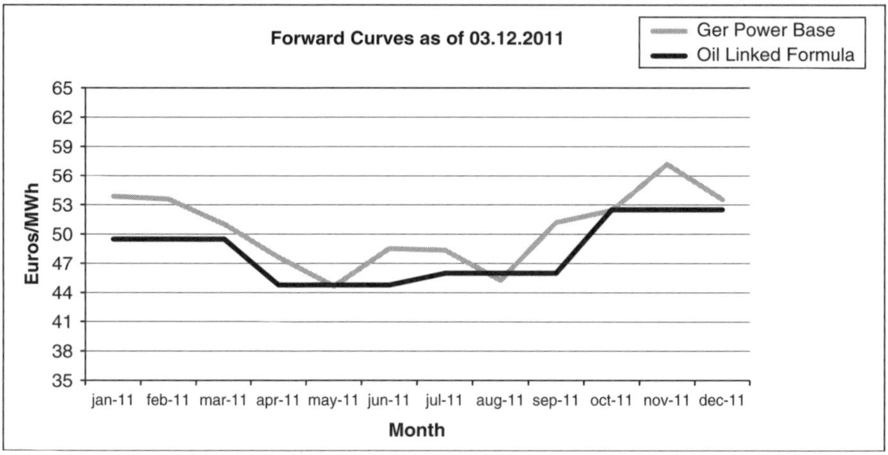

Figure 5.1 Forward curves as of 03/12/2011

to assess the full value (intrinsic and extrinsic) of the VPP under consideration and to try to determine the impact of perfect foresight on the final evaluation. A simple price evaluation using a naive "one-stage" Monte Carlo method will result in a final price of 2,478,204 euros.

We will now move on to address how to manage the risk embedded in this structure, presenting approaches on how to determine the hedging strategy. As stated, in complete and frictionless markets perfect hedges are possible via dynamic trading using standard no-arbitrage methods. For non-complete markets, like the power market, a perfect off-setting of the risks is not possible. Hence we are going to use static hedge approaches on the analyzed VPP, comparing the hedge effectiveness of two different static hedge schemes. Figure 5.2 shows the simulated payoff's distribution of the naked position on the VPP.

The "Volumetric" hedging scheme suggests hedging a volume calculated as the exposition resulting from the optimization. Using the naive Monte Carlo scheme, the exposure is the average of the hourly exercises over all the considered simulated paths. Using a "Minimum Variance" static hedging scheme (presented earlier) the optimal hedging quantities are determined as the results from a multivariate regression, where the weights in each of the available forward products are selected in order to minimize the variance of the final payoff's distribution. Figure 5.3 shows the final payoff's distribution of the naked position against distributions of hedged positions, respectively adopting "Volumetric" and "Minimum Variance" static hedging scheme.

Analysis of Figures 5.2 and 5.3 clearly shows a payoff's risk reduction for the hedged positions, assessing in this way the effectiveness of the hedging schemes under consideration.

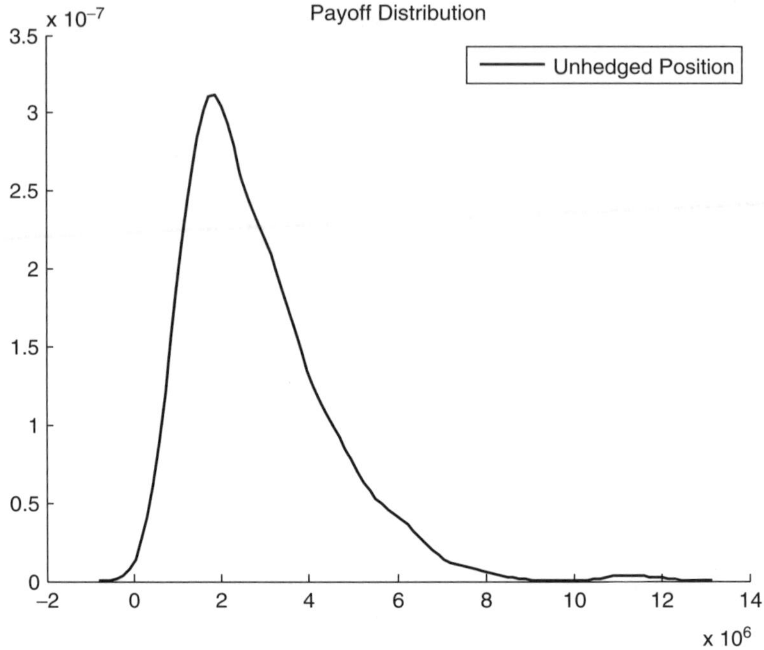

Figure 5.2 Payoff distribution of naked position

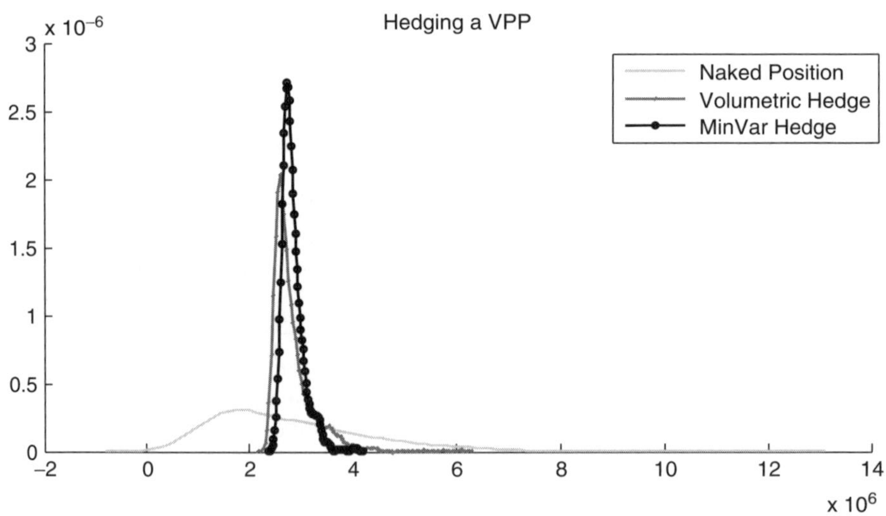

Figure 5.3 Volumetric and MinVariance hedged payoff distributions

5.5.2 Swing on Gas

We have already highlighted the importance of a contract such as swing in energy markets, which is due to the fact that the embedded flexibility really represents an important feature for energy operators who need to deal with volumetric uncertainty. In this section, after formally defining the basic structure of the contract and some important clauses, we want to practically analyze how a swing gas contract can be priced and managed taking into consideration the stochastic evolution of the prices for both the underlying and the index (the strike). The swing will be priced through a dynamic programming algorithm; prices of both, the underlying (physical gas) and the index at which the gas can be withdrawn, are modelled through a mean-reverting trinomial trees approach. The method for modelling the price evolution is the same lattice scheme suggested by Hull (2006); no correlation between gas prices and the evolution of the oil-indexed formula has been taken into consideration, which should be seen as advantageous for further extensions on the price modelling side, and will not impact the effectiveness of the pricing algorithm. An example of two possible trees, obtained for different values of a, the mean reversion speed parameters, and σ, the volatility coefficient, are given in Figure 5.4.

The space of admissible controls, the region of the admissible gas quantities taken, is derived coherently with the swing constraints (for details of admissible space set controls see also Edoli et al., 2010). Final price of the swing is calculated proceeding backward and individuating, node by node on the price's and the quantity's trees, the optimal decision comparing the value of an immediate withdrawal and the "continuation value" of a no withdrawal.

For this case study we want to price a swing contract on gas for a physical supply on the Italian market; hence the revaluation price will be PSV (Punto Virtual di Scambio), the price of the Italian hub for physical deals on gas. We have decided to model a three-year contract for the following reasons. On the one hand, the

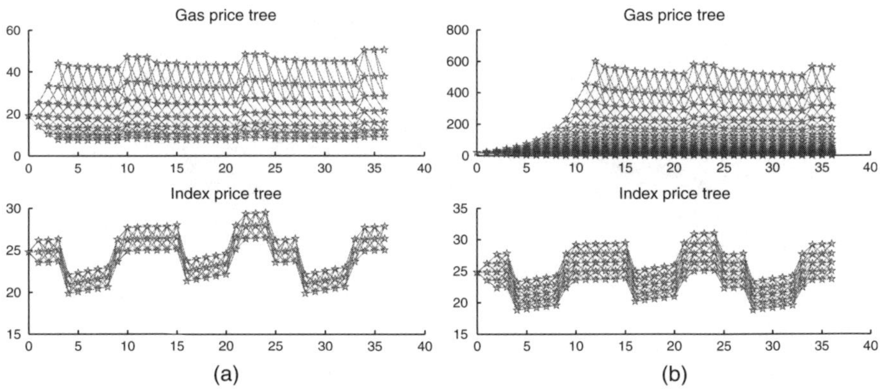

Figure 5.4 Trees for prices for different values of parameters. (a) strong mean reversion, low volatility: $a^P = 3, a^I = 10, \sigma^P = 0.3, \sigma^I = 0.1$ (b) small mean reversion, high volatility: $a^P = 0.1, a^I = 0.1, \sigma^P = 0.7, \sigma^I = 0.2$

make-up clause of a two year contract is not an interesting proposition from a modelling point of view: at the end of the first year the make-up quantity is known and this is exactly the quantity one has to call back in the second year. On a three-year contract and even if the make-up quantity of the first year is known, in the second year you still have the opportunity to nominate other make-up quantities for call-it-back in the third year, so the clause is not trivial. The prices are modelled with monthly granularity and the whole problem is treated with monthly resolution since it is not possible to get market quotes for products with higher resolution on a three years forward period. This means that the only possible evaluation, based on market prices, is to withdraw or not withdraw gas for a whole month, comparing the gas and index forward price level for that period. The swing analyzed is indexed at an oil-linked formula as is mostly done by international gas traders. In order to realize a non-trivial resolution of the problem we use an initial market price scenario with aligned forward curves of gas and oil-linked, in order to analyze an "at the money" case, as shown in Figure 5.5.

The physical parameters of the swing contracts are defined in Table 5.6.

By looking at our chosen parameters, it is possible to note a set of values for a realistic swing product with non-trivial constraints: an exercising policy that takes the daily maximum, or the daily minimum, gas quantity for all the days will not respect the contractual yearly parameters. As mentioned, the forward price curve

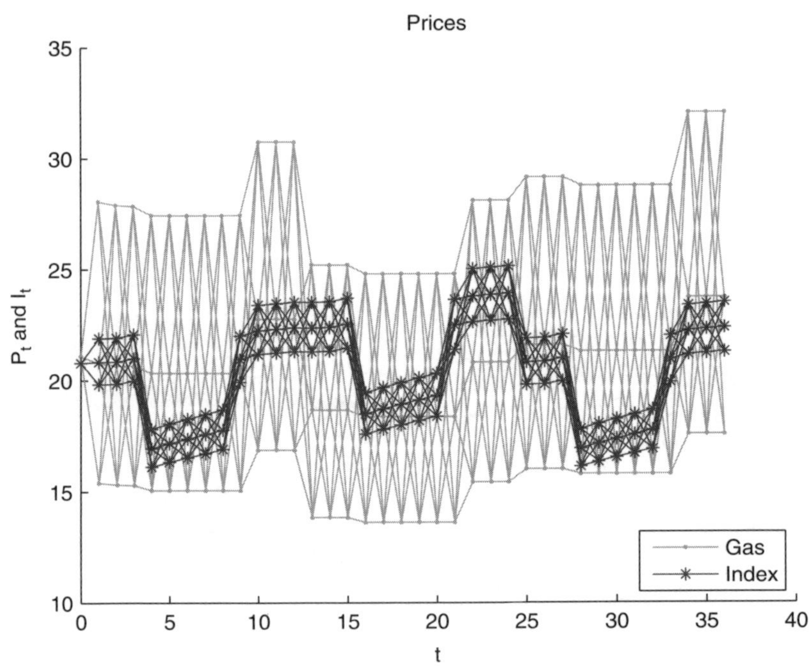

Figure 5.5 Prices term structures scenarios

Table 5.6 Swing parameters

D Number of years	3
dt Discretization	monthly
ACQ Annual Contract Quantity (smc/mil)	700
mAQ Min Annual Quantity (perc. of ACQ)	60%
MDQ Max Daily Quantity	ACQ/(0.8*365)
mDQ Min Daily Quantity (perc. of MDQ)	45%

of the oil-linked formula, the so-called Eni Gas Release used mostly in Italy, has been settled such that the levels are aligned with a PSV curve taken on 10 March 2011. The contango of the oil formula obviously weighs on the monthly shaping, but the winter and summer season medium price levels are still aligned.

The pricing algorithm gives a final price value of 48,300,000 euros as full value for the gas swing product considered. The product is in the money and, since the first year is slightly out of the money, the optimal allocation of the volume is to nominate some make-up during the first thermal year and call-it-back in the third year where the forward level for the PSV allows the make-up a better net margin against the oil formula level. An optimal allocation of volume is obviously possible if the market is liquid enough to guarantee the hedging of the whole exposure of the product up to the third year. In illiquid markets, like the Italian gas market where it is not possible to trade huge quantities for such long delivery periods, another possibility is to use a *value hedging* approach. This involves not hedging the whole exposure of the product along the forward curve, but locally hedging the market value of the contract calculating the *Deltas* with respect to movements of the underlyings. In such a case the value of the contract is exposed to the movement of each monthly forward product on the curve up to the end of the third thermal year. As a practical case study it is possible to numerically calculate, using the dynamic programming algorithm, the *Deltas* of the swing to each of the forward monthly points as the ratio between the swing price difference, calculated for the up and down shock of a forward level, and twice the value of the shock. Repeating this numerical procedure for each of the monthly forward points along the curve, we finally get a strip of *Deltas* that represent the hedging monetary values one has to buy, or sell, for each of the forward products. Figure 5.6 illustrates the calculated monthly *Deltas* for the analyzed swing: according to this hedging scheme, a trader needs to sell gas at PSV for each forward product and simultaneously buy the corresponding quantities of oil-linked formula. Obviously, the hedging quantities need to be calculated continuously along the whole life of the product since this is not a static approach, and the position needs to be restructured at discrete times (daily or weekly, according to market volatility). This approach helps to mitigate the risk of the naked position reducing the variance of the product's value distribution as highlighted in Figure 5.6.

One line shows the value distribution, in five days, of the naked swing position; one line shows the value distribution of the hedged portfolio (naked swing position

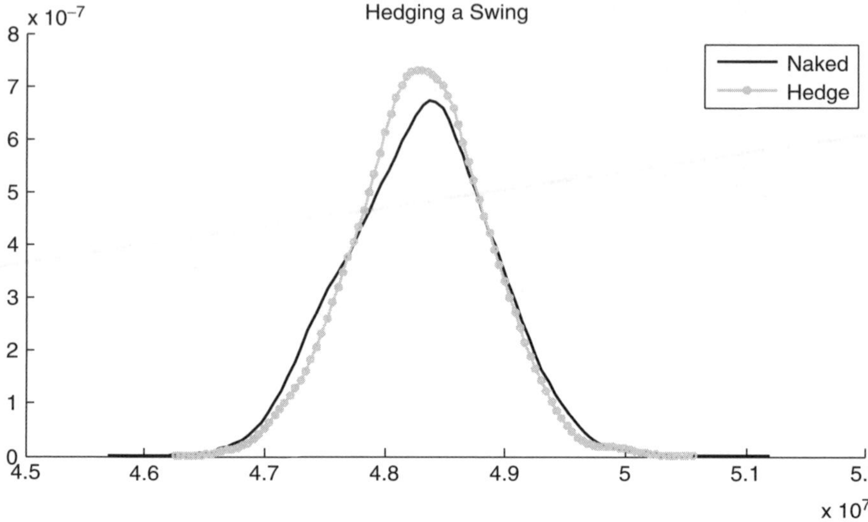

Figure 5.6 Swing hedging

plus the short and long positions respectively in the PSV and oil formula for the hedging quantities). Looking at the graph, the risk mitigation effect produced by the *value hedging* strategy adopted is evident.

5.5.3 Virtual Refinery

In this section, we propose a simulation exercise to show some numerical results on a Virtual Refinery evaluation. First, we must stress that this exercise is more a conceptual analysis than a real case application. This is because we want to infer from this numerical analysis some general results whose validity is independent of specific assumptions on model parameters or operational characteristics of the refinery asset analyzed. In particular, the simple numerical example proposed here will try to emphasize the "option nature" of the refinery asset and the economic impacts that operational constraints may have. Moreover, we will analyze also the impact that the application which our real options approach has on risk exposure calculation and hedging issues. The simulation is based on an extremely simplified case of a distillation asset capable of transforming a certain type of crude into a specific basket of products. Here we focus on valuing a refinery asset over a short period of time (3 months, 90 days); longer-period valuation can be obtained by prorating the asset valuation for a certain number of representative sub-periods. The evaluation problem is approached via a stochastic dynamic problem and is solved through backward induction by means of a lattice discretization. Some assumptions have been made in order to reduce the numerical complexity of the problem,

Table 5.7 Summary of test case characteristics

	t off (days)	t warm (days)	t on (days)	min q (thousand bbl)	max q (thousand bbl)
Case 1	1	1	1	100	300
Case 2	2	5	1	100	300
Case 3	2	5	1	200	300

although the example proposed remains realistic. In particular, the example is based on the following features and assumptions.

The spread of prices between the crude and the production basket (crack spread) is modelled by means of a binomial lattice assuming constant volatilities and correlations among the commodities involved. If we model both crude oil price and refined products prices by means of the classical mean reverting process, then any crack spread can be consistently modelled by means of the same class of stochastic processes and discretized within a binomial/trinomial scheme. We will not discuss the composition of the basket, since it is not relevant to the present application. However, inter-temporal constraints such as minimum time on, minimum time off, minimum warm time and quantity constraints such as minimum production quantity and maximum production quantity will be considered in the example. Operating decisions will be taken every day, to take into account the evolution of market conditions.

In order to determine the importance of different operating constraints on the refinery production value, we consider the three particular cases summarized in Table 5.7.

The first case represents a very flexible distillation asset, while the second and third cases are representative of more constrained refinery operations. In fact, the second and third cases differ only in their minimum production level. As outlined, the results presented focus mainly on valuation and risk management issues, ignoring purely optimization ones. In order to assess the impact of market risk on the value of the production the "worst case production value" is proposed. This measure is easily attainable by means of a lattice approach which illustrates the economic result the asset manager will obtain by operating the optimal policy in the worst possible market conditions.

From analysis of the results given in Table 5.8, and graphically represented in Figures 5.2, 5.3 and 5.4, the non-linear relation between production value and crack spread value is evident for all three cases. This is clear evidence of the "option nature" of the distillation process, as opposed to the general situation for NPV-based models. This is a numerical proof of the fact that the application of a real options methodology allows one to capture economic value where traditional deterministic approaches fail to do so. The model also associates positive production values with situations characterized by a negative implied crack spread. This

Table 5.8 Summary of test case characteristics

Crak value	−10	−5	−3	−1	0	1	3	5	10
Case 1									
Production value	0	0,001	5,1155	1246,1	8212,9	27983	80099	133480	266940
Worst case	0	0	0	0	0	823,8	9492	27003	105130
Case 2									
Production value	0	0,	4,7	1213	8045,1	27064	77399	128980	257940
Worst case	0	0	0	0	0	246,7	7144	22877	96560
Case 3									
Production value	0	0	4,5	1194,6	7995,6	27049	77398	128980	257940
Worst case	0	0	0	0	0	238,5	7144	22877	96560

is the value of uncertainty discussed in the introductory section. The positive value of market uncertainty associated with the refinery process is essentially related to the embedded industrial flexibilities which allow the refinery manager to capture favourable market upwards maximizing the production and to cut potential losses by reducing or stopping the production in adverse market conditions. Even in the short time horizon of the proposed exercise, this flexibility value is evident. As stated before, if industrial flexibilities have a positive impact on refinery production value, operational constraints have a negative one. Comparing the numerical results for Case 1 with those for Cases 2 and 3, the impacts of operational constraints, especially inter-temporal ones, can easily be assessed. The interesting fact to note is that operational constraints have the biggest impact when market conditions (crack spread levels) are neither favourable nor extremely adverse, something that can be seen by looking at Figures 5.7(a)–5.7(c).

This fact is not surprising if we consider the inter-temporal nature of most operational constraints highlighted in this exercise. In fact, inter-temporal constraints limit the capacity of the refinery manager to exercise industrial flexibilities freely, actually limiting his capacity to maximize the economic margin. When market conditions do not provide the manager with a clear incentive to commit or de-commit his refinery unit, a flexible refinery asset, able to modify its production regime in a short period of time, is much more valuable. Operational constraints are also risk sources, since they induce persistence in the decision-making process. In fact, flexibility allows the refinery manager to react promptly to sudden changes in market conditions while a lack of it may force the manager himself to commit the refinery unit (or stay off) even if it is not convenient to do so. As will become clear, the possibility and the opportunity to rapidly modify production programmes also influence the implementation of efficient hedging strategies. Based on the results obtained in the simulation exercise, the importance is clear of the correct valuation of an asset's operational flexibilities and constraints (not only those related to the distillation process) for medium-term investment decisions made on the basis of a refinery's technology. Risk exposure calculation and hedging are intimately related problems traditionally faced by oil producers and refiners. In a deterministic environment, risk factor exposure is calculated according to classical budgeting and planning tools such as scenario analysis. The resulting hedging strategy is necessarily static

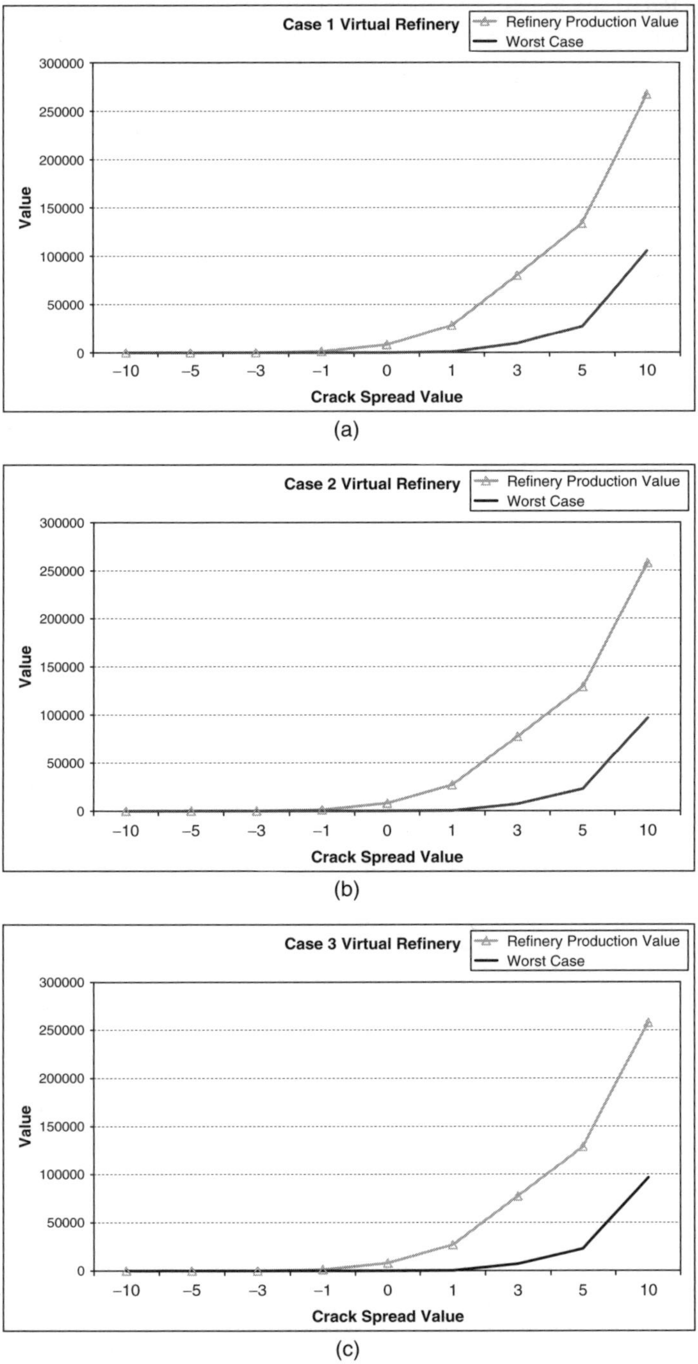

Figure 5.7 Virtual refinery case study

and not related to any kind of risk measure. This is completely unrealistic. In fact, if optimal operational policy has to be dynamically adjusted in order to be consistent with changing market conditions, then the hedging strategy should also reflect this dynamicity. Again, the application of real options methodology provides us with the tool to address the problem of exposure calculation and hedging in a dynamic way.

6 Metatrading Strategies and Capital Allocation Techniques

6.1 METATRADING DEFINITION AND FUNDAMENTAL ELEMENTS

Hitherto in this book, we have discussed energy trading issues from an internal point of view in that we have concentrated on the critical analysis of trading strategies, approaches and decision support tools assuming that a certain trading business (the energy trading business, in our specific case) already exists with a given organizational structure and rules. In other words, we have analyzed energy trading from a micro economic and business perspective. In contrast, we will dedicate this last chapter to discussion and analysis of the energy trading business from a macro perspective. In particular, we will define as "metatrading" the specific discipline whose particular goal is the correct implementation of a trading business.

If micro trading is an area of specific interest to the trader, metatrading is a subject which should be of more interest to trading managers or trading business stakeholders. Historically, a lot of effort has gone into the analysis and optimization of micro trading strategies and techniques, but rather less effort has been expended in creating the correct structuring of the trading business itself. We believe it is important to devote at least one chapter of our book to this topic since it appears more and more evident that the robust and long-lasting success of a trading business is determined more by the correct implementation of the business than by the appropriateness of particular trading decisions taken during the operational phase of the business. We saw at the beginning of the book that the more efficient and mature a market, the less likely it is for the trader to get profits out of it irrespective of the sophistication and complexity of the decision support tools used. The same cannot be said of metatrading. The correct set up and continuous adjustment of the trading business can mine and eventually facilitate the pursuit of a positive performance. Obviously, good or bad results can occur even if the business is correctly set up and continuously adjusted, but certainly only bad results will occur in the long run if incorrect metatrading decisions are taken. This is particularly true for and important in the energy sector due to its relative immaturity and its connection with typical industrial activities like energy generation, transportation and sales.

Metatrading provides the answer to generic questions like: What kind of objective should our trading business have? In which field should we concentrate our effort (energy, commodities, money market etc.)? When is the proper time to start or to quit our business? How should we organize financial and human resources in order to optimize the final result? The aim of this chapter is to set up a scientific discussion about metatrading in an attempt to emphasize its main topics, and the basic methodologies it is necessary to implement in order to create the boundary conditions for a successful trading business.

In our view, there are three main topics related to metatrading.

The first concerns the question of the proper time to invest in a trading activity and the proper field of application of the investment. To analyze and support decisions in this respect we will refer to investment-based macroeconomic theories not with the purpose of perfectly forecasting optimal investment timing and directions but with the intention of understanding macro relationships between economic variables and social phenomena.

The second important topic is the organizational one. How should we organize the allocation of economic and human resources? In this area a key factor to analyze is the correct information flow and its organizational and business implications. As we saw earlier the trading business is essentially connected with the use of private and public information and its success is linked to their optimal use.

The third area of interest is probably the most important or at least the one that most directly impacts business performance. It is the area of capital allocation and performance attribution. This is an area intimately connected to the determination of capital requirements and risk appetite. Capital allocation is not a static activity performed only at the beginning, but is dynamic and should reflect changes in prevailing economic and market conditions as past performance and risk adjusted target results.

Even more than looking for solid formal techniques to tackle metatrading problems we will stress the importance of having a clear and logical understanding of and operational approach to them. In some cases, mathematical techniques can be adopted, in others a more qualitative approach will be used. In every situation a critical revision of assumptions and the intrinsic coherence of metatrading decisions will be pursued.

6.2 MACROECONOMIC MEGATRENDS: UNDERSTANDING AND ANALYSIS

Setting up a trading business is a particular kind of investment decision. As for any investment decision an understanding of the proper time to invest is fundamental once we have selected the field of investment itself. As discussed in detail earlier in the book, the objective of a trading business is that of gaining profits by exploiting price movements of financial variables and/or commodities. In our extremely globalized world, prices of commodities and financial products are strongly influenced (if in different ways) by the same macroeconomic variables. Hence, in order to determine the proper investment time and field, it is important to have a general understanding of macroeconomic relationships. A perfect determination and forecast of economic and financial macrotrends is impossible by definition but a general understanding of the mutual impacts that macro-economic variables may have can help support investment decisions.

The simple fact that we actually consider the question of the optimal timing for performing a certain generic investment implies that we believe economic variables fluctuate periodically around a long-term growth trend allowing for an optimal investment time, just before an expansion phase starts, but also an optimal disinvestment time, just before a recession phase.

In most interpretations, classical economists such as Adam Smith maintained that the free market would tend towards economic equilibrium through the price mechanism. Modern mainstream economics points to cases where equilibrium does not correspond with market clearing but instead with unemployment. Parallel in some ways is the phenomenon of credit rationing, in which banks hold interest rates low to create an excess demand for loans, so they can pick and choose to whom to lend. Furthermore, economic equilibrium can correspond to monopoly, where the monopolistic firm maintains an artificial shortage to prop up prices and maximize profits. Finally, Keynesian macroeconomics points to underemployment equilibrium, where a surplus of labour (i.e. cyclical unemployment) co-exists for a long time with a shortage of aggregate demand. Obviously, a stable equilibrium does not allow for an optimal investment time given the absence of local expansion and recession phases.

Contrary to existing theories of economic equilibrium (self-clearing or not) there are other macroeconomic theories that postulate the existence of a business or economic cycle defined as an economy-wide fluctuation in economic activity over several months or years. These fluctuations are often measured using the growth rate of real gross domestic product. Despite being termed cycles, most of these fluctuations in economic activity do not follow a mechanical or predictable periodic pattern. In this section we will attempt to summarize the most important business cycle theories focusing mainly on those that have the investment process at their core.

Arthur F. Burns and Wesley C. Mitchell (1946) provided a definition of business cycles which is now accepted as standard. According to their definition a cycle consists of expansions occurring at about the same time in many economic activities, followed by similarly general recessions, contractions and revivals which merge into the expansion phase of the next cycle. Different business cycles can be classified according to their duration.

In 1860, French economist Clement Juglar identified the presence of economic cycles 8 to 11 years long, although he was careful not to claim any rigid regularity. Later, Joseph Schumpeter argued that a Juglar cycle has four stages: (i) expansion (increase in production and prices, low interest rates); (ii) crisis (stock exchanges crash and multiple bankruptcies of firms occur); (iii) recession (drops in prices and in output, high interest rates); (iv) recovery (stocks recover because of the fall in prices and incomes). Under this framework, recovery and prosperity are associated with increases in productivity, consumer confidence, aggregate demand and prices.

Schumpeter and others proposed a typology of business cycles according to their periodicity, so that a number of particular cycles were named after their discoverers or proposers:

- the **Kitchin inventory cycle**: is a 3–5 year cycle whose name derives from Joseph Kitchin (1923). The cycle is caused by time lags in information movements which affect decision-making by commercial firms. Businessmen extract information about the commercial situation from inventory levels and react with some time lag, adjusting their production.
- the **Juglar fixed investment cycle**: is a 7–11 year cycle often identified as "the" business cycle. Introduced by Juglar and further developed by Schumpeter, as noted above.
- the **Kuznets infrastructural investment cycle**: is a 15–25 year cycle named after Simon Kuznets (1930). Kuznets connected these medium-range economic waves with demographic processes and the changes in construction intensity which they caused, which is why he designated them *demographic* or *building* cycles/swings.
- the **Kondratiev wave or long technological cycle**: is a long range wave of 45–60 years postulated by Nikolai Kondratiev (1925). Kondratiev identified three phases in the cycle: expansion, stagnation, recession. More common today is the division into four periods with a turning point (collapse) between the first and second phases. The saturation of major markets or infrastructures (canals, railroads) creates stagnation in the economy. However, stagnation does not necessarily mean that markets are mature. The stagnation phase is characterized by a lack of good investment opportunities that leads to low interest rates and lowered credit standards which creates a speculative boom, followed by a crash and financial crisis

The effective presence of business cycles was empirically studied and sometimes also verified during the twentieth century. Here we are more interested in explaining why economic and financial fluctuations occur, what their main determinants are and how they develop through time and through different economic sectors. In particular, we are interested in all those theories that see cycles as an endogenous feature. In the end, we can state that the problem of how business cycles come about is inseparable from that of how a capitalist economy functions.

6.2.1 Keynesian Business Cycle Theory

Traditional classical and neo-classical macroeconomic theories do not allow for the possibility of economic cycles. Self-clearing mechanisms will force the economy towards equilibrium and when exogenous factors push it away from equilibrium, natural forces will lead it back without producing systematic waves or cycles. Within the classical Keynesian framework systematic cycles are also not contemplated. However, they can be accounted for by adopting simple modifications of standard theory. Roy Harrod in his theory of the trade cycle (1936), and later on in his theory of growth (1939, 1948), explored the relationships between the Keynesian multiplier and accelerator-type investment functions to explain a growing, progressive economy with and without cycles.

The principle of the multiplier, as expounded by J.M. Keynes (1936) is that if investment increases, there will be an increase in output as a result of a "multiplier" relationship between equilibrium output and the autonomous components of spending, in this case:

$$\Delta Y = \frac{\Delta I}{1 - c}$$

where c is the marginal propensity to consume, Y is output and I is investment. The principle of the accelerator was that investment decisions made by firms are at least partially dependent upon expectations of future increases in demand, which may, in turn, be extrapolated from any current or past increases in aggregate demand or output:

$$\Delta I_t = b(Y_t - Y_{t-1})$$

Thus, the multiplier principle implies that investment increases output whereas the acceleration principle implies that increases in output will themselves induce increases in investment.

Roy F. Harrod (1936) examined the dynamic properties of investment and output as they affect each other, perhaps in generating cycles and/or growth, although his analysis was purely verbal and not without some knots. John Hicks (1949; 1950) picked up where Harrod left off. Hicks' (1950) trade cycle model sought to recast Harrod's unstable "multiplier-accelerator" dynamics into cyclical ones by having explosive trajectories bang up against floors and ceilings.

These "simple" multiplier-accelerator models were among the first to tentatively incorporate economic cycles into traditional mainstream macro-economic models. Later, endogenous cycle theories appeared in which "natural" non-linearities are put in place in order to generate cycles and growth.

6.2.2 Real Business Cycle Theory

Real business cycle theory (RBC theory) constitutes a class of macroeconomic models in which, to a large extent, business cycle fluctuations can be accounted for by real (as opposed to nominal) shocks. RBC theory is associated with the Chicago school of economics in the neoclassical tradition and for that reason it is rejected and criticized by other schools within mainstream economics, notably Keynesians.

RBC theory sees recessions and periods of economic growth as the efficient response to exogenous changes in the real economic environment. According to RBC theory, business cycles are therefore "real" in the sense that they do not represent a failure of markets to clear but rather reflect the most efficient possible operation of the economy, given its structure. RBC theory differs in this way from other theories of the business cycle such as Keynesian economics and monetarism that see recessions as the failure of some market to clear.

In their seminal work *Time to Build and Aggregate Fluctuations* (1982) Finn E. Kydland and Edward C. Prescott envisioned technological shocks as the main real factor influencing an economic cycle. The general gist of their article is that something occurs that directly changes the effectiveness of capital and/or labour.

This in turn affects the decisions of workers and firms, who in turn change what they buy and produce and so eventually affect output. RBC models predict time sequences of allocation for consumption, investment, etc. given these shocks. For example, let us consider a good but temporary positive shock to productivity in a world where individuals produce goods they consume. This momentarily increases the effectiveness of workers and capital. Individuals face two types of trade-offs. One is the consumption-investment decision. Since productivity is higher, people have more output to consume. An individual might choose to consume all of it today. But if he values future consumption, all that extra output might not be worth consuming in its entirety today. Instead, he may consume some but invest the rest in capital to enhance production in subsequent periods and thus increase future consumption. This explains why investment spending is more volatile than consumption. The life-cycle hypothesis argues that households base their consumption decisions on expected lifetime income and so they prefer to "smooth" consumption over time. They will thus save (and invest) in periods of high income and defer consumption of this to periods of low income.

The other decision is the labour–leisure trade-off. Higher productivity encourages substitution of current work for future work since workers will earn more per hour today compared to tomorrow. More labour and less leisure result in higher output today, greater consumption and investment today. On the other hand, there is a contrasting effect: since workers are earning more, they may not want to work as much today and in future periods. However, given the pro-cyclical nature of labour, it seems that the above "substitution effect" trumps this "income effect".

In summary, the basic RBC model predicts that the repercussions of a temporary shock may persist for some time even after the shock disappears (propagation mechanism). It is easy to see that a string of such productivity shocks will likely result in a boom. Similarly, recessions follow a string of bad shocks to the economy. If there were no shocks, the economy would just continue to follow the growth trend with no business cycles.

It is important to note that the main assumption in RBC theory is that individuals and firms respond optimally at all times to the information available to them. In some sense, a precursor to RBC theory was developed by monetary economists Milton Friedman and Robert Lucas in the early 1970s. They envisioned the factor that influenced people's decisions to be misperception of wages. Booms/recessions occurred when workers perceived wages to be higher/lower than they really were, influencing their working and consumption trade-offs. Hence, in a world of perfect information, there would be no boom or bust (recession).

6.2.3 Austrian Business Cycle Theory

The Austrian business cycle theory (ABC theory) attempts to explain business cycles through a set of ideas held by the heterodox Austrian school of economics. The theory views business cycles (or, as some Austrians prefer, "credit cycles") as the inevitable consequence of excessive growth in bank credit, exacerbated by inherently damaging and ineffective central bank policies, which cause interest rates to remain too low for too long, resulting in excessive credit creation, speculative economic bubbles and lowered savings.

Grounded in the economic theory set out in Carl Menger's *Principles of Economics* and built on the vision of a capital-intensive production process developed in Eugen von Böhm-Bawerk's *Capital and Interest*, the Austrian theory of the business cycle remains sufficiently distinct to justify its national identity. But even in its earliest rendition in Ludwig von Mises's *Theory of Money and Credit* and in subsequent exposition and extension in F. A. von Hayek's *Prices and Production*, the theory incorporated important elements from Swedish and British economics. A popularized version of the theory is presented in Murray Rothbard's pamphlet *Economic Depressions: Their Cause and Cure*, which endeavours to explain the business cycle by focusing on excessive bank-sourced credit expansion and centralized government intervention (through the actions of a central bank). Rothbard went into much greater detail in his book *What Has Government Done to Our Money?*

According to the theory, the boom-bust cycle of malinvestment is generated by excessive and unsustainable credit extension to businesses and individual borrowers by the banks. Borrowers, in short, are misled by the bank inflation into believing that the supply of saved funds is greater than it really is. When the pool of "saved funds" increases, entrepreneurs invest in a "longer process of production", the capital structure is lengthened, especially in the "higher orders", most remote from the consumer. Borrowers take their newly acquired funds and bid up the prices of capital and other producers' goods, which, according to the theory, stimulates a shift of investment from consumer goods to capital goods industries. The Austrian school further contends that such a shift is unsustainable and must reverse itself in due course. The longer the unsustainable shift in capital goods industries continues, the more violent and disruptive the necessary re-adjustment process. The preference of entrepreneurs for longer-term investments can be explained by using any discounted cash flow model. Essentially, lower interest rates increase the relative value of cash flows that come in the future, making virtually profitable investments that do not really exist. The proportion of consumption to savings or investment is determined by people's time preferences, which is the degree to which they prefer present to future satisfactions. Thus, the natural interest rate is determined by the time preferences of the individuals in society, and the final market rates of interest reflect the pure interest rate plus or minus the entrepreneurial risk and purchasing power components.

Because of the global nature of the investment market, many entrepreneurs can make the same mistake at the same time. As they are all competing for the same pool of capital and market share, some entrepreneurs begin to borrow simply to avoid being "overrun" by other entrepreneurs who may take advantage of lower interest rates to invest in more up-to-date capital infrastructure. A tendency towards over-investment and speculative borrowing in this "artificial" low interest rate environment is therefore almost inevitable.

Austrian economists conclude that, since time preferences have not changed, people will rush to re-establish the old proportions, and demand will shift back from the higher to the lower orders. In other words, depositors will tend to remove cash from the banking system and spend it (not save it), banks will then ask their borrowers for payment and interest rates and credit conditions will deteriorate. Original investments will turn out to be errors and the malinvestment must be liquidated.

Austrian scholars assert that the boom is actually a period of wasteful malinvestment, a "false boom" where the particular kinds of investment undertaken during the period of fiat money expansion are revealed to lead nowhere but to insolvency and unsustainability. The "recession" or "depression" is actually the process by which the economy adjusts to the wastes and errors of the monetary boom, and re-establishes efficient service of sustainable consumer desires.

All Austrian theorists consider the unsustainable expansion of bank credit through fractional reserve banking as the driving feature of most business cycles. However, Murray Rothbard paid particular attention to the role of central banks in creating an environment of loose credit prior to the onset of the Great Depression, and the subsequent ineffectiveness of central bank policies, which simply delayed necessary price adjustments and prolonged market dysfunction. Under the current fiat monetary system, a central bank creates new money when it lends to member banks, and this money is multiplied many times over through the money creation process of the private banks. This new bank-created money enters the loan market and provides a lower rate of interest than that which would prevail if the money supply were stable.

The financial crisis of 2007–2010 has resulted in a revival of interest in Austrian business cycle theory. The Austrian theory is considered one of the precursors of modern credit cycle theory, which is emphasized by post-Keynesian economists and by a few mainstream academics such as Hyman Minsky and Charles P. Kindleberger. Updated credit cycle theories emphasize the role of risk, asymmetric information, moral hazard and weak regulations in credit expansion processes and in the role of banks and financial markets.

Mainstream economists strongly criticize ABC theory arguing that it requires bankers and investors to exhibit a kind of irrationality an inability to fully comprehend and forecast bank and consumer behaviour.

6.2.4 Risk-based Business Cycle Theory

The careful reader may have realized that the business cycle theories presented so far do not completely take into consideration how the modern economic world really works. This should not come as a surprise since these theories have mostly been conceived and developed in a very different economic environment. The very important role of fundamental elements of the modern economic world like financial intermediaries capital/financial markets have not been explicitly considered. Risk-based business cycle theory (RKBC) as recently developed by Cowen (1997) tries to unify the main elements of RBC and ABC by stressing the central role that "risk" plays in the entrepreneurial and banking investment decision-making process.

Entrepreneurs seek to match their production to market demands. To the extent that chosen outputs satisfy market conditions allowing for reasonable profits, consumption and production plans may be considered coordinated. Bankers do not behave differently from entrepreneurs within the market of loanable funds. The central question of a unified business cycle theory is that of explaining the reasons and the mechanism of a miscoordination between the two sides of the market. As modern financial theory teaches that risk and returns are two sides of the same coin, so they cannot be considered separately. Risky investments are characterized by long-term maturity, high reversing costs, high yielding and significant sensitivity to the arrival of new information. In contrast, safe investments are more liquid, lower yielding and less sensitive to the arrival of new information. Consumption typically represents the safer investment attainable. The essence of RKBC theory is that capital investment prices depend upon both real interest rate (nominal money growth) and risk. Changes in these variables will determine economic cyclicality or even volatility. In fact, the asymmetric effects of raising and lowering risk imply that economic busts or downturns arrive unpredictably producing jumps, rather than mere fluctuations, in the economic growth rate.

As stated above, risk and return are intrinsically connected. In the short and medium run they are positively correlated, as suggested by standard financial theory, but in the long run the relationship is inverted, perhaps due to increasing returns to scale, asset complementarities or benefits of specialization. Today's world brings higher returns than the past and probably also involves less risk. Since the earliest investments were made, the successive accumulation of risky, high return investments may have lowered long run risk for everyone at a certain social level. This time-dependent relationship between risk and returns provides a potential divider for cyclical and growth theory. The former applies to the short run while the latter characterizes the long term.

Both real and monetary factors may influence the dynamics of real interest rates and risk. In what follows, we will try to synthesize the propagation mechanism and comment on it.

Let us imagine a monetary scenario where the central bank is willing to stimulate short-run economic growth by lowering real interest rates or relaxing finance constraints. By doing so the bank will induce entrepreneurs to accept more risk and consequently will create a sectorial shift from safer to riskier investments. This will happen for two reasons: in a lower real interest rate scenario long-term investments appear to be more profitable (discounting effect); moreover, this will induce a wealth effect which will decrease risk aversion (risk aversion typically declines with wealth). The increase in risk will occur both at the individual and the aggregate level (risk multiplication principle). In the short term, before relevant uncertainty is resolved, these investments do bring higher expected returns and the whole economy will appear wealthier. But in the long run, once the risk is resolved the ex-post result may be much greater than the ex-ante impetus. Hence, the propagation mechanism will translate small ex-ante shocks into large ex-post output fluctuations. The analytical emphasis on risk implies that economic downturns are voluntary, in ex-ante terms, even though they are regretted ex-post.

Ex-ante, all capital structures can be interpreted as equilibria, if we account for risks, expectations and cost of information processing. Ex-post, capital structure disequilibria may arise to the extent that chosen investments turn out to have performed well below expectations.

Whilst this is certainly not a treatise on business cycles or macroeconomics, it is important for us to state clearly that in a risk consistent economy, money (and money or credit creation processes) is not neutral with respect to capital markets (Wicksell effect). Hence, monetary behaviours and policies (credit rationing, quantitative easing, and moral hazards in credit creation) can have real effects and contribute to the initialization, expansion or normalization of an economic wave or fluctuations.

In the end we can try to once more synthesize our discussion on macroeconomic megatrends by stressing once more the important consequences that monetary decisions can have for the short- and long-term behaviour of economic growth. Money growth and credit expansion will induce more risk in the economy, simultaneously increasing expected economic growth but also the possibility of cycles or sharp fluctuations (see Figure 6.1). The task of understanding those macro relationships, even without being able to forecast them, is fundamental to setting up and correctly running a trading business in today's energy commodity markets.

6.3 TRADING BUSINESS ORGANIZATIONAL ISSUES

Trading business is not just "luck", as we might think when observing it with a non-expert eye. Trading business success and robustness are strongly related to its organization and a bad trading framework can even compromise the positive effects of "luck".

As for almost all financial activities the trading business product is money and its industrial cost of production is almost zero (in improper terms). The main assets used to pursue the economic scope within a trading business are: human capital (talents), access to markets and to relevant information and a proper organization which allows one to exploit to the maximum the available information and perform an effective and fast decision-making process. More so than in other more traditional businesses, organizational issues can have a significant impact on the economic result.

The general scope of a good business organization is coordination of activities with maximum effectiveness and minimum cost (explicit cost is equivalent to opportunity cost for the sake of this discussion). A trading organization is made up of different traders and those whose job it is to assist traders by means of analysis, legal and back office support etc. If we focus our attention on the energy trading business, we cannot avoid discussing the potential overlaps between the activity of different traders. The dilemma in this field is how to exploit informational synergies without incurring undesired overlaps. Moreover, from the trading manager's point of view, the creation of a clear field of activity for every single trader or trading desk is the basic building block for the capital allocation process which we will discuss later in the chapter.

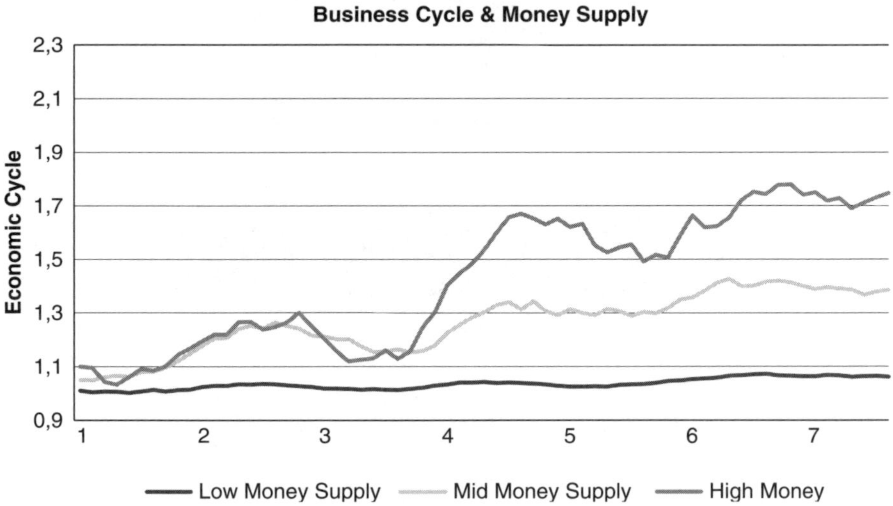

Figure 6.1 Economic cycle, risk and money supply

Among the many important organizational issues, we believe that within energy markets, two merit individual discussion: book structuring and internal market.

6.3.1 Book Structuring

In the initial phase of a business set-up, the book structure is fundamental in order for the trading manager to have a general criterion for initial capital allocation and to translate this criterion into an organizational element, defining the field of activity of every single trading desk. When the business is in the operational phase a correct and detailed book structure helps the trading manager in the recognition and allocation of the performance. In the energy trading business this is particularly important since energy commodity markets are highly inter-correlated and the risk of an inefficient capital allocation is higher than in other markets.

The book/desk structuring process operates effectively in this area. Typically, a book/desk structure is hierarchical in nature (see Figure 6.2) and tries to identify the field of activities, market tools and strategy that a certain trading desk is supposed to adopt. The general criterion that has to be followed is "independence". In fact, the more we are able to allocate capital in independent (or scarcely correlated) activities, as we will see later, the easier it will be to attribute performance (in risk adjusted terms) and to adjust capital allocation. The achievement of independence within an extremely interrelated financial segment, such as that of energy commodities, is not simple, especially considering that the dependence structure is not static but changes very rapidly in tandem with market structure changes.

Research into independence or scarce correlation is not justified solely by the general principle of diversification, but deals mainly with the capital allocation

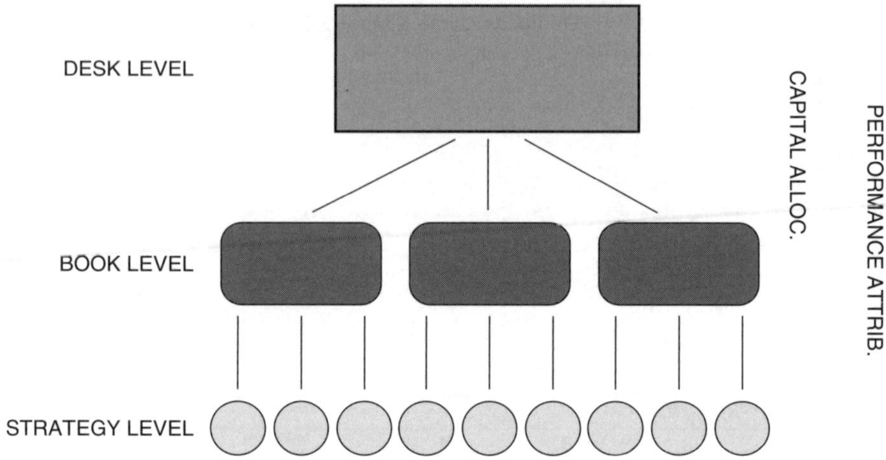

Figure 6.2 Book structure scheme

process. In fact, capital allocation is a top-down process; we know the global economic capital and we want to determine the allocation that guarantees maximum availability of capital over single desks or books without exceeding the global constraints. Obviously, the more books that are similar in terms of activity, the more they result in correlated inducing complexity in the capital division due to the strong diversification/concentration effect.

The research of statistical independence is not the unique segregation criterion we can use in order to obtain an optimal book structure (also because statistical criteria are more useful ex-post than ex-ante). Other criteria such as commodity segregation or instrument segregation can be adopted for the sake of full exploitation of information and cost minimization.

The first level of book structure hierarchy is the trading desk definition. Here decisions deal more with people than with field of activities, since a single trading desk can be considered as a separate company within the company. We should never forget that capital can only be allocated (and consequently managed by) to people and not to markets or financial instruments. Different trading styles, different instruments used to trade or simply a different trading goal (speculative, flow, asset-based) imply a different use of the same information and consequently induce the researched independence. It is not unusual in energy trading to observe a trading desk definition based on geographic markets (sometimes highly correlated markets) or specific energy commodities. As stated above, in our opinion this is not the proper criterion, since its effectiveness is subject to the evolution of market dynamics such as the increase/decrease of cross correlations between different energy markets or commodities. Moreover, the same trading style or goal applied to highly correlated products will create risk implicit concentration, which is not beneficial. It may be that market or commodity segmentation criteria induce independence as well. This is, for example, the case when we try to separate among different trading desks local energy trading business, such as gas and power, from global energy trading business such as oil or coal.

At the second level of the hierarchical structure of books we have books in the proper sense of the term. Again, different transactions should be grouped within the same book in an attempt to homogenize the risk that they contain. To take a fairly obvious example: all the hedges connected to a certain natural risk exposure (an asset or a flow business) should be put in the same book. This is particularly important for all those trading activities that have a multi-commodity exposure such as structured trading activities.

The third level of the hierarchical structure we will consider here is that of sub-books or strategies. This level is less important from the capital allocation point of view than it is from the operational one. Segregation of transactions into different strategies, even if they belong to the same trader with the same trading approach or generic goal, is important for the trader in order to really understand the profitability or capital intensity of the strategy.

While the first two hierarchical levels of the book structure should be kept relatively constant through time, the third one, since it is merely operational, should be dynamically changed in order to reflect effective business activity.

The main dilemma in book structuring is always its complexity. In some companies the book structure is extremely simplified, with only two levels and few ramifications. In others, the opposite approach is utilized. It goes without saying that it is impossible to identify the optimal size of book structure without considering contingent elements of the particular trading business we are structuring. It is nevertheless important to stress that simplicity is not always an advantage and that, on the other hand, a complex book structure may induce a complex capital allocation (and allocation re-adjustment) process that has to be properly supported and analyzed in order not to incur mistakes or misevaluations.

6.3.2 Internal Market

The "market" (a free and competitive one) is not just the virtual place where supply and demand meet. It is primarily the site where information is exchanged and created by means of largely unconscious processes put in place by market operators.

One of the most influential and important economists and sociologists of the twentieth century, the Austrian Friedrich von Hayek, used to define the "market" and the price formation mechanism taking place within it as the principal tool for actions coordination among different economic agents. Without referring explicitly to financial markets (note: it is nevertheless evident that financial markets nowadays represent the brightest examples of a competitive market), Hayek believed that the unconscious coordination process attainable via the market price formation mechanism is almost certainly superior to any other centralized coordination imposed by authority. The reason for this superiority is related to a better exploitation of available information of single operators with respect to any other centralized authority. Individual information is then made available to the whole market community through a price formation mechanism.

If the market mechanism is important as a coordination tool from the macroeconomic point of view (coordination among different companies), we believe it can also play a similar role from the microeconomic point of view (coordination within the company). This is particularly true in the trading business where a transparent price mechanism is available and even more in the energy sector where the exigency to coordinate different activities (trading, generation, sales) related to the same underlying markets is extremely significant.

Traditionally, energy trading companies (and trading companies in general) try to limit access to outside markets to a few desks for the sake of minimization of execution and transaction costs. Coordination between execution desks and the rest of the company is then obtained via a rigid and complex network of internal transactions, that do not always reflect market prices. In power markets, the case of difficult interactions between trading and sales or generation departments is typical. Of course, transaction cost minimization is a goal that has to be pursued and attained by any company but without incurring the risk of organizational miscoordination.

As an example of miscoordination risk we can cite the bad investment decisions that can arise when a market-based internal transfer pricing rule is ignored for the sake of vertical integration and conversely, the inefficiencies that can materialize in execution desks when market access monopolies are imposed from above.

The internal market concept and system have been developed to resolve the dichotomy, described above, between cost efficiency and informational efficiency. The principle of an internal market is extremely simple and consists in limiting access to the outside market to a unique execution desk, basically working as an internal broker, allowing all the other desks to see all the external orders and transactions but also to express their orders (buy or sell) looking for an internal match. If the internal match is attainable it is performed automatically without the intervention of the execution desk, otherwise the internal order is transferred outside and potentially executed by the execution desk.

This framework allows internal desks to coordinate implicitly their activities by using market prices as an unconscious coordination tool, and to take their operational decisions using the maximum available information. In fact, in a relatively illiquid market such as the energy one (power and gas in particular) the possibility to observe market dynamics directly (even without accessing it directly) represents a significant increase in the information set for portfolio managers or asset managers compared to the simple observation of end of day closing prices. In respect of transaction costs minimization, the internal market represents an optimal solution given the limitation of the access to external platforms and the maximization of netting opportunities it allows.

Trading business is highly contingent on the quality and efficiency of its human capital. Highly skilled resources should be put in the right position to provide their performance. Organizational integration and access to information sources are the essential elements in performance, but for its part the company should optimize costs and allocate capital where the expected reward is highest.

6.4 CAPITAL MANAGEMENT PRINCIPLES

6.4.1 Economic Capital Definition and Initial Allocation

As previously stated the trading business is not only made up of good investment decisions, but also of capital allocation (reallocation) and performance attribution processes. Questions such as: How much capital is required to cover potential losses arising from the risk we are facing? What is the risk-adjusted performance produced by each trading desk and strategy? How much capital should be allocated along trading desks in order to maximize the overall performance? are fundamental for any trading company. Obviously, in order to answer these questions, the notion of "capital" should first be properly defined.

Unlike banks and other financial institutions, energy trading companies are not subject to specific regulatory capital requirements, hence we will focus directly on the concept of economic capital as opposed to concepts of available capital and invested capital. Economic capital represents an internal estimate of the capital the company needs to run its business covering, all potential losses it may face during a predefined future time horizon. Its main components are net working capital and risk capital. While net working capital is an effective component of the liquid capital the company should be able to access in order to face the natural mismatch between its economic and financial cycles, risk capital is not necessarily reflected in the available capital especially when no regulatory requirements are enforceable. This is typically the case within the energy trading business. Nevertheless, a grasp of the concept of economic and risk capital is essential for any analysis and understanding of the performance of our trading business. From this point of view the difference between economic capital and invested capital is evident. In fact, available capital can be partially composed of equity and debt with different opportunity costs.

Our aim in this section is to analyze capital management techniques as a performance optimization tool, hence the capital measure we are interested in is obviously the more comprehensive notion of economic capital. In fact, if capital management is aimed at risk-adjusted performance optimization a distortion in the capital measurement (as the use of a non-risk comprehensive notion of capital) may potentially bias management decisions.

Capital management decisions can be divided into a theoretical loop composed of initial capital allocation, performance measurement and attribution (in a risk-adjusted fashion) and capital reallocation. Initial capital allocation is typically performed by means of heuristic processes based on current measurement of risk capital employed plus a certain security buffer. Obviously, this possibility is only allowed when regulatory constraints are not imposed and in any case cannot be considered theoretically coherent since it does not start from the definition of the overall economic capital as an absolute constraint to subsequent business set-up decisions. On the other hand, as suggested in the previous section, an ex-ante division among desks of a certain amount of economic capital (risk capital in particular) is not simply due to unpredictable diversification effects. Here, effective desk and book structuring is important and helpful to avoid potential superposition of a company's different entities.

At the level of performance measurement and attribution, risk measurement and integration is an essential activity. Risk-adjusted performance measures are then the instrument used by managers to periodically engaging capital allocation revisions.

6.4.2 Risk Measurement and Integration Approaches for Energy Portfolios

Traditional risk and performance assessment techniques have been adapted to also work properly in the energy field and nowadays almost all the major energy trading companies control their business by means of very sophisticated risk policies and tools.

However, complex tools and policies are often implemented without a preliminary and critical assessment as to the appropriateness of the tool with respect to the kind of portfolio currently being managed. The proper risk representation techniques of a pure energy trading company are different from those of a vertically integrated energy one and both differ from those of a purely financial subject. The difference is not only related to the model we use to simulate relevant risk drivers or to the level of sophistication we want to reach in our analysis: the difference is often related to the actual use we make of a certain risk measure. Moreover, we need to consider that energy traders are also often energy producers and retailers and for those structures risk integration is a primary challenge. For the sake of risk capital determination a coherent approach to the market, credit and operational risks is necessary as is a robust approach to risk integration problems.

The scope of the present section does not include the proposal of methods and tools for calculating portfolio's risk, VaR or exposure again. Rather we want to focus the reader's attention on more "qualitative" risk issues which nevertheless have a tremendous impact on the correct implementation of a proper risk assessment and management strategy.

Value-based market risk measures

In this section, we will concentrate on synthetic risk measures for portfolios made up of liquid physical or financial energy products. In this situation, as portfolio managers, we have at any moment the possibility to liquidate or modify the composition of our portfolio without incurring large financial costs. Hence, the economic performance of this kind of business is determined mainly by fluctuation in the value of the portfolio itself rather than by the financial payoff of the deals that compose it. Hence, the risk we run is represented by the maximum potential drop (or some function of it) in terms of market value our portfolio may incur within a given time horizon.

Synthetic risk measures that emphasize this aspect of portfolio risk are called "value based risk measures". Of course, we will start by discussing the classical Value at Risk.

Value at Risk. Value at Risk has come to be widely used and popular among banks and financial institutions since the beginning of the 1990s. For this reason in the energy field it was also natural from the earliest instances of trading activity to evaluate the risks embedded in open trading positions by means of VaR.

Value at Risk effectively measures the market price risk exposure of an open position, condensing risk factors such as market price volatility and correlation of relevant energy commodities and potentially currency and interest rate risks.

It is usually defined as the minimum potential loss that a trading portfolio may have over a holding period of m days, in $x\%$ worst cases. This means that we may expect to lose more than the VaR figure, in the given holding period of m days, only in $x\%$ of cases (see Figure 6.3 for a graphical representation of VaR, ES and CVaR).

VaR is a simple and intuitive measure that depends on two main arguments:

- the duration of the holding period (number of days);
- the confidence interval's level $x\%$.

The holding period usually reflects the number of days necessary to liquidate completely the position without incurring additional costs, hence it should be established proportionally to market liquidity. Usually, for portfolios of exchange traded instruments this period is something between one and fifteen days. The level of the confidence interval reflects how conservative the measure is. In fact, the closer $x\%$ is to one, the higher the risk measure and, consequently, the probability of having a worse economic result is low.

From the statistical point of view, VaR is a percentile measure. It measures the percentile of the portfolio value variations corresponding to the selected confidence level. Formally, if X defines the portfolio fair value we have that

$$\mathrm{VaR}(x) = \left\{c \in \mathbb{R}^+ | \mathbb{P}(-\Delta X > \mathrm{VaR}(x)) = 1 - x\right\}$$

Typical confidence levels are 95%, 97.5% or 99% since they correspond to well-known values in the Gaussian distribution tables.

As mentioned, VaR calculation is based on the concept of fair value (market value) of the portfolio. Hence, VaR calculation methodologies are highly related to portfolio valuation methods especially when options and non-linear derivatives are present in the portfolio.

Traditional VaR calculation methods can be divided into two groups: analytical and numerical (simulation based) methods.

Analytical methods were the first presented and used in traditional financial applications of VaR and they are essentially based on some theoretical assumptions, the main one being that of joint "normality" of asset returns. The normality assumption is essential to obtain closed formulas for VaR calculation when we manage a large and well diversified portfolio of financial assets but it is not always realistic for energy markets. However, the relaxation of this assumption makes the development of an analytical calculation method much more difficult and sometimes non-attainable. For this reason numerical methods are to be preferred even if calculation time may be much higher.

The best way to circumvent problems of analytical models is by means of simulations. Using Monte Carlo simulation methods we can price a wide range of derivative products and consequently we can obtain a fairly accurate estimate of a portfolio's potential value changes. We can simulate a large number of scenarios for the relevant risk drivers (essentially forward prices and volatilities) and for every scenario we can obtain a potential value change for the portfolio itself. Given the large number of scenarios performed, a probability distribution function can be estimated by means of either parametric or non-parametric methods and the selected percentile measure can be extracted.

If the portfolio is mainly composed of linear positions, the VaR calculation may be quite quick since the simulated scenarios will reflect only forward curve shocks, while in the case of highly structured portfolios the calculation may slow down significantly, especially when portfolio dimensions are big.

Realistic modelling of the joint stochastic behaviour of the relevant risk drivers is not a simple task. The main difficulty is modelling the dependence structure relating risk variables, and unfortunately there is no simple benchmark solution for this.

The problem of simulating random draws from a multivariate and complex distribution may be solved by substituting historical simulation for Monte Carlo simulation.

The historical simulation method consists in estimating VaR by means of historical daily market variables movements over a quite large and significant time horizon. Knowing the actual composition of the portfolio, it is possible to compute the VaR calculating the theoretical portfolio value for every single day of the historical sample. The main advantage of the historical VaR method is that of being based on an accurate estimate of the empirical distribution of the major risk factor. Hence, all the problems mentioned above regarding the correct simulation of realistic risk drivers dynamics and dependence structure disappear. However, a number of disadvantages arise. The first is the size of the historical sample. In order to have a robust estimation of portfolio value change distribution a consistent database of historical prices is necessary but not always available. Secondly, this approach can only be applied for portfolios of liquid financial instruments, traded on organized exchanges, since only for that kind of asset are historical time series available. The third important disadvantage concerns the fact that historical VaR is a backward looking measure, and we know that the past does not always give us a good indication of the future.

Expected shortfall and conditional VaR. Value at Risk is definitely the risk measure adopted as best practice in the finance industry but this does not mean that it always represents the best possible synthetic indicator of the economic risk embedded in our portfolio.

There are some important mathematical and practical reasons that lead us to think that VaR may be inappropriate to measure a portfolio's risk in some particular conditions. When the loss density function of our portfolio (left tail of portfolio value changes density function) is particularly thick, non monotonically decreasing or eventually discontinuous, the percentile value selected for the VaR calculation may not be highly representative of the real risk that the portfolio owner faces. This is mainly due to the fact that, in this case, a rare and extreme event can potentially occur (with a probability lower than that implicit in VaR measure) provoking a sensible drop in portfolio value. As stated above, energy portfolios quite often have non-standard distributions.

Expected Shortfall was the first risk measure alternative to VaR proposed in the literature and used for practical purposes. It is considered the best risk measure both for its mathematical properties and its straightforward interpretation.

While VaR is a percentile measure of a statistical distribution, Expected Shortfall (ES) is its conditional mean. If VaR is a threshold which is fallen short of in a certain percentage of cases, ES is the expectation of losses under the condition that the same threshold will indefinitely be fallen short of. Formally, we have that if

$$\mathrm{VaR}(x) = \left\{c \in \mathbb{R}^+ | \mathbb{P}(-\Delta X > \mathrm{VaR}(x)) = 1 - x\right\}$$

then

$$\mathrm{ES}(x) = \left\{d \in \mathbb{R}^+ | \mathbb{E}(-\Delta X | -\Delta X \geqslant \mathrm{VaR}(x))\right\}$$

ES is always, by construction, a more conservative risk measure than the VaR, and has also nice mathematical features such as being a "coherent" risk measure.

Conditional Value at Risk (CVaR) was proposed by Rockafellar and Uryasev (2002) as a measure which combines the positive feature of ES with the familiar concept of VaR.

CVaR is essentially a linear combination of VaR and ES, with a combination parameter which should reflect portfolio manager risk attitude. Formally

$$\mathrm{CVaR}(x) = \gamma \mathrm{VaR}(x) + (1 - \gamma)\mathrm{ES}(x) \quad 0 \leqslant \gamma \leqslant 1$$

Rockafellar and Uryasev mainly emphasize the nice mathematical features of CVaR, with a particular focus on portfolio optimization with risk–reward constraints. However, the idea of combining the information contained in two different risk measures like VaR and ES also has a reasonable market explanation. In fact, while the VaR measure is particularly suitable to budget a risk-adjusted performance value for our portfolio in "normal" market conditions, ES may be used to assess the survival probability of our trading activity.

Flow-based risk measures

The economic performance of a portfolio made up exclusively of liquid products is fully determined by its day-by-day value change. This is so because every single day it is possible to dynamically modify the structure of the portfolio itself, closing some positions or opening new ones without incurring enormous transaction costs. When we manage a heterogeneous portfolio of non-standard physical or financial

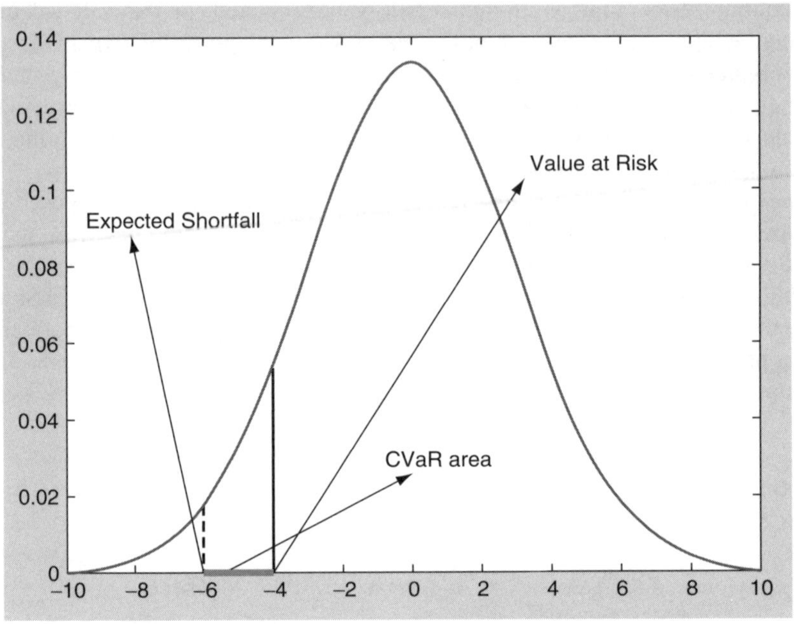

Figure 6.3 VaR, ES and CVaR graphical representation

deals, it is often not possible to liquidate a position without incurring expensive penalties or high liquidity costs. Hence, a non-profitable deal cannot be closed upfront, realizing a negative mark to market, but should be held in the portfolio until its natural maturity. The natural consequence of this fact is that the economic performance of the portfolio is not related to day-by-day portfolio value changes but is determined by its realized margin. As a consequence, the risk of the portfolio cannot be expressed by the potential drop in the portfolio value over a short period of time, but should be measured by some indicator of the uncertainty which characterizes portfolio expected payoff over the whole portfolio tenor. Flow-based risk measures do this job.

Profit at Risk. The feature that characterizes PaR is that it assumes that markets are illiquid, and for that reason open positions are held to maturity. A formal definition of PaR may be given as follows: the minimum potential loss that a portfolio may suffer in the $x\%$ worst cases if held to maturity (see Figure 6.4 for a graphical representation of PaR and CFaR).

The focus is clearly on the economic flow produced by the portfolio and not on its value.

As mentioned earlier, PaR is a risk measure suitable for monitoring and managing portfolios generated by medium to long-term structured contracts. PaR time horizon should be chosen according to the purpose for which it is intended. Usually, the economic year is chosen by the management for a better comparison with budget values and balance sheet results.

PaR calculation requires the assessment of economic margins coming from business activity that will generate the economic result in the future. Typically, for the calculation of PaR analytical methods are not available and scenario-based simulation approaches are used. Its assessment is carried out by simulating spot price scenarios related to portfolio commodities, evaluating their path evolution up to the selected time horizon. We then calculate the portfolio margin relative to each of these scenarios and a probability distribution of the portfolio's margin can be obtained.

Since PaR measures the risk embedded in a portfolio of non-standard products, market risk variables may not be the only relevant drivers that should be simulated. Volumetric clauses and constraints should be properly considered for a fully comprehensive picture of the portfolio's overall risk.

According to its calculation, PaR is a suitable risk measure for all continuative activities for which the possibility to unwind the position quickly is not simple. It may also be considered for measuring the risk of real asset management activities such as power generation, fuel procurement and storage, and origination, but in this case we have to remember that economic performance and risk are not affected exclusively by market risk driver changes but also by management strategy. Hence, PaR calculation should be based on simulation models that are also able to capture the impact of operational and strategic decisions (real option models). PaR is a fundamental control tool for the whole value creation chain, measuring risk exposure and potential limit overruns, impacting on tactical decisions for risk reduction and hedging implementation. Moreover, it may be used as an indicator for top management in risk assessing medium to long-term investment decisions and commercial deals. PaR represents a coherent framework for strategic decisions.

Cash Flow at Risk. The Cash Flow at Risk (CFaR) approach answers the question of how far the deviation between actual cash flow and the planned value (or that used in the budget) is due to changes in underlying risk factors. Effectively, it is a quite similar measure to PaR in terms of calculation methodology and time horizon, but it focuses on cash flow depreciation instead of economic margin depreciation. Sometimes the time delay which characterizes the economic and financial manifestation of the events which characterize the firm's life determines the choice between PaR and CFaR as the most appropriate risk measure.

Of course, also in the case of CFaR, analytical calculation methodologies are not available and simulation approaches (Monte Carlo or historical) prevail. Obviously, VaR is still the most widely used synthetic risk measure, but it is clear that flow measures can make a significant contribution to the risk analysis of complex energy portfolios.

Credit risk for energy portfolios

In general, credit risk can be defined as the risk arising from an unexpected deterioration in the credit quality of one or more counterparties.

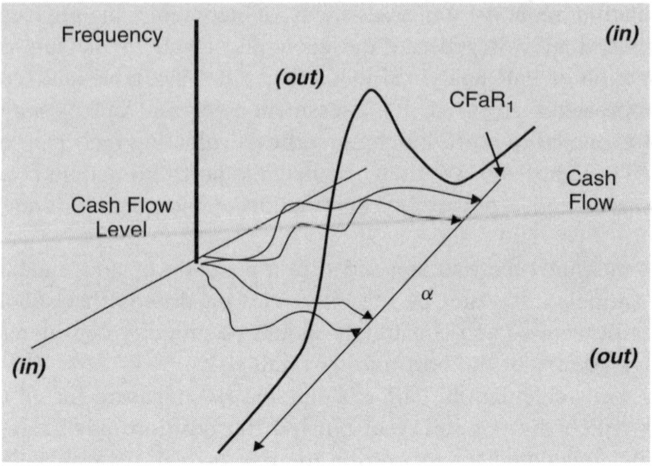

Figure 6.4 PaR and CFaR graphical representation

Credit risk measurement and management is one of the main issues today for industrial and financial companies and it is not only related to trading activity.

The consolidated approach for measuring credit risk is simply expressed by the equation used to calculate the so-called expected loss, that is *(Loss Given Default)* × *(Default Probability*). It can also be reformulated as *Expected Loss* = *(Loss Given Default - Collateral)* × Default Probability.

Loss given default (LGD) is technically the amount of money (exposure) we lose if my counterparty defaults today. In the energy sector, especially when we deal with a portfolio made up of physical and financial positions, this quantity is typically composed of the settlement exposure and the replacement exposure. The settlement exposure is the equivalent of the monetary value of energy delivered but not yet paid for and is related to the fact that financial settlement and invoice payment of a deal are usually temporally displaced with respect to physical energy delivery. If our counterparty faces bankruptcy today, it may be the case that there are invoices related to past deals not yet executed. Settlement exposure is related to the payment terms of contracts and may be significant, especially for physical transactions we are involved in sellers.

Replacement exposure is related to the situation where my counterparty defaults and the market value of the deal we are involved in with him is positive for me. This means that we have to face a drop in the P&L figure if our counterparty defaults the contract. In physical contracts this amount is called replacement exposure because it represents the opportunity cost we face for replacing the physical energy bought or sold in the market. If settlement exposure is independent of market prices since it only depends on contracts price, replacement exposure is related to the mark to market of the defaulted contract. Hence, at least theoretically, the replacement exposure should be zero at the moment of the deal closing.

Replacement exposure measures today's market value of a specific contract or of a bunch of contracts with a particular counterparty, but it does not reflect the potential value this contract may reach at its natural maturity. In order to consider this dimension of the credit risk we need to replace the concept of replacement exposure with the concept of "potential future exposure" (PFE). PFE expresses a measure of how things can go well against a certain counterparty and it is somehow related to the concept of Profit at Risk. In particular, it is a measure of the other tail of the profit distribution!

Here, sticking to the approach followed in this chapter, we will not spend time analyzing PFE calculation methodologies. Obviously, the coherence in the way we calculate market risk measures (PaR, VaR) of our portfolio and PFE should be guaranteed.

Using PFE instead of replacement exposure we obviously reach a higher value of expected loss, just because we are considering a risk dimension not considered previously.

Independently of the way it is calculated, LGD can be mitigated considering collaterals that potentially guarantee a part of the portfolio or recovery amounts. Recovery amounts are highly uncertain in size and time of effective settlement, hence, prudentially, it is better not to consider them. Collaterals that can be executed upon request in case of contract default reduce proportionally the exposure at default and consequently lower the overall expected loss.

We will not discuss here the other important component of the expected loss, which is the default probability, since calculation methodologies are not specific issues for the energy sector. One thing to point out here is that in the energy sector more than in any other financial or non-financial field many typical trading or commercial counterparties are not big listed companies. Hence, traditional quantitative methods for the computation of the probability of default, like credit metrics or credit+, cannot be straightforwardly used. More commonly internal rating systems have to be employed, but this issue is outside the scope of the present discussion.

Risk integration problems: risk capital assessment

So far we have discussed how different types of risk can be separately measured and monitored. In relation to market risk we have analyzed value risks and flow risks, and we have briefly discussed credit risk, although we did not explicitly consider operational risks.

However, in order to support top management decisions related to capital allocation and optimal management we need an integrated picture of risk that can also be clearly understood by non-specialists.

The challenge of different risk measures aggregation is in this sense very important and unfortunately not very developed and analyzed in terms of its theoretical and practical implications. Many market players, not only in the energy field, use sophisticated methods to analyze individual risks in depth but then very little effort is expended in looking for a more coherent risk aggregation technique. Clearly, best practices do not exist at the moment.

Understanding the benefits of diversifying risk among different books, business units, and commodities and being able to control and maintain the right proportion between market risks (core business risks) and credit/operational risks (non-core business risks) is a fundamental issue for correct economic capital allocation.

Risk aggregation can be performed across different dimensions up to the complete synthesis of the overall risk into a unique number representing the Risk Capital of the company, that is the capital necessary to face all potential risks that may arise in a given period of time (usually the business year).

The first task to tackle is the aggregation of market risk into a unique measure. Previously, we have used VaR to measure the market risk of the liquid (standard) part of our portfolio and PaR, or another flow measure, for the market risk of its non-standard components. Naturally, the aggregation of market risk should be performed by measuring the PaR of the overall portfolio, since we need a measure of the overall market risk under the assumption of a continuative business during the reference business period. If it is also not technically difficult to calculate PaR for liquid instruments, this may lead to a serious overestimation of the overall market risk depending on the operating rules we actually apply in a "limit brake situation".

In fact, if our policy is that of stopping business activity once the cumulated loss reaches the initial VaR allocation, the maximum negative impact that liquid assets can have on the overall profit of the portfolio is exactly equal to the initial VaR allocation. In this situation the integration between PaR and VaR is obtained simply by summing the PaR figure with the initial VaR allocation (initial limit). This aggregated number is by definition less or equal to the global PaR. For that reason we mention risk overestimation.

Obviously, if we do not have a precise rule by which to regulate the VaR limit brake situation, an objective market risk aggregation may be difficult.

In order for PaR to be a comprehensive market risk measure we need to be able to calculate PaR over a certain time horizon for the whole bunch of books and business units that compose the entire company. The integration of market risk among different business units is not a simple task if we consider large vertically integrated energy companies or diversified energy trading ones. We can simply obtain representative figures for trading books, but generation books or sales books are not always completely integrated into the risk analysis. This is not even an easy task for those companies that are highly diversified from the geographical point of view. All the subsidiaries have their own systems, which work perfectly well, but an overall enterprise-wide aggregation is difficult to perform.

In all those situations characterized by objective problems in the way of risk aggregation, practical shortcuts may be considered. In fact, P&L individual figures of a portfolio's components (books or BUs) can be used to estimate directly a correlation matrix of the performance of the different components, and overall PaR can be simply obtained or at least approximated.

Alternative market risk aggregation techniques, more sophisticated from the theoretical point of view, can be used but with a bigger effort and with no guarantee of improvement in terms of final performance (see Saita (2007) for further details).

The further step on the way to complete risk integration is integration between market and credit risk (operational risk integration can also be performed at a more qualitative level).

The main difference between a market risk limit structure and a credit risk limit structure is the representation in terms of capital allocation of the limit structures themselves. If a VaR or PaR limit structure can be easily translated into an amount of capital allocated to a certain profit centre, counterparty limits are jointly used by the whole company. Hence, it is difficult to consider a credit limit structure as a proper capital allocation.

What we can do is to adopt a "credit charge technique". This approach entails monitoring credit exposure by counterparties, as usual, on an enterprise-wide level but then charging every single business unit or desk for the proportional credit risk created by it.

The charging process can take place by means of a P&L deduction of a certain fixed proportion of the global credit risk associated with a certain profit centre or through a direct deduction of the overall credit risk created from the market risk limit (VaR or PaR).

This practical way of integrating market and credit risks run by the company has various theoretical pros and cons that do not warrant discuss in this short presentation. However, this simple approach provides two fundamental benefits namely,

- budget and control of credit risk at a corporate level;
- it disincentivizes business units from carrying too much counterparty risk.

We must, however, bear in mind that there is an important difference between credit and market risk quality in energy companies. In fact, if running its own market risk is the core business for every industrial company, to run counterparty risk over a certain physiological level is philosophically wrong for companies that are not banks or insurance companies. An industrial company should decide a priori the proportion of the overall Capital at Risk it is willing to dedicate to credit and only afterwards implement a reasonable way to split this amount among all its business counterparties. At the same time different business units should participate in the life of the company and its goals.

Obviously, unsolved issues persist, such as:

- What is the right proportion between market risk and credit risk?
- What happens if a counterparty limit is reached and the use of the limit is not homogeneously split among different business units? Someone will be unfairly penalized!

In general, risk integration issues are an open field of research and discussion. No clear benchmarks are yet in place and each company is looking for its own self consistency. Good sense, in this situation, is always the best tool with which to come equipped.

6.4.3 Performance Assessment

Performance assessment is an extremely important topic for many players involved in energy trading. Essentially, to assess the performance of any trading activity means measuring the economic performance scaled by the risk run in order to produce it; for this reason we usually refer to risk adjusted performance measurement. Performance assessment is important for traders as an ex-ante support for pricing; it is important for managers in order to evaluate how the risk capital should be allocated among desks (before trading activity has started) and in order to remunerate traders fairly for the economic value added with respect to the risk capital allocated and effectively used.

Performance assessment is traditional for all those trading activities characterized by high market liquidity, pretty standard trading instruments and simple long/short trading strategies. As we have seen so far, energy trading does not always exhibit the aforementioned characteristics. Hence, performance assessment issues should be revisited in order to work properly in our field and represent a valid management tool.

The specific issue we want to analyze in this section is the difference between absolute and relative performance measures. Absolute measures aim to assess the absolute economic performance produced by an instrument or a portfolio in a given interval of time. Relative performance measures aim to assess whether the economic performance is higher or lower (sufficient or insufficient) with respect to some predefined benchmark.

Both measures can be expressed as a risk-adjusted return (% rate of the economic capital employed) or in terms of risk-adjusted profit or economic value added (absolute money).

Both instruments can be separately or jointly used by different trading players to infer different information and support different decisions. Typically, traders are not as interested in relative performance as shareholders are, while managers should be interested in a joint analysis of the two.

Performance measures should definitely be simple to calculate and to understand for all users otherwise they risk being misused or even not used at all. If we do not use risk-adjusted performance we have a biased view of the economic performance produced by our trading activity and we do not have any instrument to understand if and how the invested capital, or rather the risk capital, has been optimally allocated. Big profits arising without a proper risk assessment cannot be fully understood and consequently they tend not to be robust in their time evolution.

Absolute performance measures. The need to compare the performance of different portfolios and business units with respect to the risk capital allocated or to the relative risk is not new and is not typical only for energy trading.

Traditionally, the reward to risk ratio of undiversified portfolios is measured by CAPM derived indicators, like *Jensen alpha*, *Treynor ratio* or *Sharpe ratio*.

The Sharpe ratio is certainly the most popular. It is defined as the ratio between the portfolio expected excess return and its return's standard deviation:

$$\mathrm{SR} = \frac{\mu - r}{\sigma}$$

The Sharpe ratio scales the overall performance of the portfolio on its systematic and idiosyncratic risk. It measures the performance as a percentage return on the capital employed.

Similar performance measures scale the economic return only on the systematic part of the overall risk, but basically are constructed on the same theoretical framework.

The general problem with these measures is that since they lead to dimensionless numbers they do not allow one to assess and compare the absolute economic performance and hence they are not particularly helpful for risk-adjusted capital budgeting and control issues. Moreover, as we have seen in our discussion of capital constrained trading strategies, it is not always possible to achieve a linear relationship between absolute expected performance and risk capital (see Section 2.4.5). For this reason absolute Risk Adjusted Performance Measures, like *RaRoC*, tend to be preferred.

There are many definitions of Risk Adjusted Return on Capital; in trading environments the most commonly accepted one is the following:

$$\mathrm{RaRoC} = \frac{\text{Expected Return}}{\text{Economic Capital}} \tag{6.1}$$

where the expected return is the monetary assessment of the economic margin generated during a certain time horizon (typically the budget year) and the economic capital, as defined, is the amount of money needed to secure business survival in the worst case scenario. Economic capital should take into consideration all the components of the capital employed especially the most important one, the risk capital which should consider all the relevant risks such as market, credit and operational risks, and, of course, working capital.

Assuming that we are able to condense all the risk capital requirements into a Profit at Risk measure, and that the size of working capital is negligible with respect to that of PaR (which is not always the case) the expression, (6.1) becomes:

$$\mathrm{RaRoC} = \frac{\text{Expected Return}}{\text{PaR}}$$

The attractive thing about RaRoC is that it provides a uniform measure for assessing the performance of single deals, portfolios, desks and even entire companies irrespective of how heterogeneous the range of traded products included.

By using RaRoC, the management can assess the business return in a fully consistent way with respect to the established risk limits and corresponding capital allocation/requirements.

The ultimate goal of a company is to increase its shareholder value, since the shareholders provide the capital and effectively have the alternative of diverting their capital to other projects. Hence, it is not enough to guarantee that RaRoC is positive – it also has to be adequate.

We can introduce a hurdle rate to bear directly into the RaRoC definition so that we can directly estimate the pure economic value added:

$$\text{RaRoC} = \frac{\text{Expected Return} - (\text{Cost of Capital}) \times \text{PaR}}{\text{PaR}}$$

Determining the Cost of Capital is not easy and there are several approaches to this problem. In our opinion neither subjective nor accounting methods are satisfactory since, as stated, shareholders are more focused on opportunity cost of capital employed. How to establish in a scientific way a fair hurdle rate for our business or project leads us to the concept of relative performance measures.

Relative performance measures. The scope of a relative performance measure (always risk-adjusted) is that of measuring the additional economic value (or disvalue) generated compared to that of similar and alternative investments. Obviously, by similar we do not mean here necessarily similar in sector or structure but similar only in terms of the embedded risk profile. Whenever we evaluate our private investments we try to understand precisely which one is the best among a set of alternatives which reflect more or less the same risk profile, which should be our risk profile.

The traditional way to estimate the appropriate hurdle rate, according to the methodology described above, is based on the CAPM theoretical framework.

Using the standard CAPM equation and the concept of beta, we can obtain our target return rate:

$$\mathbb{E}\left[r_{CC}\right] = \text{rf} + \beta(\mathbb{E}\left[r_M\right] - \text{rf})$$

where $\mathbb{E}\left[r_{CC}\right]$ is the *hurdle rate* and $(\mathbb{E}\left[r_M\right] - \text{rf})$ is the *excess market return*.

This approach is obviously extremely theoretical and assumes a perfect and frictionless capital market. In reality, the debt to equity ratio matters considerably in the definition of the cost of capital and consequently the hurdle rate. CAPM and classical option pricing theory can be integrated in order to obtain a more realistic determination of the expected return on equity capital.

$$\mathbb{E}\left[r_{CC}\right] = \text{rf} + \mathcal{N}\left(\frac{\ln\left(\frac{V}{\text{DC}}\right) + \left(\text{rf} + \frac{\sigma^2}{2}t\right)}{\sigma\sqrt{t}}\right)(\bar{r} - \text{rf})\,\frac{V}{\text{EqC}}$$

where:

$$\mathrm{EqC} = V \cdot \mathcal{N}\left(\frac{\ln\left(\frac{V}{\mathrm{DC}}\right) + \left(\mathrm{rf} + \frac{\sigma^2}{2}t\right)}{\sigma\sqrt{t}}\right) - e^{-\mathrm{rf}\cdot t} \cdot \mathrm{DC} \cdot \mathcal{N}\left(\frac{\ln\left(\frac{V}{\mathrm{DC}}\right) + \left(\mathrm{rf} - \frac{\sigma^2}{2}t\right)}{\sigma\sqrt{t}}\right)$$

and V is the company's value, DC is the debt capital and $\bar{r}$ is the average return of investment.

Nevertheless, we still have a very theoretical approach with a wide set of parameters that are difficult to estimate in an objective way. In any case, both the approaches proposed can be interpreted as decision support tools to be used in parallel with respect to internal and subjective evaluations.

Even if we accept the limitations of the two proposed approaches we haven't solved all the problems. Once we have estimated the overall hurdle rate (company wide) we still have the problem of converting it into hurdle rates for different desks (characterized by different trading activities and strategies). If CAPM-based approaches are suitable for unidirectional trading activities (e.g. long fund), we need to remember that energy trading is more complex and put together dynamic long/short positions and also directional positions in market movements not directly related to price level (e.g. long/short volatility or correlations). How can we benchmark this kind of trading activity?

Benchmarking using passive trading strategies (ad-hoc constructed) may be the solution and makes evident the individual contribution to overall economic performance.

A benchmark performance index based on passive trading strategy can be derived using the major futures contracts to which our business is exposed (power, gas, oil, fx, CO_2, etc).

Once underlying assets have been established we need to determine index weights in order to be sure that the same dollar risk (unitary risk) is associated with each of the relevant market drivers and that the same weights are revised periodically to reflect the relevant changes in product volatility. In particular, in order to ensure that equal risk is allocated to each of the commodities present in the book, the percentage of indexation ($x(i)$) of each of the n commodities should be equal to $x(i) = \frac{1}{n}\frac{1}{\sigma(i)}$. Finally, long/short position in each of the commodities can be determined by the simplest possible momentum trading rule (e.g. if the cumulated return of the last week is positive buy or else sell).

However, these kinds of passive trading rule are linear and may not work well for benchmarking highly non-linear trading strategies based on options or structured energy products. At least we can have an idea of the added value extracted by structured energy trading with respect to more standard trading strategies.

The last issue to tackle is related to the best way of using all those performance measures. In essence, risk-adjusted performance measures can be used for two different purposes: ex-post performance measurement and rewarding; ex-ante capital allocation.

Obviously, the two are extremely linked. Ex-post performance evaluation can be done on the ex-ante allocated capital or on the effectively used one. Ex-ante capital allocation is typically based on historical performance. On the one hand we can state that allocated capital (ex-ante) should be used to calculate performance, on the other we can argue that only utilized capital is representative of the effective risk run. Theoretically, capital allocation is an activity that should ideally precede performance measurement, hence allocated capital should drive the performance assessment. Using this approach gives people the incentive to use all the capital allocated even if it is not really efficient to do so.

But we don't want to give an answer to this dilemma, we merely want to focus the reader's attention on it. The proper solution is to be found situation by situation; nevertheless knowledge of the pros and cons of each approach is fundamental irrespective of our final decision.

6.4.4 The Dynamics of Capital Allocation (Capital Reallocation Process)

The optimization through time of economic capital allocation among a company's business units and desks is one of the main objectives and ultimate aim of an enterprise-wide risk management system. Unfortunately, that is no simple task and, moreover, we have no benchmark to follow as we do for risk measurement and portfolio management issues. The absence of strong theoretical benchmarks in this field not only affects the energy trading business but the entire universe of financial entities.

A few cornerstones can nevertheless be established.

The capital reallocation process is not disjointed from strategic planning or budgeting, for when a change in strategy occurs capital needs to be addressed in consequence.

Capital reallocation should reflect the way we assess risk-adjusted performance and the way we decide to set up individual targets and incentive schemes in terms of ex-ante and ex-post results. In the capital reallocation decision-making process, top managers should not be influenced by absolute results, but, as mentioned earlier, effective capital employed (especially risk capital) should be properly considered.

The link between the capital reallocation process and the planning/budgeting process is a contested issue among academics and practitioners. Quite often the frequency of change decisions required in order to have an optimal and efficient allocation of the capital employed is not consistent with the typical timing of the planning process. Hence, inconsistencies may arise and in any case compromises should be found in order to make this relationship realistic and effective. On the other hand, a too frequent change in risk limit structure does not benefit economic performance either from the psychological or the financial point of view. In fact, as we have pointed out when analyzing both directional and relative trading strategies, every single strategy needs a certain minimum time to provide the expected results. Hence, a too frequent change in the allocated capital (risk limit) will reduce the probability of reaching expected (desired) results. Again, no theoretical support to combine optimally allocated capital and rebalancing period with expected performance is available. As shown in Section 2.4.5, a risk limit means capital usage in a given time horizon and the relationship between allocated capital and expected performance is not a trivial one.

The capital reallocation process is usually undertaken basing decisions on past performance since expected returns and risks are assessed on historical records. This way of approaching the problem is pretty natural but may be misleading. A good balance of historical performance quantitative assessment and a more qualitative analysis of it may prove helpful in fine-tuning an optimal capital reallocation approach. For example, the analysis of the average level of operational activity (number of trades per period) or average risk limit usage may be informative in order to judge the merit and the performance of a trading activity. To obtain a certain performance by means of an intense trading activity and a deep usage of risk limits (even with some occasional losses) has, of course, a different meaning with respect to the same performance obtained with just a few trades and no activity for the rest of the time. The role of luck in this case can be predominant. The same conclusion can be reached if the performance is obtained with a significant non-homogeneous usage of risk limit.

In summary we may conclude that allocating capital is not like choosing the right assets in our investment portfolio. It has an impact on the overall strategy of the company and, moreover, it deals with people, internal organization and incentive schemes. Certainly, it cannot be treated as a purely technical exercise, but coherence should be pursued throughout the decision-making process involving initial capital allocation, ex-ante performance target setting and risk measurement, ex-post performance assessment and attribution and capital reallocation.

Throughout this chapter we have sought to analyze energy trading activity from a macro perspective, identifying the main pillars on which good trading activity should be based. We have defined as metatrading strategy the way a manager decides to set up his trading business. In our opinion, the most important metatrading decisions deal with business cycle identification and interpretation, optimal organization of information flows and business activities and capital allocation/reallocation processes. We have also emphasized how important it is to support metatrading decisions with the proper mix of qualitative and quantitative decision tools, avoiding a rigid and unilateral approach.

Obviously, metatrading is a subject that needs to be further analyzed and expanded since there is virtually nothing in the current literature on the topic, especially focusing on energy and commodity trading. Our contribution has aimed rather to initiate and stimulate discussion on this topic than to establish benchmarks. Indeed, we would go so far as to say that a metatrading approach may be even more important than specific micro trading approaches since it represents the prerequisite for transforming a pure gambling activity into a robust and professional trading business.

Bibliography

Ané, T. and Geman, H. (2000). Order low, transaction clock and normality of asset returns. *Journal of Finance*, 55(5): 2259–2284.

Basak, S. and Chabakauri, G. (2008). Dynamic hedging in incomplete markets. Submitted paper.

Basak, S. and Shapiro, A. (2001). Value-at-risk-based risk management: optimal policies and asset prices. *Review of Financial Studies*, 14(2): 371–405.

Benth, F. E. and Karlsen, K. H. (2005). A note on Merton's portfolio selection problem for the Schwartz mean-reversion model. *Stochastic Analysis and Applications*, 23(4): 687–704.

Benth, F. E., Koekebakker, S., and Benth, J. S. (2008). *Stochastic Modelling of Electricity and Related Markets*. World Scientific.

Björk, T. (2004). *Arbitrage Theory in Continuous Time*. Oxford Finance.

Breusch, T. S. and Pagan, A. R. (1979). Simple test for heteroscedasticity and random coefficient variation. *Econometrica*, 47(5): 1287–1294.

Brigo, D., Dalessandro, A., Neugebauer, M. and Triki, F. (2009). A stochastic processes toolkit for risk management: Geometric Brownian motion, jumps, GARCH and variance gamma models. *Journal of Risk Management in Financial Institutions*, 2: 365–393.

Brigo, D. and Mercurio, F. (2006). *Interest Rate Models – Theory and Practice*, 2nd edition. Springer.

Burns, A. F. and Wesley, C. M. (1946). *Measuring Business Cycles*. NBER (National Bureau of Economic Research).

Campbell, J. Y., Lo, A. W., and MacKinlay, C. (1997). *The Econometric of Financial Markets*. Princeton University Press.

Clark, P. K. (1973). A subordinated stochastic process with finite variance for speculative prices. *Econometrica*, 41(1): 135–156.

Clewlow, L. and Strickland, C. (2000). *Energy Derivatives: Pricing and Risk Management*. Lacima Publications.

Cowen, T. (1997). *Risk and Business Cycles: New and Old Austrian Perspectives*. Routledge, London.

Cox, J., Ross, S., and Rubinstein, M. (1979). Option pricing: A simplified approach. *Journal of Financial Economics*, 7: 229–64.

Cuoco, D., Hua, H., and Sergei, I. (2008). Optimal dynamic trading strategies with risk limits. *Operations Research*, 56: 358–368.

Cuthbertson, K. and Nitzsche, D. (2004). *Quantitative Financial Economics. Stocks, Bonds & Foreign Exchange*. John Wiley & Sons.

Dickey, D. A. and Fuller, W. A. (1979). Distribution of the estimators for autoregressive time series with a unit root. *Journal of the American Statistical Association*, 74: 427–431.

Duffie, D. and Richardson, H. R. (1991). Mean-variance hedging in continuous time. *The Annals of Applied Probability*, 1(1): 1–15.

Edoli, E., Fiorenzani, S., Ravelli, S., and Vargiolu, T. (2010). Modeling and valuing *make-up* clause in long term gas swing contracts. Submitted paper.

Engle, R. F. and Granger, C. W. J. (1987). Co-integration and error correction: Representation, estimation and testing. *Econometrica*, 55: 251–276.

Fama, E. F. (1970). Efficient capital markets: A review of theory and empirical work. *Journal of Finance*, 25(2): 383–417.

Fiorenzani, S. (2006a). Financial optimisation and risk management in refining activities. *International Journal Global Energy Issues*, 26(1–2).

Fiorenzani, S. (2006b). *Quantitative Methods for Electricity Trading and Risk Management*. Palgrave Macmillan.

Gatheral, J. (2006). *The Volatility Surface*. John Wiley & Sons.

Geman, H. (2005). *Commodities and Commodity Derivatives*. John Wiley & Sons.

Geman, H. (2008). *Risk Management in Commodity Markets*. John Wiley & Sons.

Hagemann, H., Nishizawa, T., and Ikeda, Y. (2010). *Austrian Economics in Transition: From Carl Menger to Friedrich Hayek*. Palgrave Macmillan.

Harrod, R. F. (1936). *The Trade Cycle: An Essay*. Clarendon Press.

Harrod, R. F. (1939). An essay in dynamic theory. *Economic Journal*, XLIX, 14–33.

Harrod, R. F. (1948). *Towards a Dynamic Economics*. Macmillan, London.

Henderson, V. (2005). Valuing the option to invest in an incomplete market. Princeton University, working paper.

Hicks, J. R. (1949). Harrod's Dynamic Theory. *Economica*, 16: 106–21.

Hicks, J. R. (1950). *A Contribution to the Theory of the Trade Cycle*. 1956 reprint of Oxford, Clarendon Press.

Hull, J. C. (2006). *Options, Futures and Other Derivatives*. 6th edition. Prentice Hall.

Johansen, S. (1991). Cointegration and hypothesis testing of cointegration vectors in Gaussian vector autoregressive models. *Econometrica*, 59(6): 1551–1580.

Kahneman, D. and Tversky, A. (1974). Judgment under uncertainty: heuristics and biases. *Science*, 185(4157): 1124–1131.

Kahneman, D. and Tversky, A. (1979). Prospect theory: an analysis of decision under risk. *Econometrica*, 47(2): 263–292.

Keynes, J. M. (1936). *The General Theory of Employment, Interest and Money*. 1st edition, Macmillan Cambridge University Press, for Royal Economic Society.

Kitchin, J. (1923). Cycles and trends in economic factors. *Review of Economics and Statistics*, 5(1): 10–16.

Kondratiev, N. D. and Stolper, W. F. (1935). The long waves in economic life. *Review of Economics and Statistics*, 17(6): 105–115.

Kuznets, S. (1930). *Secular Movements in Production and Prices. Their Nature and their Bearing upon Cyclical Fluctuations*. Houghton Mifflin.

Kydland, F. E. and Prescott, E. C. (1982). Time to build and aggregate fluctuations. *Econometrica* 50(6): 1345–1370.

Littlechild, S. (1990). *Austrian Economics*. Edward Elgar.

Longstaff, F. and Schwartz, E. (2001). Valuing american options by simulation: A simple least squares approach. *Review of Financial Studies*, 14(1): 113–147.

Markowitz, H. (1952). Portfolio selection. *The Journal of Finance*, 7(1): 77–91.

Menger, C. (1981). *Principles of Economics*. Originally published in 1871. Translated by Dingwall, J. and Hoselitz, B. F., with an introduction by Hayek, Friedrich A., New York University Press.

Merton, R. C. (1969). Lifetime portfolio selection under uncertainty: The continuous-time case. *Review of Economics and Statistics*, 51(3): 247–257.

Monroe, I. (1978). Processes that can be embedded in Brownian motion. *Annals of Probability*, 6(1): 42–56.

Pascucci, A. (2008). *Calcolo Stocastico per la Finanza*. Springer, Milan.

Pascucci, A. and Runggaldier, W. J. (2009). *Finanza Matematica*. Springer.

Pilipovic, D. (2007). *Energy Risk: Valuing and Managing Energy Derivatives*. McGraw-Hill Professional.

Roberts, H. (1967). Statistical versus clinical prediction of the stock market. Unpublished manuscript.

Rockafellar, R. T. and Uryasev, S. (2002). Conditional value at risk for general loss distributions. *Journal of Banking and Finance*, 26: 1443–71.

Rodrigues, A. and Armada, M. R. (2006). The valuation of real options with the least squares monte carlo simulation method. Working paper available at www.fep.up.pt/conferencias/pfn2006/Conference%20Papers/540.pdf.

Rothbard, M. N. (1969). *Economic Depressions: Causes and Cures*. The Libertarian Forum.

Rothbard, M. N. (1980). *What Has Government Done to Our Money*, original 1969, acquired by The Ludwig von Mises Institute.

Nobel Prize Committee, Time-series Econometrics: Cointegration and Autoregressive Conditional Heteroskedasticity, No 2003-1, Nobel Prize in Economics documents, Nobel Prize Committee

Rudloff, B. and Chabakauri, G. (2005). Convex hedging in incomplete markets. *Applied Mathematical Finance*, 14(5): 437–452.

Saita, F. (2007). *Value at Risk and Bank Capital Management*. Academic Press (Elsevier, UK).

Schumpeter, J. A. (1939). *Business Cycles: A Theoretical, Historical, and Statistical Analysis of the Capitalist Process*. 1st edition, McGraw-Hill Book Company.

Schwert, W.G. (1990). Stock volatility and the crash of '87. *Review of financial studies*, 3, 77–102.

Svensson, L. E. O. and Werner, I. M. (1993). Non traded assets in incomplete markets. *European Economic Review*, 37: 1149–1168.

Taleb, N. (1997). *Dynamic Hedging*. John Wiley & Sons.

Tepla, L. (2000). Optimal hedging and valuation of non-traded assets. *European Finance Review*, 4: 231–251.

Thaler, R. (1999). Mental accounting matters. *Journal of Behavioural Decision Making*, 12(3): 183–206.

de la Vega, J. P. (1688). *Confusion of Confusions*. Sonsbeek Publishers.

von Böhm-Bawerk, E. (1980). *Capital and Interest*. Translated by Smart, William, Macmillan. (1959) (reprint). Available online at: http://www.econlib.org/library/BohmBawerk/bbCI.html)

von Hayek, F. A. (1935). *Prices and Production*. Routledge and Sons. (1931). 2nd edition, Routledge and Kegan.

von Mises, L. (1953). *The Theory of Money and Credit; Translated from German Version of 1912 by H.E. Batson*. Yale University Press: New Haven.

Index

Note: Page references in *italics* refer to Figures; those in **bold** refer to Tables

absolute performance measures 188–90
accelerating processes 15–17
adaptive expectations 44
additive smoothing 45
ADF test 92–3, **93**, 94, 96, **97**
adopted stochastic control 129
adopted stochastic process 129
aggregated supply and demand 38–9, *38*
Alpha 125
ambiguity, aversion to 14
American call option 102
American put option 102
anchorage 14
arbitrageur 112
Arithmetic Brownian Motion 28, 29
ARMA model 45–6
Asian option 107–8
asset 109
asset allocation with capital constraints 76–80
Augmented Dickey-Fuller (ADF) test 10, 19, **20–3**, 26, **27**
Australian business cycle (ABC) theory 168–70
autoregressive process of order n (AR(n)) 45–6
auxiliary option 121
availability (heuristic behaviour) 14
average strike Asian 108
aversion to ambiguity 14

barrier options 106–7
behavioural finance 13–14
Bellman's optimality principle 136
benchmark performance index 191
Benth-Karlsen problem 61–2
Bernoulli partial differential equation (PDE) 66
binomial lattice 159
binomial model 118
binomial tree *71*
Black-Scholes model 119, 142
Bollinger Bands 49, 50
book/desk structuring 173–5, *174*
Breusch-Pagan test 20, 22
Brownian motion 73, 119
building cycles 166
business cycles 166
butterfly spreads 111
buy/sell and hold strategy 54, 56

calendar spreads *52*, 111
Candlestick Indicators (Japanese Candlestick) 49
capital allocation 173–4, 177
  dynamics of 192–3
capital asset price model (CAPM) 190, 191
Capital at Risk 187
capital management principles 177–93
capital reallocation 177
  dynamics of 192–3
carbon markets 17
carry forward clauses 146
Cash Flow at Risk (CFaR) 183
certainty effect 15
CES 57
Charm 121
charts (technical analysis) 49
Chebyshev polynomials 139

cointegration 84–9
cointegration of order (*d*, *b*) 86
cointegration order one 86
commodity segregation 174
conditional expectations 5–7
Conditional Value at Risk (CVaR) 180–1
constant relative risk aversion (CARA) 57, 151
consumption goods 114
contango 95
continuation value 138
continuous time dynamic hedging framework 122–6
contract of wager 101
contracts for differences (cfd) 35
control variables 136
convenience yields 114–15
correlation 84
Cost of Capital 190
Cowles-Jones (CJ) test 10–11, 24–5, **24–5**
crack spread 81, 83, 159
credit charge technique 187
credit rationing 172
credit risk for energy portfolios 183–5
cross commodities spread trading 81, 92–5
CRRA 57

Dark Clouds 50
debt to equity ratio 190
Delta 120, 121, 157
delta hedging 120, 125–6
  delta-neutral position 128
demographic cycles 166
deterministic trend 46–9, *48*
Dickey-Fuller test 87
directional trading 33–57
  fundamental trading models 37–42
  market products for 35–7
  price trend determination 37–57
  statistical trading models 42–9
  technical trading models 49–51
  timing in 33–4
discrete delta 122–3
diversification 173
do nothing trading signal 53
domestic demand 39
Double No Touch option 107
double smoothing 44
down-and-in Barrier options 107
down-and-out Barrier options 106
downwards spread strategies 110–11
dynamic hedging 120, 140

ECM representation 88
economic capital definition and initial allocation 177–8
economic cycles 165
efficient frontier 59
efficient market 85
Efficient Markets Hypotheses 1–3, 82
  in energy commodities markets 19–27
  informational and mathematical implications 3
  mathematical framework 3–7
  subordination, trading volume and 27–8
  trading implications 2–3
  violations of 13–15, 18
Elliot waves 49
energy commodities markets 17–19
  Efficient Markets Hypotheses in 19–27
Engle-Granger test 87
Eni Gas Release 2007 (ENIGRO7) 52, *52*
equilibrium error 86
equilibrium price 54
equivalence 116
European call option 101
European put option 101–2
ex-ante capital allocation 192
excess Market return 190
exotic options 105–9
  features of 106
exotic option traders 125
expected loss 184
expected return on equity capital 190–1
Expected Shortfall (ES) 181
expected utility maximization problem 59
expected utility principle 14–15
expiry date 101
exponential smoothing 44
exponential weighted moving average (EWMA) 44–6
extra-information 6
extreme market moves 122–3

fair game 7
feedback loop processes 16, 17
figures (technical analysis) 49
filtration 3, 5
flow based risk measures 181–3
forward contracts 35, 36
Fourier series 139
full requirements contracts 134–5
fundamental trading models 37–42
  case study 54–7, *56*

future contracts 35, 36
futures vs options 102

Gamma 120–1, 123–4
  Shadow 123–4
  surface 123, *124*
gas demand/supply drivers 39–40, *39*, 41–2
Gauss Markov assumptions 91
Gaussian Kernel methods 31–2
Gaussian white noise 94
Girsanov theorem 71, 73
Greeks 106, 119–22, 125

Hamilton-Jacobi-Bellman approach 61, 62–6
Hammer 50
Hanged Man 50
hedge 101
  delta 120, 125–6
  dynamic 120, 140
  in incomplete markets 149–51
  myopic 140, 150
  proxy 150
  static 140
  swing *158*
  with forwards 139–140
hedgers 104
hedging error 140, 150
Hermitte polynomials 139
heuristic behaviours 14
Hilbert space 139
hurdle rate 190

implied volatility surface 124
in & out trading 51, 54, 56
in the money 103
industrial demand 39
information asymmetries 15–17
information set 3–5
instrike 106, 107
instrument segregation 174
inter-temporal asset allocation problems 59–62
  mean-reverting asset: Benth-Karlsen problem 61–2
  traditional 60–1
internal market 175–6
investment goods 114
isolation effect 15
Iterated Expectations, Law of 3, 7
Ito's formula 75

Japanese Candlestick 49
Jensen alpha 188
Johansen test 87, 88–9
Juglar cycle 165, 166

Keynesian business cycle theory 166–8
Kick in 107
Kick out 106
Kitchin inventory cycle 166
Knock out 106
Knocked out options 107
Kolmogorov-Smirnov test 20, 22, 32
Kondratiev wave 166
Kuznets infrastructural investment cycle 166

Lagrange multipliers 70
Lagrangian function 71, 72
Lagrangian method 59
lattice approach method 138
Law of Iterated Expectations 3, 7
law of X 4
Least Squared Monte Carlo (LSMC) 138–9, 152
Legendre-Fenchel transform 72
Leguerre polynomials 139
line chart 50
linear dependence 84
liquidity 35
location spread 81–2, 90, 91, *95*, 96–8, **97**, *97*, **98**
long memory process *46*, 47
long-run equilibrium 86
long-run level 51
long technological cycle 166
long wave 86
Lookback option 108
loss given default (LGD) 184, 185

MACD 49
macroeconomic megatrends 164–72
make up clause 146–9
Margrabe formula 142
market, definition 175
market efficiency, weak and strong forms 1–2
market makers 104, 105
market risk premium 140
market segmentation 19, 24
martingale hypothesis 7–11, 69–76, 116
  market incompleteness 76
martingale measure 116
maturity 101

mean reversion *83*, 89, *90*, 93, 94, 97, 98
measurable space 4
merchant trading (asset backed trading) 132
merit order 41
metatrading 79, 163–93
  definition and fundamental elements 163–4
micro trading 163
minimum variance of hedging error 151
minimum variance static hedging scheme 151, 153
miscoordination risk 176
Momentum 49
Monte Carlo simulation 180
  Least Squared Monte Carlo (LSMC) 138–9, 152
  naive Monte Carlo simulation 137–8, 152, 153
moral hazards in credit creation 172
Morning Star 50
moving average process of order q (MA(q)) 45–6
multiplicative smoothing 45
multiplier, Keynesian 166–7
multiplier-accelerator models 167
myopic hedge 140, 150

naive Monte Carlo simulation 137–8, 152, 153
naked position 127
net option buyers 104, 105
net option sellers 104, 105
net working capital 177
no-arbitrage hypothesis 15, 112–14, 116, 117–18
no touch option 107
non-linearity 101–5
non stationarity 84–9

oil-based options 105
one touch option 107
optimal hedging ratio 125
optimal strategic asset allocation techniques 82
optimal value function 63
optimal way 57
option pricing 115–19, 190
option traders 104–5
options 101–29
  Asian 107–8
  Barrier 106–7
  case study 126–9
  combinations 109–12
  continuous time dynamic hedging framework 122–6
  definition 101
  energy option markets 105
  exotic 105–9
  factors influencing value 103–4
  interest rate and 103
  Payout 107
  Quanto 108–9
  storage cost and convenience yield 114–15
  time to maturity 103
  underlying price and strike 103
  value bounds and parity relationship 112–15
  volatility 103
  vs futures 102
ordinary least squares (OLS) regression 87, 91
Ornstein-Uhlenbeck process 62, 93
out of the money 103
outstrike 106, 107
over the counter (OTC) markets 106

Parabolic SAR 49
partial differential equation (PDE) 64, 66
path-dependence 117
path-independence 117
pay as bid markets 38
Payout options 107
peak-shaped industrial load 42
perfect foresight 137, 152
performance assessment 188–92
  absolute performance measures 188–90
  relative performance measures 190–2
Pivot Point 49
point and figures technique 50
portfolio value 126, 127
  delta-neutral position 128
  naked position 127
potential future exposure (PFE) 185
power demand/supply drivers 40–2, *43*
power series 139
premium 101
probability space 4
profiled forward contracts 133–4
Profit at Risk (PaR) 182–3, 185, 186
Profit at Risk limitation 77
progressively measureable process 70
proxy hedge 150
put-call parity 113

quantitative easing 172
Quanto option 108–9

Radon-Nikodym variable 71, 73
random variable 4
Random Walk Hypothesis 8–10, 26, 27
Random Walk with drift model 47, 48
real business cycle (RBC) theory 167–8
rebalancing, portfolio 117
reference period 60
reflection effect 15
relative performance measures 190–2
Relative Strength Index (RSI) 49, 50
relative (value) trading strategies 81
replacement exposure 184–5
residual Normal fit 20, 21–3
retail structured products 133–5
Risk Adjusted Performance Measures 189
Risk Adjusted Return on Capital (RaRoC) 189–90
risk aggregation 186
Risk-based Business Cycle (RKBC) Theory 170–2
risk capital 177
risk capital assessment 185–7
risk integration 185–7
risk measurement and integration approaches 178–87
risk multiplication principle 171
risk reduction strategies 100
risk reversal strategy 107

Saddle Point Theorem 70, 71
Schwartz model 62
self financing condition 60, 61
self-financing portfolio 117
semi-strong efficient market 5
settlement exposure 184
Shadow Gamma 123–4
Sharpe ratio 188, 189
short time measure 84, 85
σ−algebras 3–5
similarity (heuristic behaviour) 14
Simple Moving Averages (SMA) 50
single period asset allocation model 58–9
single smoothing 44
Spark spread 81, 83, *84*, 91, *91*, 92–5, **93**, **95**
spot trading 35
spread trading 81–100
  cointegration 84–9
  combining directional and 98–100
  definition and identification 82–4
  energy spread trading strategies 89–91
  energy spreads and spread trading strategies 92–8
  non stationarity 84–9
spreads 109–11
stack curve 41
state variables 136
static hedge 140
statistical independence 174
statistical performance 51
statistical ratio 53
statistical trading models 42–9
  case study 51–4
  sample window 52
  structural market change 52
  time horizon 51
Stochastic Dynamic Programming 66–9
Stochastic Optimal Control 61, 62, 126
stochastic process 4, 5
stochastic trend 46–9, *48*
stochastic variables 136
straddles 111–12, *111*
strangles 111–12, *111*
straps 111–12
strategic asset allocation methods 57–80
  asset allocation with capital constraints 76–80
  dynamic programming 62–76
  inter-temporal asset allocation problems 59–62
  single period asset allocation model 58–9
  traditional asset allocation models 57–8
strike price 101
strips 111–12
strong efficient market 1–2, 5
structured products on energy 125–6
  case study 152–62
  main typology 131–3
  retail 133–5
  wholesale 135–49
subordination 28–32
  Efficient Markets Hypothesis and 27–8
swaps 35
swing contracts 146–9
swing hedging *158*
synthetic risk measures 178–81
System Marginal Price 38

take or pay contracts 133
technical analysis 49–51, 50–1
technical trading models 49–51

theorem of asset pricing
  first 116
  second 118
Theta 121, 125
time spread 81, 82, 90, 91, 95–6, **96**
timing in directional trading 33–4
Tolling contracts 140
trade cycle model 166, 167
trading business organizational issues 172–6
trading desk definition 174–5
traditional asset allocation models 57–8
trajectory of X 5
trend stationary process 46, 47
Treynor ratio 188
trigonometric series 139
trinomial model 118–19

underemployment equilibrium 165
underlying 101
up-and-in Barrier options 107
up-and-out Barrier options 106
utility functions 57

Value at Risk (VaR) 77, 78, 79, 80, 179–80, 186
  Conditional (CVaR) 180–1
value based market risk measures 178–81
value hedging approach 157, 158
Vanna 121, 125
Variance Ratio 25, **25–7**
Variance Ratio tests 11–13
vector auto regressive (VAR) system 87, 88
Vega 121–2, 124–5
Verification Theorem 63, 66
vicious circle 17
virtual asset 135, 139
Virtual Gas Storages (VGS) 139
  structure and pricing techniques 144–6, **145**
Virtual Power Plants (VPP) 139, 152–4
  structure and pricing techniques 140–2, 145
Virtual Refineries 139, 158–62
  structure and pricing techniques 142–4
volatility surface movements 124–5
Volga 125
Volumetric static hedging 153

weak efficient market 1–2, 5
weighted average sourcing price (wasp) 55, 56
wholesale structured products 135–49
  general pricing 135–40
  swing contracts and *make-up* clause 146–9
  virtual gas storage 144–6
  virtual power plants 140–2
  virtual refinery 142–4
Wicksell effect 172
Wiener process 93

zero drift martingale 82